Shakespeare in the Theatre: Sarah Siddons and John Philip Kemble

SERIES EDITORS

Peter Holland, Farah Karim-Cooper and Stephen Purcell

Published titles
Patrice Chéreau, Dominique Goy-Blanquet
The American Shakespeare Center, Paul Menzer
Mark Rylance at the Globe, Stephen Purcell
The National Theatre, 1963–1975: Olivier and Hall,
Robert Shaughnessy
Nicholas Hytner, Abigail Rokison-Woodall
Peter Sellars, Ayanna Thompson
Trevor Nunn, Russell Jackson
Cheek by Jowl, Peter Kirwan
Peter Hall, Stuart Hampton-Reeves
Yukio Ninagawa, Conor Hanratty
The King's Men, Lucy Munro
William Davenant and the Duke's Company, Amanda Eubanks
Winkler and Richard Schoch

Forthcoming
Phyllida Lloyd, Elizabeth Schafer
Satoshi Miyagi, Mika Eglinton
Tina Packer, Katharine Goodland
Kathryn Hunter, Stephen Purcell

Shakespeare in the Theatre: Sarah Siddons and John Philip Kemble

Fiona Ritchie

THE ARDEN SHAKESPEARE
LONDON • NEW YORK • OXFORD • NEW DELHI • SYDNEY

THE ARDEN SHAKESPEARE
Bloomsbury Publishing Plc
50 Bedford Square, London, WC1B 3DP, UK
1385 Broadway, New York, NY 10018, USA
29 Earlsfort Terrace, Dublin 2, Ireland

BLOOMSBURY, THE ARDEN SHAKESPEARE and the Arden Shakespeare logo are trademarks of Bloomsbury Publishing Plc

First published in Great Britain 2023
This paperback published 2024

Copyright © Fiona Ritchie, 2023

Fiona Ritchie has asserted her right under the Copyright, Designs and Patents Act, 1988, to be identified as the author of this work.

For legal purposes the Acknowledgements on p. ix constitute an extension of this copyright page.

Series design by Dani Leigh
Cover image: John Philip Kemble, Sarah Siddons (© Courtesy of the Garrick Club, London)

All rights reserved. No part of this publication may be reproduced or transmitted in any form or by any means, electronic or mechanical, including photocopying, recording, or any information storage or retrieval system, without prior permission in writing from the publishers.

Bloomsbury Publishing Plc does not have any control over, or responsibility for, any third-party websites referred to or in this book. All internet addresses given in this book were correct at the time of going to press. The author and publisher regret any inconvenience caused if addresses have changed or sites have ceased to exist, but can accept no responsibility for any such changes.

Library of Congress Cataloging-in-Publication Data

Names: Ritchie, Fiona, author.
Title: Sarah Siddons and John Philip Kemble / Fiona Ritchie.
Description: London ; New York : The Arden Shakespeare, 2022. | Series: Shakespeare in the theatre | Includes bibliographical references.
Identifiers: LCCN 2022026610 | ISBN 9781350073289 (hardback) | ISBN 9781350352421 (paperback) | ISBN 9781350073302 (ebook) | ISBN 9781350073296 (epub) | ISBN 9781350073319
Subjects: LCSH: Siddons, Sarah, 1755-1831. | Kemble, John Philip, 1757-1823. | Theater–England–History–18th century. | Theater–England–History–19th century. | Shakespeare, William, 1564-1616–Stage history–1625-1800. | Shakespeare, William, 1564-1616–Stage history–1800-1950. | Shakespeare, William, 1564-1616–Dramatic production.
Classification: LCC PN2598.S5 R58 2022 | DDC 792.02/8092 [B]–dc23/eng/20220718
LC record available at https://lccn.loc.gov/2022026610

ISBN: HB: 978-1-3500-7328-9
PB: 978-1-3503-5242-1
ePDF: 978-1-3500-7330-2
eBook: 978-1-3500-7329-6

Series: Shakespeare in the Theatre

Typeset by Deanta Global Publishing Services, Chennai, India

To find out more about our authors and books visit www.bloomsbury.com and sign up for our newsletters.

To
Michael Ritchie
and
Emile and Margot Stoten-Ritchie
with love

CONTENTS

List of Figures viii
Acknowledgements ix
A note on the text xi
Series preface xii

Introduction: Debuts (1775, 1782, 1783) 1

1 Acting together (the 1780s) 19

2 Producing Shakespeare at Drury Lane (1788–96, 1800–2) 49

3 *Vortigern* (1796): 'A most audacious impostor' 75

4 *Macbeth* and unrest: Covent Garden management (1803–12) and the OP Riots (1809) 99

5 Sibling *Hamlet* 125

Conclusion: Retirements (1812, 1817) 147

Appendix: Siddons's and Kemble's performances together in London 165
Notes 174
Bibliography 218
Index 235

FIGURES

Cover. Thomas Beach, *John Philip Kemble and Sarah Siddons in Macbeth* (1786). G0390. Courtesy of the Garrick Club, London.

1 Reproduction of a playbill for 12 February 1767 documenting an early performance by Siddons and Kemble with their parents' company in Worcester 3
2 *Mrs. Siddons as Constance* (late eighteenth century?) 23
3 John Sartain after George Henry Harlow, *Trial of Queen Katharine* (nineteenth century) 57
4 Richard Westall, *Volumnia Pleading with Coriolanus* (*c.* 1800) 66
5 Joseph Stadler after Joseph Barrow, *Pizarro Act 4 Scene 1* (1800) 71
6 Playbill for the production of *Vortigern* at the Theatre Royal Drury Lane (2 April 1796) 76
7 James Gillray, *Theatrical Mendicants, Relieved* (1809) 108
8 Isaac Cruikshank, *Is This a Rattle Which I See Before Me?* (1809) 110
9 Mary Sackville Hamilton, *Mrs. Siddons's Dress as Hamlet. Act I Scene II* 133
10 Henry Dawe after Thomas Lawrence, *John Philip Kemble as Hamlet* (1827) 143
11 John Flaxman and J. E. Hinchliffe, *Statue of John Philip Kemble as Cato* (1826) 163
12 Thomas Campbell, *Statue of Sarah Siddons* (1845) 164

ACKNOWLEDGEMENTS

I am enormously grateful to the editors of the Shakespeare in the Theatre series, Bridget Escolme, Peter Holland and Farah Karim-Cooper, for inviting me to write this book. I appreciate their confidence in me and have learnt a great deal in completing this volume. I thank Peter Holland for his supportive, generous and constructive feedback on the manuscript at various stages. Sincere thanks are also due to my editors at the Arden Shakespeare, Lara Bateman and Mark Dudgeon, for their patience and support throughout the process of writing this book.

Colleagues in the fields of Shakespeare studies and eighteenth-century theatre history have assisted me in crucial ways in preparing this manuscript. Michael Burden, Jeffrey Kahan, Jack Lynch and Daniel O'Quinn generously shared materials that were foundational to this study. Antonia Forster, Michael Gamer and Damian Walford Davies kindly sent me copies of their publications when I was unable to access libraries at the beginning of the Covid-19 shutdown. My sincere thanks go to them, as well as to Mattie Burkert, Kate Flaherty, Marcie Frank, Lisa Freeman, Trevor Griffiths, Tony Howard, Edel Lamb, Elaine McGirr, Heather McPherson, Lucy Munro, Chelsea Phillips, Leslie Ritchie, Diana Solomon, Tiffany Stern and David Taylor, all of whom have influenced my thinking during the writing of this book. Colleagues in the Department of English at McGill University have been unfailingly supportive, especially Erin Hurley, Michael Nicholson, Derek Nystrom, Peter Sabor, Denis Salter, Myrna Wyatt Selkirk, Alanna Thain and my compassionate Department Chair, Trevor Ponech. I am deeply indebted to the staff of several libraries and archives for their help with research queries, permissions and so on. Special thanks to Erin Blake (Folger Shakespeare Library),

Dale Stinchcomb (Harvard Theatre Collection) and Lonnie Weatherby (McGill University Library).

I have benefited enormously from working with some outstanding research assistants in completing this study. Charlotte Boatner-Doane, Catherine Quirk and, especially, Willow White made important contributions at various stages of the research and writing process, and the final product has been strengthened by their input. I thank the undergraduate and graduate students with whom I have shared my research and my writing process for their enthusiastic response.

This book would not have been completed without the encouragement of various (largely female) writing communities. I am particularly grateful to Meghan Clayards, Aparna Nadig, Monica Popescu, Cecily Raynor and Katie Zien, the members of my McGill writing group, for providing much-needed motivation through the ups and downs of combining writing, teaching, service, parenting and more. The Any Good Thing writing challenge was an important part of this monograph from start to finish.

Friends including Steve Day, Natalie Doyle, Martine Habra, Louise King, George Mogg, Brigitte Pientka, Dirk Schlimm, Lucie Sutherland and many others have offered practical and emotional support to keep me afloat, particularly during the last, difficult months of finishing this volume. Special thanks go to Jen Drouin, my respected Shakespeare colleague, dear friend and all-round partner in crime. I am also deeply grateful to all of the Spencers for nurturing a family connection that is incredibly important to me.

This book is dedicated to my brother, Michael. Reflecting on the fact that he is almost the same number of months younger than me as Kemble was than Siddons has helped me to appreciate the nature of their relationship. My brother's ongoing and unconditional love and support are a daily testament to the way siblings can nourish and sustain each other. And to my children, Emile and Margot: may you also flourish through mutual love and support, always.

A NOTE ON THE TEXT

Daily newspapers are cited by date only. References to weekly and monthly periodicals include the volume and issue number (where available), date and page number. I have consulted primary source materials through a number of electronic databases, including Eighteenth Century Drama and Eighteenth Century Journals (Adam Matthew Digital), Gale Primary Sources, Google Books, the HathiTrust Digital Library and the Internet Archive. Quotations preserve the spelling of the original source, including the variant spellings of Shakespeare's name used during the period. Throughout the text I cite frequently from the *Biographical Dictionary of Actors, Actresses, Musicians, Dancers, Managers & Other Stage Personnel in London, 1660-1800* and the online edition of the *Oxford Dictionary of National Biography*, abbreviated as *BD* and *ODNB*. For performance information, I reference two electronic resources: the *London Stage Database* for performances until the end of the 1799–1800 season and the *London Stage Calendar* for performances from the 1800–1 season onwards, abbreviated as *LSD* and *LSC*.

SERIES PREFACE

Each volume in the *Shakespeare in the Theatre* series focuses on a director or theatre company that has made a significant contribution to Shakespeare production, identifying the artistic and political/social contexts of their work.

The series introduces readers to the work of significant theatre directors and companies whose Shakespeare productions have been transformative in our understanding of his plays in performance. Each volume examines a single figure or company, considering their key productions, rehearsal approaches and their work with other artists (actors, designers, composers). A particular feature of each book is its exploration of the contexts within which these theatre artists have made their Shakespeare productions work. Thus, the series not only considers the ways in which directors and companies produce Shakespeare but also reflects upon their other theatre activities and the broader artistic, cultural and sociopolitical milieu within which their Shakespeare performances and productions have been created. The key to the series' originality, then, is its consideration of Shakespeare production in a range of artistic and broader contexts; in this sense, it decentres Shakespeare from within Shakespeare studies, pointing to the range of people, artistic practices and cultural phenomena that combine to make meaning in the theatre.

Series editors: Peter Holland, Farah Karim-Cooper
and Stephen Purcell

Introduction

Debuts (1775, 1782, 1783)

In a January 2022 article for the BBC which explores Lady Macbeth as a character who has been widely misunderstood, Hanna Flint evokes Sarah Siddons's interpretation of the role over 200 years ago as one that 'broke the mould' and shaped the performances of subsequent generations of actors.[1] That influence can still be felt today. In Joel Coen's 2021 film, Frances McDormand plays the character not as 'overtly "evil"' but as a woman convinced her 'murderous actions are for the good of her hard-working husband'.[2] In discussing her preparation to act the part in an upcoming Broadway production, Ruth Negga describes her desire to counter 'the long-standing demonisation' of Shakespeare's 'fiend-like queen'.[3] Whether or not McDormand and Negga are conscious of their famous predecessor, both of these interpretations have their roots in Siddons's approach to Lady Macbeth, which aimed to create sympathy without condoning the character's immoral actions. Siddons's Lady Macbeth has become iconic, a performance remembered even now as though we had seen it for ourselves. Her brother, John Philip Kemble, acted opposite her as Macbeth, constructing his version of the character through careful textual and historical investigations. He then transferred this approach to his work as theatre manager, becoming the first modern British director (though the word was not used at the time). Kemble's meticulous research and attention to detail (including costume, scenery, music, acting and the blocking of supernumeraries) ensured that his Shakespeare productions were governed by a clear and cohesive directorial vision in a way that was previously unusual but that we now take for granted. Celebrated in their own time, Siddons and Kemble live on in our cultural and theatrical memory. This book analyses their careers to demonstrate how they achieved their status as great Shakespeareans.

Provincial debuts

The story of the careers of Sarah Siddons (born 5 July 1755 in Brecon) and John Philip Kemble (born 1 February 1757 in Prescot) begins with a playbill dated 12 February 1767 announcing a performance of *King Charles the First* (Figure 1). This play, written in imitation of Shakespeare's histories, was acted by Roger Kemble's company of comedians in Worcester. The venue was not a purpose-built theatre but, rather, an inn, the King's Head, and in order to evade legislation that restricted where and how performances could take place, the play was acted free of charge between parts of a musical concert, circumstances which speak to the lowly status of this performance. But although this production was a far cry from what was to be seen on the lofty London stages, two members of its cast would subsequently become the most famous actors of the late-eighteenth-century and early-nineteenth-century stage. The pre-teen performers Miss Kemble, who played the young Princess Elizabeth, and her brother Master J. Kemble, who acted James, Duke of York, would later make their names as Sarah Siddons and John Philip Kemble, the most renowned British actors of their generation, and would be celebrated for their powerful and definitive interpretations of Shakespeare.[4]

The cast of the 1767 performance of *King Charles the First* also featured Sarah and John's parents, Roger and Sarah Kemble, and their younger sister, Frances, as well as the actor William Siddons, who would later marry the young Sarah Kemble. Sarah and John (hereafter referred to as Siddons and Kemble for the sake of simplicity) were born into a formidable

> APPENDIX.
>
> (A).
>
> *Worcester, February 12th, 1767.*
>
> Mr. Kemble's Company of Comedians.
>
> At the Theatre, at the King's Head, this Evening, will be performed, A CONCERT OF MUSICK, to begin exactly at Six o'Clock.
>
> Tickets to be had at the usual places.
>
> Between the parts of the CONCERT, will be presented, *gratis*, a Celebrated Historical Play, (never performed here), called
>
> KING CHARLES THE FIRST.
>
> The Characters to be dressed in ancient habits, according to the fashion of those times.
>
> | | |
> |---|---|
> | The part of *King Charles*, | Mr. Jones. |
> | *Duke of Richmond*, | Mr. Siddons. |
> | *Marquis of Lindsay*, | Mr. Salisbury. |
> | *Bishop Juxon*, | Mr. Fowler. |
> | *General Fairfax*, | Mr. Kemble. |
> | *Colonel Ireton*, | Mr. Crump. |
> | *Colonel Tomlinson*, | Mr. Hughes. |
> | The part of *Oliver Cromwell*, | Mr. Vaughan. |
> | *Servant*, | Mr. Butler. |
>
> *James, Duke of York*, (afterwards King of England), Master J. KEMBLE.
>
> The *Duke of Gloucester*, (King Charles's younger Son), Miss Fanny Kemble.
>
> *Serjeant Bradshaw*, (Judge of the pretended High Court of Justice), Mr. Burton.
>
> The young *Princess Elizabeth*, Miss Kemble.
>
> *Lady Fairfax*, Mrs. Kemble.
>
> The part of the *Queen*, Mrs. Vaughan.
>
> Singing between the Acts by Mrs. Fowler, and Miss Kemble.
>
> To which will be added, a Comedy, called
>
> THE MINOR.
>
> And on Saturday next, the 14th inst. will be again presented the above Tragedy, with a Farce that will be expressed in the Bills for that day.
>
> *** The days of Performance, are Mondays, Thursdays, and Saturdays.

FIGURE 1 *Reproduction of a playbill for 12 February 1767 documenting an early performance by Siddons and Kemble with their parents' company in Worcester.* From An Authentic Narrative of Mr. Kemble's Retirement from the Stage *(London: John Miller, 1817), 72. Digitized by the Internet Archive, original held by the University of California Libraries.*

theatrical family. Roger Kemble met and married Sarah Ward while performing with her parents' touring company in the Midlands, and he eventually took over that troupe in 1766. The siblings may have acquired their penchant for Shakespeare from their grandparents, whose company staged a fundraising performance of *Othello* on 9 September 1746 to restore the memorial to Shakespeare in the Holy Trinity Church, said to be the first recorded performance of a Shakespeare play in Stratford-upon-Avon. The older Sarah Ward was the daughter of Stephen Butcher and his wife (name unknown) who were also provincial performers, and it was apparently from this side of the family that Siddons and Kemble inherited 'their aristocratic bearing, their Roman features, and their theatrical genius'.[5]

Roger and Sarah Kemble had a total of twelve children (Siddons and Kemble were the eldest), all born at various locations to which their theatre company toured. The Kembles apparently did not want their offspring to take to the stage, though all of the surviving children did, and all but one married performers. To remove them from the world of the theatre, Siddons was sent to work as a lady's maid in 1770 (primarily in an attempt to separate her from William Siddons as the Kembles did not approve of his relationship with their daughter), and Kemble was dispatched to Douai, France, to train as a Catholic priest in 1771. While both learned skills that would be important for their stage careers in these professions (aristocratic deportment for Siddons and classical declamation for Kemble), their time outside the theatrical world was short-lived. Following her marriage to William, Siddons made a name for herself among the aristocratic elite while acting at Cheltenham in the summer of 1774. Siddons encouraged Crump and Chamberlain, the managers of the provincial company with which she had been acting, to engage Kemble in early 1776, following his return from France.

Eighteenth-century Britain boasted a vibrant provincial theatre scene. Strolling companies toured regions of the country, performing in halls, inns and even barns. Roger Kemble's troupe was one such company, acting throughout the West Midlands. These theatrical circuits allowed citizens of even relatively small towns to see performances on a regular basis. Larger towns had purpose-built performance venues and from the 1760s onwards many of these received the designation Theatre Royal, indicating that they had government approval to stage drama, and further developing and elevating regional performance. The London theatre world was also tightly controlled. There were only three patent theatres, the Theatres Royal of Drury Lane and Covent Garden, which operated from September to June, and the Haymarket, which opened in the summer months when the two main theatres were closed. By the time that Siddons and Kemble made their names, it was common for star actors to tour the provinces over the summer, allowing audiences outside London to experience their celebrated performances and further cementing their fame. The London theatre world generally looked down on performance outside the capital, particularly that of itinerant companies, as unsophisticated. For example, Henry Bate, sent by Drury Lane manager David Garrick to observe Siddons at Cheltenham in the summer of 1775 with a view to recruiting her to act at Drury Lane, wrote of observing the actress play Rosalind in 'a barn about three yards over and consequently under almost every disadvantage'.[6] He expressed surprise that she 'had contracted no strolling habits', despite having 'been up on the stage from her cradle', instead noting the refinement of 'her ease, figure and manner'.[7] In fact, the experience Siddons and Kemble had obtained both through their many early provincial performances and by observing at first-hand the workings of touring theatre companies was crucial to their later success.

Siddons's London debuts

Siddons's first appearance at Drury Lane on 29 December 1775 as Portia in *The Merchant of Venice* was not the stuff of legend. Indeed, this great Shakespearean actress did not immediately excel in a Shakespearean role in the capital and, despite her later fame, she did not take the London theatre world by storm straightaway. At the end of the season, she was dismissed and did not appear in London again until 1782. Siddons's personal circumstances must have made it challenging to make such an important career move at this time. She had given birth to her second child just a few weeks before and had then moved her family to London and begun rehearsing with Garrick's company. Furthermore, Drury Lane was very different from any of the venues in which Siddons had previously performed. It seated about 2,000 spectators, compared to the few hundred at most that the converted malt house in Cheltenham could have accommodated, and therefore necessitated a different acting technique.

Several other reasons have been posited for Siddons's failure in this first season, and examining these gives us some sense of both her acting style and audience taste early in her career. First of all, the character of Portia was deemed an unsuitable one. The actress's early negotiations with Garrick included a list of twenty-three roles in her command, six of which were marked as ones she favoured, including Portia, suggesting an early preference for this part.[8] However, in her recollections, quoted by her biographer, Thomas Campbell, Siddons claimed, perhaps with the benefit of hindsight, that Portia was 'a character in which it was not likely that I should excite any great sensation'.[9] Another biographer, James Boaden, felt that while Siddons had Portia's 'taste, her sensibility, her reflecting dignity, her unexpected powers of almost masculine declamation', the role contained 'nothing to alarm, to excite, to fire with indignation, or subdue by tenderness'.[10] Thus, as Portia, Siddons could only 'convince the reason', whereas the actress needed 'to raise an interest by piercing the heart'.[11] Boaden suggests that Siddons already excelled in the declamatory style for which she later became famous when performing Shakespearean heroines. He also implies not that Siddons could not move her audience but, rather, that the part chosen for her did not allow her to do so, suggesting she had also begun to make pathetic roles a central component of her repertoire. These affective parts proved enduringly popular. Such characters, generally found in the Restoration and eighteenth-century tragic repertoire, were placed in highly moving situations and generated an extremely emotional response from the audience. A further problem for Siddons was that the Drury Lane company already featured several important actresses who, in line with the theatrical tradition of the period, owned these emotive roles, thus effectively barring the new actress from performing them. Mary Ann Yates and Elizabeth Younge were the current stars and occupied 'all that was worth doing in tragedy and sober comedy', whereas Frances Abington excelled in 'the sparkling gaiety or pungent satire' of lighter comedy.[12] Siddons would have to wait until Yates and Younge left Drury Lane at the end of the 1770s in order to achieve greater prominence on the London theatre scene.

Theatre history has treated Siddons's Portia as her debut on the London stage but in fact her first performance in the capital had occurred a few days earlier. Critical attention now tends to focus on the mainpieces acted in the period, the full-length plays that made up the bulk of an evening's entertainment. However, theatres at this time staged a bill of performances each night which combined a mainpiece with an afterpiece – a brief, often comic play – along with other forms of entertainment (such as entr'acte songs and dances). Although afterpieces were shorter than mainpieces, they were not necessarily less important to the audience and often proved to be the most popular element of the playbill. One such afterpiece was *The Jubilee*, which Garrick revived on 26 December, casting Siddons as Venus, and which had many more performances that season.[13] *The Jubilee* was a farce written by Garrick himself that both poked fun at the Shakespearean celebration that he had organized in Stratford-upon-Avon in 1769 and staged for a London audience the procession of Shakespearean characters that was rained off during the notoriously wet weekend in the Midlands. The piece culminates with the crowning of Shakespeare's statue by Tragedy and Comedy, and a celebratory roundelay sung by assorted graces and muses, including Venus. Siddons was not chosen to embody a Shakespearean character in the pageant at the heart of *The Jubilee* because these parts were already identified with members of the Drury Lane company who acted them when the plays themselves were performed. The role of Venus, however, did connect Siddons with Shakespeare in the public imagination as she participated in this theatrical celebration of the dramatist.

Siddons's only other Shakespearean role that season was as Lady Anne to Garrick's Richard III, which she acted three times. Given her later reputation as a tragedienne, the actress might have been expected to excel in this part, but the *London Magazine* described her as '*lamentable*'.[14] Although Siddons later struck her spectators with terror, for example as Lady Macbeth, her biographers' claims that she was intimidated by Garrick's ferocity as Richard are plausible given Frances Burney's comments on a performance just a few years earlier: 'Garrick was sublimely horrible! – Good Heaven – how he made me shudder whenever he appeared!'[15] Siddons's performance must also have been overshadowed by the fact that the celebrated Garrick was acting the character (with which he was closely identified) for the final time in his long career. The actress also created the role of Emily in Hannah Cowley's new play *The Runaway*, which had a successful run of seventeen performances that season. In this play she showcased her skills in comedy, but Campbell suggests that a moment in the play in which the heroine is 'accused of having been a strolling player' would have been 'mortifying' for Siddons.[16]

Siddons returned to the provinces after her dismissal from Drury Lane not as a strolling player but, rather, as a member of established regional companies. She acted with Joseph Younger and George Mattocks's company at Liverpool and Manchester and on Tate Wilkinson's Yorkshire circuit before engaging at Bath in the autumn of 1778. It was at Bath and Bristol that she honed her craft, mastering over one hundred roles, including many that she later made famous on the London stage. When she left Bath in 1782 to return to Drury Lane (now under the management of Richard Brinsley Sheridan), she delivered a farewell speech to the audience in which she offered 'Three Reasons – for her quitting this theatre', bringing her three children onto the stage.[17] When Siddons appeared again in London on 10 October 1782, her choice of role, the title character in the successful pathetic tragedy *Isabella; or, The Fatal Marriage* (written by Thomas Southerne in 1694 and adapted by Garrick in 1757), was apparently more judicious than choosing Portia in 1775. Furthermore, Siddons's oldest child, Henry, acted alongside her. In contrast to her earlier London debut, the actress had now begun to foreground her maternal status in performance, a strategy which contributed to her success this time around: as Campbell noted, 'with her beautiful little son, Henry, in her hand, she looked the very personage'.[18] From Boaden's comment that in this play Siddons acted 'with pathos that will never be excelled', we can deduce that the problem identified with her performance of Portia – that it focused on declamation at the expense of passion – was rectified with this choice of role.[19] Indeed, the rest of the actress's parts that season were largely in the same pathetic vein. With Yates and Younge now acting at Covent Garden, Siddons was free to take up the lead female roles in the recent and contemporary repertoire that she had played in the provinces. In fact, she did not perform any Shakespearean parts in the 1782–3 season.

Siddons's next part was Euphrasia in *The Grecian Daughter* (Arthur Murphy, 1772) on 28 October. In this tragedy, 'she assumed the graces of filial piety' rather than Isabella's wifely obedience and showcased 'a royal loftiness . . . and a look of majesty' which later came to be hallmarks of her performance of some Shakespearean heroines.[20] The fact that Yates was brought out at Covent Garden in the same role in a deliberately competitive move suggests that Siddons was now seen as a major threat. She then tackled the principal characters in two of Nicholas Rowe's she-tragedies (dramas focused on the sufferings of the central female character and designed to move the audience), Jane Shore in the play of the same name (1714) on 8 November and Calista in *The Fair Penitent* (1702) on 29 November. Boaden recorded the powerful effect Siddons had on her spectators when she acted Jane Shore: 'I well remember (how is it possible I should ever forget?) the *sobs*, the *shrieks*, among the tenderer part of her audiences; or those *tears*, which manhood, at first, struggled to suppress, but at length grew proud of indulging.'[21] Campbell noted of Siddons's Calista that 'her success in the character was another large step in her popularity'.[22] On 14 December she played Belvidera in the perennially popular tragedy *Venice Preserved* (Thomas Otway, 1682). She had acted the role at Cheltenham in 1774, when a group of fashionable playgoers had attended in anticipation of 'a treat of the ludicrous, in the misrepresentation of the piece' by a provincial company.[23] But instead of laughter, Siddons's performance provoked such weeping in the group of playgoers 'that they were unpresentable in the morning, and were confined to their rooms with headachs'.[24] Although doubtless exaggerated, this anecdote confirms the emotional power of Siddons's performance in this character. The actress's ability to portray strength and pathos as Belvidera, who plays an active role in the political plot but eventually goes mad at her treatment by her husband, Jaffier, made the role a huge success for her on the London stage as well: the *Morning Post* went so far as to claim that 'there did not appear a *single error* in her performance'.[25] On 18 March 1783, Siddons tackled Zara in William Congreve's only tragedy, *The Mourning Bride* (1697), another character that she had acted successfully in the regions before bringing her interpretation to the London stage. William Godwin later pronounced that 'her magnificence in the part was inexpressible' and 'not inferior even to her *Lady Macbeth*'.[26]

There were a number of markers of Siddons's success on the occasion of her reappearance at Drury Lane in 1782: a fashion apparently sprang up at that time for breakfasting near the theatre 'in order to be among the first to queue up for seats'; visitors 'thronged' to see William Hamilton's portrait of Siddons as Isabella, which also featured her son Henry, even before the painting was finished; Queen Charlotte appointed Siddons 'reading preceptress' to the princesses (her daughters with King George III); and she was 'highly gratified' by being given Garrick's dressing room as a result of her accomplishments.[27] Towards the end of the season, the *Morning Herald* reported on Siddons's financial success: originally engaged by the managers at £10 per week, she was subsequently allowed 'to fix her own terms in future', said to be £20 per week for the following season.[28] Siddons's major achievements were a result of both talent and hard work. She acted on half of the roughly 190 nights of performance of that season, including 22 appearances as Isabella, 14 as Jane Shore, 14 as Calista, 13 as Belvidera and 11 as Euphrasia.[29]

Robert Shaughnessy's comment that 'there could hardly have been a greater contrast between Siddons's ignominious departure from Drury Lane in 1776 and her triumphant return there six years later' is typical of the way in which biographers have portrayed the actress's return to London in 1782 as the polar opposite of her ill-fated 1775 debut.[30] Siddons herself characterized this second appearance as a triumph over her earlier failure, describing the 'nervous agitation' and 'dreadful suspense' she experienced before her 'fiery trial' and contrasting these emotions with the 'reiterated shouts and plaudits' with which her performance was greeted.[31] Another aspect of this contrast lies in the fact that, unlike in her first London season, Siddons did not attempt any Shakespearean roles. Instead, the characters in which she triumphed were those of the Restoration and the eighteenth-century repertoire. Campbell pronounced Southerne, Otway and Rowe, the authors of several of these dramas, as 'entitled to our respect' as successors of Shakespeare, and Boaden drew a link between Southerne's *Isabella* and *King Lear*.[32] Thus, although the plays in which Siddons was successful in this second London season may seem utterly un-Shakespearean to us, perhaps eighteenth-century audiences saw a connection. Furthermore, these roles remained central to the actress's repertoire: Isabella, Euphrasia and Belvidera were performed as part of the selection of Siddons's best characters in her final season on the stage.

Kemble's London debut

When John Philip Kemble made his Drury Lane debut on 30 September 1783, one year after Siddons's return to the capital, the London audience was well prepared for his arrival by the popularity of his older sister. According to Boaden, the actress took an active interest in promoting her brother: 'Mrs. Siddons had, with becoming zeal, prepared her friends to welcome her elder brother; and as she had herself acted repeatedly with him, there could be no reasonable doubt of the opinion she expressed of his talents.'[33] Siddons had supported her brother's burgeoning career in the provinces, encouraging Younger and Mattocks to hire him at Liverpool and Manchester in 1777 (and apparently also bailing him out when he found himself imprisoned for debt), and her success on Tate Wilkinson's circuit inspired the Yorkshire manager to employ Kemble in 1778 in the hope of reaping a similar financial reward from his acting.[34] Just as Siddons had submitted a list of her roles to Bate to share with Garrick, Kemble sent Wilkinson a catalogue of sixty-eight tragic and fifty-eight comic parts, twenty-nine of which were marked as his favourites, demonstrating mastery of an impressively varied repertoire.[35] Kemble then spent two seasons acting in Dublin and elsewhere in Ireland, appearing alongside Siddons in the summer of 1783 as he had done in Liverpool and Manchester a few years earlier. However, Kemble's first appearance in London was in no way as sensational as Siddons's second debut as Isabella in the preceding season: 'The impression that he did make at first was not of the brilliant and overwhelming character which attended on his more gifted sister.'[36]

When Kemble stepped onto the Drury Lane stage, audiences immediately recognized the family resemblance, exclaiming 'how very like his sister!'[37] But each actor had a different impact on the audience: 'She swept after her all hearts, passions, sympathies; he had gained admiration and intellectual interest.'[38] Ultimately, 'the advantage was with her' and Siddons's emphasis on passion won out over Kemble's focus on intellect for the audience at this time.[39] Kemble perhaps deliberately adopted a somewhat different style than Siddons in order to differentiate himself from his sister in an attempt to achieve success on his own terms. But the relationship remained perceptible to spectators: in a review of his debut London performance, the *Morning Chronicle* pronounced Kemble 'a true brother of Mrs. Siddons' who 'proves his relationship to his sister, in ability as well as in blood' and was therefore 'a valuable acquisition to the theatre'.[40]

Kemble's debut role was Hamlet, a part which became one of the most important of his career. Boaden noted the difficulty of performing such a famous character: 'If he agreed with his predecessors and contemporaries, it would be said that he wanted originality; if he differed essentially, in either conception or execution, he was open to the charge of self-sufficiency and presumption.'[41] This is borne out by the fact that while Kemble did in fact introduce several new elements to the part, his critics derogatorily called these changes, particularly those made to the text or the actor's interpretation of it, 'NEW READINGS'.[42] The alterations made by Kemble, including vocal delivery, physical action and costuming, will be discussed in Chapter 5 of this volume, as will Siddons's interpretation of Hamlet. Kemble's sensitivity to criticism of the presumptuousness of his innovations is evidenced by the fact that he originally omitted Hamlet's advice to the players' speech, 'upon the modest principle, that he must first be admitted a master in the faculty, before he presumed to censure the faults of others'.[43] He later restored the lines. Proof of the success of his performance is seen in the same way as with Siddons: John Henderson was brought out as Hamlet at Covent Garden in order to compete, and the rival actor in fact even adopted some of Kemble's innovations.[44] Kemble faced the same issue as Siddons in terms of access to roles because senior actors such as William Smith, John Palmer and William Brereton 'were unwilling to give up the major parts they were accustomed to play and by tradition could not be deprived of them'.[45]

Like Siddons, Kemble's other parts this season were largely non-Shakespearean. He next played the title role in *Edward the Black Prince* (William Shirley, 1750), a play described as a 'strange rhapsody of tragic shreds and patches' from Shakespearean dramas such as *Hamlet* and *Richard III*.[46] Given his burgeoning career as a Shakespearean actor, Kemble might have been expected to succeed in such a work but, instead, he was considered uneven in the title role: 'In the impassioned scenes he was nervous, and dignified; but in those less interesting, offensively emphatic, and monotonous.'[47] This irregularity was particularly evident in his attempts to manage the emotional tone of the play, in distinction to Siddons, who was praised for the pathetic dimension of her acting. As the comic villain Sir Giles Overreach in *A New Way to Pay Old Debts* (Philip Massinger, c. 1625), Boaden found him inferior to Henderson: 'He had not the bustle, the ardour, the grasp of the man; and his exultation was not so triumphant.'[48] On 28 April 1784, Kemble acted Cato in Joseph Addison's 1713 tragedy, one of the Roman roles that would become so central to his career, the most famous of which, Coriolanus, will be discussed in Chapter 2.

Kemble's Shakespearean parts in his debut London season included Richard III, which he acted for the first time in the capital on 6 November 1783. Boaden claimed that this role improved later in Kemble's career: 'It had then, by no means the effect, which he subsequently gave to it.'[49] Furthermore, audiences remembered 'the dreadful energy of Garrick' in the part that had startled Siddons several years earlier when she acted Lady Anne.[50] However, Kemble's Richard displayed 'greater *subtlety*' than his predecessors.[51] He also played Shylock on 22 January 1784, and the following day the *Morning Chronicle* reported that he 'was very favourably received', further noting that, as in the other roles he had played that season, he 'displayed a mixture of merit and extravagance, but less of the latter than in any other part we have seen him play'.[52] Kemble's 'extravagance' seemed to lie in the 'new readings' he proposed, just as he had done in *Hamlet*.[53] Hamlet, Richard and Shylock were parts he had played in Dublin, where, as 'his admired sister' had done in London, Kemble had 'made tragedies once more the fashion'.[54]

In describing his success in Dublin, a critic in the *Gentleman's Magazine* praised Kemble's ability 'to give scenes, particularly Shakspeare's, a new and more emphatical grace than I have ever known imparted to them by any other performer'.[55] Once he was able to take over the major Shakespearean roles from established London actors, Kemble would bring these skills to the capital as well.

Debuting together

Siddons and Kemble appeared together for the first time on the London stage on 22 November 1783, acting wife and husband in the lead roles of Edward Moore's *The Gamester* (1753). In this affective domestic tragedy, Mrs Beverley strives to save her husband, who is essentially good though addicted to gambling, but despite her efforts Beverley eventually poisons himself in despair. Although denigrated by some critics as too bourgeois (purists still believed that tragedy should focus on the fortunes of eminent figures), *The Gamester* was extremely popular with playgoers because of its focus on figures drawn from everyday life and the strong emotions their situation provoked. Campbell writes of Siddons's and Kemble's performance that 'their success was brilliant' and explains that when they acted together, 'there was a pleasing harmony in their manner, although hers was the more natural; and, side by side, they appeared the two noblest specimens that could be produced of the breed of England'.[56] Although Mrs Beverley was another pathetic character 'of fond suffering virtue', Siddons was able to incorporate flashes of the power and grandeur for which she later became famous: Boaden describes her refutation of the nefarious Stukely's attempts to arouse her suspicions and jealousy, in which 'her eye . . . "flamed amazement"'.[57] Kemble's performance both showed 'his critical judgment of the meaning of each sentence', paying the same close attention to the text as he had done in *Hamlet*, and 'gave to Beverley points of superior efficacy in stirring the bosom', demonstrating that he could also perform passionate roles.[58] The popularity of *The Gamester* paved the way for the siblings' first joint London appearance in a Shakespeare play, *King John*, on 10 December 1783, a production that will be discussed in Chapter 1.

Kemble chose *The Countess of Salisbury* (Hall Hartson, 1767), a tragedy based on Thomas Leland's 1762 medieval romance novel *Longsword*, for his benefit on 13 April 1784 in order to act alongside his sister. As part of their contract, actors were accorded one benefit night per season, an evening on which they kept the night's profits, minus the house production costs. Benefit nights were designed to showcase actors' popularity and performers usually chose either roles in which they had already been successful or parts they had not yet attempted that would provide playgoers with some novelty, in the hope of drawing large audiences to the theatre and thereby maximizing their profits. When Siddons had appeared as the Countess of Salisbury opposite Smith on 6 March, the *Morning Chronicle* reported that 'even her great acting could not keep it up from ridicule'.[59] However, when she performed with her brother, Kemble's benefit took a very respectable £290 15s.[60] Siddons's status was already so high that, unusually, she received two benefit performances each season, the first of which was 'clear', that is, free of house charges. In 1783–4, for her first benefit Siddons played Lady Randolph in John Home's tragedy *Douglas* (1756) on 22 December 1783. This choice of role was perceived as a direct challenge to one of her rivals, Ann Crawford (formerly Barry). Siddons excelled in depicting the character's maternal grief and the receipts for the performance were £303 8s. 6d. For her second benefit on 24 April 1784, she chose a drama in which Kemble could appear alongside her, *Tancred and Sigismunda* (James Thomson, 1745). In this tragedy, Siddons played a character torn between a sense of duty to her father and her love for Tancred. The *New Spectator* pronounced that the siblings played the lead roles 'with such happiness of expression, as to leave few, if any, dry eyes in the house'.[61] The performance earned £324 1s., the highest amount taken for a benefit at Drury Lane that season. While Boaden and Campbell felt that *The Countess of Salisbury* and *Tancred and Sigismunda* were beneath the actors, especially Siddons, these were roles that Siddons and Kemble had played to great acclaim outside London earlier in their careers.[62] Siddons had acted both the Countess and Sigismunda at Bath and had performed the latter role even earlier, at Manchester in 1778. When *The Countess of Salibsury* was advertised for Kemble's benefit night, the press noted that 'those who have seen Mr. Kemble at York and in Dublin, speak of his Earl Alwin as a very capital performance'.[63] It is notable that both actors decided to appear together for their benefits this season, suggesting that they believed the power of a joint performance would be a draw for playgoers and would earn them more money. As we have seen, the Drury Lane accounts demonstrate that this was the case. Acting together was an important foundation for Siddons and Kemble, as I will explore further in the next chapter.

1

Acting together (the 1780s)

The play in which Siddons and Kemble had first appeared together on the London stage, *The Gamester*, remained an important part of the siblings' repertoire. It had nine performances in 1783–4 and was chosen for Siddons's first and Kemble's second appearance of the next season on 5 October 1784. But this performance met with 'strong opposition, on account of some reports having been circulated to [Siddons's] disadvantage, concerning her conduct during her last visit to Dublin'.[1] Ellen Donkin explains that during a summer trip to Ireland, Siddons 'had been accused (unjustly, as it turned out) by two fellow actors, West Digges and William Brereton, of first refusing to perform in their benefits and then of charging an exorbitant sum for appearing'.[2] Siddons was received with 'a very distinguished mark of disapprobation' and she and her brother were forced to leave the stage.[3] She was eventually allowed to address the audience to offer some explanation but then needed to compose herself backstage, delaying the start of the play for 'a considerable period of time'.[4] When she did appear, the audience 'could perceive that the lady supported herself with a great degree of firmness under this very awful trial – a trial which, in a great measure, determined her future fame'.[5] Donkin characterizes this event as marking a 'power shift' in relations between actress and audience in which Siddons ensured that her 'terms for appearing onstage without harassment were unconditionally accepted'.[6] She further notes that 'Brereton (correctly) felt himself in danger of being replaced' by Kemble as Siddons's stage partner.[7] The incident thus suggests that these joint performances had high stakes for the theatrical culture of the day.

A significant factor that contributed to Siddons's and Kemble's choice of roles in both Shakespearean and eighteenth-century drama early in their careers was the theatrical convention of actors' ownership over specific roles. This explains why the siblings were unable to perform in London all of the parts they had identified as comprising their repertoires in the lists they sent to Garrick and Wilkinson early in their provincial careers. By the time of her second London debut, Siddons's main competitors, Yates and Younge, were no longer acting at Drury Lane, whereas Kemble had to wait until the late 1780s for his rivals to leave the stage. This aspect of stage practice meant that Kemble was not always 'permitted to strengthen either himself or his sister by acting with her' at the beginning of his career.[8] A case in point is *Macbeth*, in which the siblings eventually delivered perhaps their most significant joint performances. Siddons first played Lady Macbeth at Drury Lane for her benefit on 2 February 1785 with William Smith as Macbeth. Kemble chose the same piece for his benefit on 31 March 1785, performing alongside his sister. But he subsequently acted the part of Macduff until 16 October 1788, when he could finally take over the lead role on the retirement of its previous owner.

King John

King John was the first Shakespeare play in which the siblings appeared together on the London stage. While not often performed today, it was a popular piece in the eighteenth century. Major actresses found in Constance a strong role as her fight for her son Arthur's claim to the crown and her grief at his death allowed them to perform the powerful emotions so highly regarded at the time. Although they had acted alongside one another in other Shakespearean dramas such as *Hamlet* and *Othello* in Liverpool and Manchester in 1777 and 1778,

Siddons and Kemble had not appeared together in *King John* in the provinces. According to the *London Stage*, coincidentally, the siblings had both appeared in the play for the first time on the same date but at separate locations: Kemble as King John in Dublin and Siddons as Constance in Bath on 18 April 1782. Their first joint London performance of *King John* took place on 10 December 1783 by royal command. Campbell wrote of George III's 'wish to see the Siddons and the Kemble together, in the tragedy of "King John"', but the choice of play may have been down to the manager rather than the King.[9] Kemble's rival, Henderson, had acted the part several times during his career and as recently as 29 March of that year at Covent Garden in a benefit for Siddons's competitor, Yates, who appeared as Constance. Thus by bringing out his rising stars in this play, Sheridan was attempting to compete directly with the rival theatre.

The *Morning Herald* noted that Sheridan's staging showed 'an unusual stile of splendor' and implied that it must have been expensive, suggesting that the manager wanted to put special emphasis on this production.[10] But despite the care taken over the performance, the reception of *King John* was somewhat mixed. The *Public Advertiser* claimed that Siddons's Constance produced in the audience 'no kindred Emotion' and that Kemble '*failed*'.[11] The *General Evening Post* was more positive, praising the 'conspicuous talents' that Siddons brought to the role and stating that Kemble 'appeared to great advantage in King John'.[12] Campbell expressed some surprise about such 'truculent' reviews of the 1783 production and considered it possible that Siddons 'was not at this period the same perfect *Lady Constance*, such as I saw her some ten years afterwards'.[13] Here he gets at an important historiographical problem in the writing of performance history: that an actor's rendition of a character will, of course, change over time. This is particularly significant in the case of a long theatrical career, such as those of Siddons and Kemble. Indeed, Campbell wrote of Siddons's 'boast, that she gradually improved in all her characters, and that she never repeated her performance of any part, without studying it anew to the utmost of her power and leisure'.[14] The theatre historian therefore must be attentive to the specificities of each performance of the same role at different points in time. Biographies such as Boaden's and Campbell's that synthesize descriptions of particular roles over many years can be supplemented with newspaper reviews of the specific performance in question. Siddons, however, may have been unusual in her continued engagement with the parts she played, as eighteenth-century actors generally did not expect to change their performances much from year to year. David Rostron notes that 'Kemble seems to have arrived at a conception of a role or of a play, and then to have fixed it almost immutably for the rest of his career', as demonstrated by a comment in the *Times* in 1815: 'It is the necessary consequence of having maturely studied a given part, and arrived at a high degree of excellence in performing it, that the portrait, once finished, admits no novelty which is not a defect.'[15] Discussions of Siddons's and Kemble's acting in this volume seek to remain attuned to the nuances of specific moments of performance while also exploring the roles across the actors' careers.

Kemble revived *King John* in 1800 as manager of Drury Lane and again in 1804 during his first season at Covent Garden. Much of the extant commentary and scholarship examines these productions. Maarten Van Dijk explains why the play became a key component of the repertoire under Kemble's management, noting that it 'lent itself to the occasional grand revival, with new costumes and sets, which were a Kemble speciality'.[16] In evaluating their performances in this play across Siddons's and Kemble's careers as a whole, Campbell and Boaden suggest that they were ultimately successful in *King John* because they each assumed a role particularly suited to their individual strengths as performers. Campbell described Siddons as 'the embodied image of maternal love and intrepidity; of wronged and righteous feeling; of proud grief and majestic desolation'.[17] Much of this characterization can be seen in an image of Siddons as Constance from the first half of her career (Figure 2).

FIGURE 2 Mrs. Siddons as Constance *(late eighteenth century?)*. ART File S568 no.54 (size S), image 27865. *Used by permission of the Folger Shakespeare Library.*

Boaden praised Kemble's 'cold-blooded, hesitating, cowardly and creeping villainy'.[18] Siddons demonstrated her strength in performing grief and indignation, whereas Kemble assumed an air of dignified treachery. *King John* offered roles in which each actor could excel while in fact limiting the interaction between Siddons and Kemble on stage. The fact that the dominant current of feeling in this play is not romantic may also have aided the siblings' success.

The two actors not only performed very different characters but also relied on distinct methods to realize their interpretations. In her account of performing Constance, Siddons described how she achieved and, more importantly, given her character's sporadic appearance, sustained the emotions necessary for the part:

> Whenever I was called upon to personate the character of *Constance*, I never, from the beginning of the play to the end of my part in it, once suffered my dressing-room door to be closed in order that my attention might be constantly fixed on those distressing events which, by this means, I could plainly hear going on upon the stage, the terrible effects of which progress were to be represented by me. Moreover, I never omitted to place myself, with *Arthur* in my hand, to hear the march, when, upon the reconciliation of England and France, they entered the gates of Angiers to ratify the contract of marriage between the *Dauphin* and *Lady Blanche;* because the sickening sounds of that march would usually cause the bitter tears of rage, disappointment, betrayed confidence, baffled ambition, and, above all, the agonizing feelings of maternal affection to gush into my eyes. In short, the spirit of the whole drama took possession of my mind and frame, by my attention being incessantly riveted to the passing scenes.[19]

Siddons needed to remain connected to the play, even while her character was not on stage, in order to deliver an affectively striking performance. This immersive approach to acting was not common in the eighteenth century: in 1763, Susanna Cibber, one of Siddons's most significant predecessors, was criticized for dropping character while on stage by curtseying to ladies in the boxes during a performance of *Hamlet*.[20]

Kemble took a more studious approach to his preparation of the role. He was instructed by Thomas Sheridan (himself previously successful as King John) who read the part to

Kemble 'very nearly as he used to play it'.[21] Sheridan was known as an orator as well as an actor (and the father of the Drury Lane manager), and his focus on oral delivery was appreciated by Kemble. The younger actor also took up his mentor's focus on 'the leading trait, or passion, of John's character', and Kemble made the 'mental conflict ... between a desire to get the murder [of Arthur] done, and the desire not to think or talk of it' central to his interpretation.[22] Though they used different means to attain their goals, both Siddons and Kemble achieved powerful emotional effects. And both evoked the same imagery in their performance, though to different ends: Siddons appeared as 'desperate and ferocious as a hunted tigress in defence of her young', while Kemble employed a 'tiger-like prowl to and fro ... as he eyed his young victim'.[23]

Siddons's method of keeping the dressing room door open in order to receive the emotional impact of the action taking place on stage while she was off it was key to her ability to render the 'terrible surprise' of the opening lines of Act III ('GONE to be married! gone to swear a peace! / False blood to false blood joine'd! Gone to be friends!'), when Constance learns that the French King has abandoned her cause and that peace will be brokered with the English through the marriage of Blanche to the Dauphin.[24] When later in the scene she '*Throws herself on the ground*' with the lines 'here I and sorrow sit; / Here is my throne, bid kings come bow to it', critics recognized the moment as a high point of the play.[25] Actress, playwright and critic Elizabeth Inchbald, for example, wrote that when uttered by Siddons, these lines seemed 'like a triumphant reference to her own potent skill in the delineation of woe'.[26] When, on the subsequent entrance of the new allies and the announcement of the marriage of Blanche to the Dauphin, Constance declares this 'A wicked day, and not a holy day!', Siddons gave, according to Boaden, an unequalled impression.[27] The actress herself described it as a 'frantic and appalling exclamation'.[28] Her cursing of Austria as a coward was full of 'withering contempt, that clogged the very *name* of Lymoges', and was accompanied by an unforgettable look, action and tone.[29] Siddons, however, wrote of the 'difficulty . . . of representing with tempered rage and dignified contempt the biting sarcasm' directed at Austria.[30]

In her description of the final scene, Siddons makes clear why the character appealed to her and why, perhaps, it appealed to the audience. Although Constance is thought of as ambitious, she is, according to the actress, 'ambitious only for her son'.[31] Arthur is her only motivation for pursuing hereditary sovereignty: 'Not one regret for lost regal power or splendour ever escapes from her lips . . . all other considerations are annihilated in the grievous recollections of motherly love.'[32] Maternal passion was considered much more properly feminine than naked ambition and so this role was in one sense a relatively straightforward one for Siddons to play. She could build on the audience's knowledge of her own maternity and did not have to wrestle with the morality of female ambition, as she later did with Lady Macbeth.[33] Campbell pointed to apparent contrasts in the actress's performance: 'With what unutterable tenderness was her brow bent over her pretty *Arthur* at one moment, and in the next how nobly drawn back, in a look at her enemies that dignified her vituperation.'[34] However, Siddons saw these two types of action as of a piece, as her comments quoted earlier make clear: her scorn for her enemies is entirely motivated by her love of her son.

Critics noted two significant scenes in Kemble's performance of this play. In the first, when King John discusses the killing of Arthur with Hubert (3.3), William Hazlitt noted that the audience 'saw instantly, and before a syllable was uttered, partly from the change of countenance and partly from the arrangement of the scene [Arthur was visible downstage as his fate was being discussed], the purpose which had entered his mind to murder the young Prince'.[35] The remainder of the scene, however 'wanted the filling up, the true and master-touches, the deep piercing heart-felt tones of nature'.[36] At the end of his career at least (the review is from 1816), Kemble acted the part 'finely' but did not 'harrow up the feelings' of the audience.[37] Other commentators noted a 'hesitation of his manner' as 'afraid to name his wish, and longing every moment to have the words taken, as it were, out of his mouth, his pauses were admirably thrown in' in this scene.[38] As usual, Kemble had prepared his part with careful study: the 'depiction of hesitancy in relation to guilt was . . . based on established critical principles'.[39]

King John's death scene (5.7) also drew considerable critical commentary. Inchbald writes that no spectator could hear the monarch describe the effect of the poison on his body 'and not feel for that moment parched with a scorching fever'.[40] When he later developed his own production, Kemble placed a couch upstage centre and played the scene from there which enabled him to show 'the deep and unaffected sinking of the whole man'.[41] He died with a final exhalation 'expressive of more than the mere parting of the spirit, and almost telling in its long and lamenting sound the agony of a fallen king'.[42] Van Dijk notes that Kemble emphasized the agony of King John's death in order to give his audience greater moral satisfaction at the monarch's demise, but the actor also sought to elicit sympathy for King John, not least through his final tragic sigh, in order to 'elevate a villain to the level of sublime pathos'.[43]

The siblings would later use a similar technique in their performances in *Macbeth*, as I shall demonstrate in Chapter 4, as they portrayed the lead roles more sympathetically than their predecessors while still allowing for moral critique of the characters' actions. Whereas in that play Siddons and Kemble appeared together on stage in multiple scenes and developed and conveyed their interpretation of the lead characters together, in *King John* they did not really act cooperatively. The play may have been chosen in order to showcase each actor's strengths, but it did not serve as a vehicle for them to perform together. The scenes discussed previously in which each of them shone reveal the actors performing alone or with other actors, rather than working collaboratively. An analysis of *King John* demonstrates that the idea of Siddons and Kemble acting together can be interpreted more broadly than is suggested by an examination of some of the other plays (discussed in the Introduction) in which they acted together in 1783–4.

Developing a joint Shakespearean repertoire

Following the success of *King John*, Siddons and Kemble began to appear together in other Shakespeare plays. They acted *Othello* for the first time in the capital on 8 March 1785. While this joint appearance may have seemed novel for London audiences, it represented established practice for the siblings, who had previously performed the play in the provinces, for example, at Manchester on 29 January 1777 for Kemble's first appearance in that city. In London, the principal character was somewhat unusual as 'a part which Mr. Kemble was permitted to retain' and that 'gave him one striking opportunity of acting with Mrs. Siddons'.[44] The play had been performed only a handful of times at Drury Lane following Siddons's joining the company in 1782. The lead role was generally taken by William Farren, who left for Covent Garden at the end of the 1783–4 season, and Desdemona was played by Sarah Ward, who subsequently yielded the part to Siddons. *Othello* was initially staged at Drury Lane to showcase Kemble rather than Siddons; indeed, Boaden claimed that the role of Desdemona 'was little calculated to serve' the actress and Campbell struggled with the contrast between the 'sublime and energetic' Lady Macbeth, the Shakespearean role Siddons had performed immediately prior to *Othello*, and the 'gentleness' of her Desdemona.[45] But Siddons in fact appears to have been more successful in *Othello* than her brother. While the *Morning Post* admitted that 'the soft, the tender, the gentle character of *Desdemona* is not so exactly agreeable as many others to the genius of Mrs. *Siddons*', the critic pronounced that she nevertheless 'acquitted herself in a very pleasing manner'.[46] Siddons wrote to her friends, the Whalleys, to express her gratification about the public response to her Desdemona: 'You have no idea how the innocence and playful simplicity of the latter have laid hold on the hearts of the people. I am very much flattered by this, as nobody ever has done anything with that character before.'[47] Kemble, on the other hand, was damned with faint praise in being deemed to have 'succeeded better than could be expected' and critiqued for having 'carried vehemence into the confines of brutality', thereby making Othello too ferocious.[48]

Othello was performed four more times before the end of the 1784–5 season, including by command of the royal family on 12 March. The play then opened the next season at Drury Lane on 17 September 1785 with the siblings again in the lead roles. Boaden describes the foregrounding of the theatre's 'greatest talent' in this way as a 'sound policy'.[49] Thus even if neither actor was particularly well suited to their roles in *Othello*, the play appears to have been chosen once again to allow them to appear in the same piece, and in this drama they acted together more substantially than they had done in *King John*. Siddons drew praise for her intercession for Cassio ('beyond measure winning') and the virtue she displayed in reacting to Othello's accusations of infidelity.[50] For example, when Othello takes his wife's hand and muses on the presence of 'a young and sweating devil . . . / That commonly rebels', Siddons clearly showed Desdemona's struggle to perceive his meaning and its implications: 'The surprise arising to astonishment, a sort of *doubt* if she heard aright, and that being admitted, what it could *mean*; a hope that it would end in nothing so unusual from him as *offensive* meaning' slowly gave way to 'slight relief' when Othello proclaimed her hand a good and frank one.[51] 'All this commentary', said Boaden, 'was quite as legible as the text'.[52] Siddons's skill as Desdemona lay in reacting to the lines delivered to her and the press deemed roles such as this one, 'which require no violent exertion', suitable for the actress in the third trimester of her sixth pregnancy.[53]

By September 1785, Kemble was deemed to have made an 'astonishing improvement' as Othello, now demonstrating his 'power to wring the heart' as well as 'accuracy of conception, subtlety of discrimination, and unrivalled elegance of action and deportment'.[54] While he had developed his ability to perform pathos, Kemble did not lose the ferocity of which he had earlier been accused: in his performance of the final scene, 'terror was very highly wrought indeed'.[55] This horror may have been augmented by the fact that the woman he had to murder onstage at the play's conclusion was his sister. At this point in the siblings' careers, the audience unanimously recognized 'that they had two great tragedians upon the same stage'.[56] But Kemble did not study or research the role of Othello to the degree that he usually did: 'Without looking away from the page of Shakespeare, to enquire what might be the native properties of the African, Mr. Kemble's Othello was a high poetical impersonation, and from his first entrance to his last, he wrapped that great and ardent being in a mantle of mysterious solemnity, awfully predictive of his fate.'[57] The careful exploration of geographical and temporal milieu that Kemble applied to ancient Rome, which we will see in the next chapter's discussion of *Coriolanus*, apparently did not extend to the investigation of non-European contexts. Kemble created a grand character but performed Othello as a European, not an African (the latter itself, of course, a term greatly lacking in specificity).

Siddons and Kemble performed regularly in *Othello* until 1797 at Drury Lane. Kemble then revived the play when he became manager of Covent Garden, with the addition of George Frederick Cooke as Iago. Charles Kemble played Cassio, as he had done in 1797. The production premiered on 20 January 1804 and was described as being performed 'in great stile', the characters 'pourtrayed with an excellence almost equal to that with which they were originally conceived'.[58] From 1805, Sarah Smith took over the role of Desdemona and from 1809, Kemble ceded Othello to Charles Mayne Young. Neither Siddons nor Kemble included *Othello* in the performances of their retirement seasons as by this point Siddons was deemed too old to act Desdemona, and Edmund Kean had caused a sensation as Othello. Nevertheless, the play was important to the creation of a joint Shakespearean repertoire early in their careers.

While *Othello* was originally staged to showcase Kemble but allowed his sister to shine, on 21 January 1788 *King Lear* was performed for Siddons's benefit but proved to be more advantageous to her brother. Campbell wrote of the siblings: 'Their magnificent acting was always the more acceptable for being conjoined on the stage; though, when comparison was instituted, it leaned almost invariably in favour of the sister's genius. In this play, however, I believe I shall not contradict the general recollection of all surviving spectators, when I say that the brother was a more memorable player than the sister.'[59] It is perhaps curious that Siddons chose to foreground Kemble in her benefit night performance, but she earned an impressive £343 12s. 6d., clear of house charges, from this decision.

Campbell recorded that Siddons considered Cordelia 'a secondary part, which she would not have performed, but for the benefit of her brother', suggesting that she intended to profit from his acting, rather than showcase her own.[60] This dismissal might be surprising but Campbell justified it by reminding the reader that during this period, the play was performed in versions largely derived from Nahum Tate's 1680 adaptation, which added a love story between Edgar and Cordelia, both of whom remain alive at the end of the play (as does Lear) to rule over the kingdom. Boaden noted that without this addition, the role of Cordelia 'would hardly have been deemed of sufficient importance to call upon the talents of a great actress'.[61] From 1792 onwards, Kemble worked with his own version of *King Lear*, but it was one that was largely based on Tate's adaptation; indeed, it abandoned much of the Shakespearean text restored by Garrick (who had reinstated the language but kept Tate's plot) and maintained the love story and the happy ending for the virtuous characters. Kemble removed some of Tate's less palatable elements, such as the amorous interactions between Edmund, Goneril and Regan, and had the blinding of Gloucester occur offstage. In privileging Tate's adaptation,

Kemble was following the period's taste for a less morally ambiguous version of the play, a preference that would persist among audiences until William Charles Macready restored Shakespeare's *King Lear* to the stage in 1838.

Like her Desdemona, Siddons's Cordelia was notable for the performance of selfless virtue. Boaden praised Siddons's delivery of a particular speech in Tate's adaptation 'with a filial tenderness, an ardour and a piety highly impressive'.[62] After Lear and Cordelia have been reunited at the end of Act IV, Cordelia vows to fight for her father:

> Oh, for an arm
> Like the fierce thunderer's, when the earth-born sons
> Storm'd heaven, to fight this injur'd father's battle! –
> That I could shift my sex, and die me deep
> In his opposer's blood! – But, as I may,
> With women's weapons, piety and prayers,
> I'll aid his cause.[63]

It is clear why Siddons would excel in delivering these lines, which balance force and femininity. For the most part, however, Cordelia's submissiveness, like Desdemona's, was deemed at odds with the power Siddons depicted in roles such as Constance and Lady Macbeth for which the actress was becoming famous.

The high point of Kemble's performance of Lear was his denunciation of Goneril, which was praised 'with a remarkable degree of unanimity' across his career.[64] Boaden writes of the delivery of the curse in Kemble's London debut in the role, that it 'harrowed up the soul: the gathering himself together, with the hands convulsively clasped, the encreasing fervour and rapidity, and the suffocation of the conclusive words, all evinced consummate skill and original invention'.[65] A review of a much later performance described this scene in more detail: '*Lear* paused for a moment, with his eye fixed on the ground, as if winding himself up for some great solemnity; he then with one rapid glance at his daughter, rushed to the front of the stage, dropped to his knees, and with his hands strongly clasped, and his eyes straining upwards, began the imprecation.'[66] At the end of the speech 'he seemed overwhelmed with a father's feelings; his strength failed, his head drooped, his eye wandered, and his voice sunk and quivered, and faded, till it became almost inaudible'.[67] However, Kemble's own physical weaknesses made the part of Lear a challenging one for him. His recurrent asthma rendered his voice 'his weakest technical instrument', and this made some of Lear's speeches challenging for the actor to deliver.[68] Leigh Hunt complained that the famous speech beginning 'Blow winds and crack your cheeks' ('burst your cheeks' in Kemble's text) was delivered 'with a gloomy carelessness'.[69] But rather than the actor being casual about the delivery, it is more likely that the physical power required for this monologue, which needs to recreate the storm in vocal form, eluded Kemble. Rostron explains that this made Kemble 'husband his resources for the great climaxes of each role', hence his emphasis on a series of 'points' (such as the cursing of Goneril).[70]

The extant commentary unfortunately gives us no sense of how Siddons and Kemble performed together in their early London appearances in this play. Kemble's later promptbooks, however, contain annotations that demonstrate how Lear and Cordelia interacted physically on stage that may apply to the earlier performances as well. For example, in the scene in which Lear divides his kingdom (1.2), as Cordelia delivers the lines 'Now comes my trial. – How am I distress'd, / That must, with cold speech, tempt the cholerick King', Kemble notes that 'Lear, assisted by Kent L. and Gloster R. descends from the throne, and comes forward into the Centre'.[71] Thus Kemble carefully planned Lear's movement to augment the sense of fear and apprehension experienced by Cordelia as she prepares to defy her father. In the play's denouement, as Lear delivers the lines beginning 'Cordelia then shall be a queen', the annotations state that 'the King runs towards Cordelia, who meets him in the centre of the stage, & throws herself at his feet' in a picture of filial piety.[72] With Lear's injunction to Edgar to take Cordelia 'crown'd, / The imperial grace fresh blooming on her brow', at which 'the King leads Cordelia into the centre of the stage – Edgar flies to meet her – they both kneel at the King's feet', we see how Kemble managed to keep himself centre stage through the positioning of the actors, despite the fact that the adaptation's ending ostensibly focuses on the triumph of Edgar and Cordelia.[73] In 1808, the *Universal Magazine* declared that 'on the whole, we do consider Mr. Kemble's *Lear* as one of those characters in which he stands alone'.[74] Kemble performed the part many times over the course of his career, certainly more times than Siddons acted Cordelia. While she gave up the role after 1801, probably because she faced sexist criticism about which characters were appropriate for a middle-aged actress, Kemble performed Lear intermittently from 1808 to 1810, though the mental illness of King George III meant that the play had to be withdrawn from the stage thereafter as depicting the madness of a ruler was a sensitive issue. This was, then, a play that benefited the brother more than the sister.

In addition to building a tragic Shakespearean repertoire, the siblings also appeared in Shakespearean comedies. Kemble chose *The Merchant of Venice* for his benefit on 6 April 1786 and acted the part of Bassanio, with Siddons as Portia. He had played Shylock early in his career in the provinces and on a few occasions at Drury Lane in 1784 (with his sister, Elizabeth Kemble, as Portia) when Thomas King, the actor who usually played the part, was absent. The *Morning Chronicle* cited the fact that he now took on 'the more trifling part of Bassanio, even on the night of his own benefit' as 'a very eminent proof of modesty' and pronounced his performance 'beautiful'.[75] Kemble played Shylock on 17 January 1789 during his first season as actor-manager and performed it at Drury Lane every season from 1792 to 1802, ceding the part to Cooke when he moved to Covent Garden.

Siddons's earlier 'failure' as Portia at Drury Lane must have preyed on her mind as she tackled the role again in 1786, but this time she triumphed. The *Morning Chronicle* wrote that she was 'beyond comparison better than any of her predecessors' and particularly praised her delivery of 'the famous speech on mercy' which she gave in an innovative way: 'From every other Portia, it has always appeared as a *recitation* of a beautiful sentiment, *prepared for the occasion*, not as naturally arising from, and replicatory to the words of Shylock, but as if totally unconnected and independent.'[76] Siddons, however, made sure that the speech was organically linked with the rest of the play. Godwin singled out what he called a 'light' scene in Act V in which Portia perplexes Bassanio 'by persisting that he had given his ring to a woman, and not to a man' as particularly significant for Siddons: 'There was something inexpressibly delightful in beholding a woman of her general majesty condescend for once to become sportive.'[77] Siddons's imposing gravity gave her a surprising advantage during this moment of performance, and the playfulness may have been augmented when she acted with her brother as Bassanio. Siddons continued to play Portia throughout her career and the play also became an important one in the Shakespearean readings that she gave following her retirement from the stage (discussed in the Conclusion to this book).

In fact, Kemble might have intended to showcase his comic acting with the afterpiece that followed *The Merchant of Venice*, rather than with the 'trifling' role of Bassanio. *Catharine and Petruchio* was a popular adaptation of *The Taming of the Shrew* by Garrick in which Kemble took the male lead, delivering a performance that 'was among the best acting we ever saw for boldness, originality, insight into character, and the power of affording entertainment. It proved Kemble's comick talents beyond all dispute'.[78] Catharine on this occasion was played by Mary Ann Wrighten, but Siddons performed the part in another benefit performance for Kemble on 13 March 1788 (the mainpiece was *Jane Shore*) and for her own benefit night that season on 5 May (the mainpiece was *All For Love*, John Dryden's version of *Antony and Cleopatra*). Boaden dismissed Catharine as unsuitable for the actress ('there never could be an atom of farce in the composition of Mrs. Siddons') and Campbell thought she played the role 'for her brother's benefit, certainly not for her own', but the *World* pronounced the siblings' comic acting in this piece 'equal to any of their efforts' and they continued to act the play occasionally.[79]

Portia, who appears dressed as a lawyer in the trial scene, was undoubtedly Siddons's most successful breeches role but she also attempted some of Shakespeare's other cross-dressing heroines, with her brother acting alongside her. On 18 February 1786 they appeared together in *As You Like It*. Siddons had played Rosalind the previous season, but the part of Orlando was now taken by Kemble for the first time. The play was occasionally repeated with this casting that season and early in the next, but Siddons soon gave up Rosalind to her rival, Dorothy Jordan, though Kemble continued to act Orlando until 1791, when he switched to the role of Jaques. It was as a result of an early performance of Rosalind at Cheltenham that Siddons had been engaged to act at Drury Lane in 1775. Bate reported to Garrick: 'I know no woman who marks the different passages and transitions with so much variety and at the same time propriety of expression.'[80] Bate had to use his imagination somewhat, however, in evaluating the actress, remarking that 'her figure must be remarkably fine, when she is happily delivered of a big belly, which entirely mars for the present her whole shape'.[81] Siddons's cross-dressing as Rosalind came in for criticism: her costume was described as 'injudicious' by Anna Seward because the actress's 'scrupulous prudery of decency produced an ambiguous vestment that seemed neither male nor female'.[82] Siddons shied away from exposing her legs in such cross-dressed roles, but her attempts at modesty in costuming were not accepted by the audience.

There was also resistance to the idea of Siddons as a comic actress. Boaden wrote of 'the common objection to her comedy, that it was only the smile of *tragedy*' but claimed that Siddons in fact revealed the true nature of Rosalind as 'her vivacity is understanding, not buoyant spirits'.[83] Another commentator pinpointed the actress's shortcomings in this part: 'Her *Rosalind* wanted neither playfulness nor feminine softness; but it was totally without archness – not because she did not properly conceive it; but how could such a countenance be arch?'[84] While such critiques are largely filtered through Siddons's later reputation as a tragedienne, William Windham noted of Siddons in response to a 1786 performance of Rosalind that 'the highest praise that can be given to her comedy is, that it is the perfection of art; but her tragedy is the perfection of nature'.[85] Kemble's biographers failed to comment on his appearances in this play, so it cannot have been a significant part of his acting repertoire.

On 29 January 1787, Siddons and Kemble acted Posthumus and Imogen in *Cymbeline* for Siddons's benefit and the play was performed five times more that season.[86] Boaden notes that Siddons's benefit nights 'usually presented some interesting novelty to the public' and so this performance was somewhat experimental in nature, though Siddons had played Imogen during her time at Bath and both brother and sister had included these roles on their lists of favourite characters early in their careers.[87] This experimentation seems again to have been in providing a less revealing costume for the cross-dressing part of the play. She wrote to the painter William Hamilton requesting that he 'make her a slight sketch for a boy's dress, to conceal the person as much as possible' for the role of Imogen as she had given the one he made her for Rosalind to another actress.[88] Again, there was critical complaint about 'the delicate style of her male attire', which Boaden refuted: 'It was exactly the strait, or frock-coat and trowsers of our modern beaux; and you saw, as you ought in fact to see, the attempt at the opposite sex not quite successful.'[89] He acknowledged that some actresses had been more effective as Fidele, the male aspect of the role, but declared Siddons 'the only perfect Imogen that I have ever seen'.[90]

Campbell's assessment is that Siddons's success as Imogen was due to the fact that 'she gave greatness to the character, without diminishing its gentleness'.[91] Boaden singled out the key scene with Iachimo as one never equalled:

The variety of her manner and expression was quite astonishing: the reluctant reception of the imputations as to her lord's fidelity, the detection of the villainy, the scorn of her virtuous indignation, and the dignity with which she called upon Pisanio, to relieve her from the wretch who had too long 'abused her credulous ears,' were triumphs even for Mrs. Siddons.[92]

Boaden was also effusive about Kemble's success, declaring him 'by a thousand degrees, the best Posthumus of my time'.[93] His performance was 'learned, judicious, and in the fine burst upon Iachimo at the close, a most powerful effort; and such it continued through his theatric life'.[94] The press reported that Siddons had earned 'about 650 or 700' pounds from the 1787 benefit performance of *Cymbeline*, though Imogen did not become a mainstay of her repertoire.[95] Kemble continued to act Posthumus and included it in the selection of major roles he played in his retirement season. Given their later reputation as tragic actors, it might seem incongruous to see Siddons and Kemble achieving success in a play that we would now consider a romance or even a comedy. But Kemble's promptbook noted the use of the green stage cloth that signified tragedy, suggesting the play's genre was perceived differently by early-nineteenth-century audiences. Siddons's experimentation with cross-dressing was here used to explore how the device might be employed in tragedy rather than comedy, just as it was in her performances of Hamlet, as we shall see in Chapter 5.

Acting together in non-Shakespearean drama

The siblings' success in tragedy is demonstrated by the creation of new plays for them in this genre such as Richard Cumberland's *The Carmelite*, an original drama with roles written for the actors which debuted on 2 December 1784. Siddons played Matilda, the Lady of St Valori, and Kemble acted Montgomeri, her son. The play was said to benefit the dramatist who wrote it more than the performers for whom it was created, but with fourteen performances it was the most successful new drama of the season and was revived again on 20 November 1787.[96] The creation of new roles also avoided the issue of more senior actors blocking access to parts through their ownership of particular characters. However, *The Carmelite* was regarded as too similar to other plays in which Siddons had appeared, notably Home's *Douglas*, in which she had acted Lady Randolph in the previous season and even a few weeks earlier than the première of Cumberland's new tragedy, on 13 November 1784.[97] Both plays relied on the pathos of maternal affection, but *The Carmelite* offered a happy ending that preserved poetic justice: Matilda is reunited with her husband and her son survives, in stark contrast to Lady Randolph's suicide following the death of her son, Norval. Unlike the revised ending of Tate's *King Lear*, the denouement of *The Carmelite* was critiqued as improbable on the grounds that 'happiness and tragedy seldom will unite, and the great efficacy of the stage is the tear for expiring virtue'.[98] Whereas in *King Lear* Kemble had appeared as the father and Siddons as the daughter, the roles were now reversed as Kemble's character, Montgomeri, was the son of Siddons's Matilda. When St Valori (played by Smith), who has been presumed dead, returns disguised as a Carmelite and observes his wife, he becomes jealous of Matilda's esteem for Montgomeri (whose identity as Matilda's son is unknown to everyone except his mother). In this element of the plot, Cumberland built on 'the hint of such indecent passion given by Home in *Douglas*'.[99] But the relationship between Siddons and Kemble in this play did not elicit commentary on these insinuations of incest but, rather, on the probability of the actors performing mother and son. In his *Memoirs*, Cumberland recounted that the play's original audience saw 'merit in Mr. Kemble, who ... appeared in the character of the youthful Montgomeri' and 'did not think the worse of him because he had reached the age of manhood'.[100] Boaden wrote that in watching such plays, 'the relative ages of the parties is always judiciously forgotten', and the *Public Advertiser* pronounced that in all mother and son scenes in which Siddons appeared, 'if, for no other reason, though reasons there are many, [than] from similitude of countenance, Kemble should constantly be the son'.[101] Boaden simply commented that the scenes in which they appeared together 'were very finely acted'.[102] The audience was willing to accept the fiction of the siblings appearing in filial and spousal relationships.

On 8 March 1787, Siddons joined Kemble in Robert Jephson's *The Count of Narbonne*, a play in which Kemble had had great success in Dublin before debuting in London. The performance was staged in order to drum up enthusiasm for the dramatist's new play *Julia*, which he had written for the siblings.[103] Jephson's *Julia* debuted on 14 April 1787 with Siddons in the title part and Kemble as Mentevole, who is accused of murdering Julia's husband and ends the play by stabbing her. The *Morning Herald* noted the drama's 'evident imitation of *Shakspear*'s phraseology and manner' and further commented that the character of Mentevole 'is drawn with the greatest force and novelty' so that '*Julia* takes a second place', although Siddons 'raised it by her fine acting, to a deserved pre-eminence'.[104] Boaden felt that 'the dark designing subtlety' of Mentevole made it 'a part very truly calculated for [Kemble's] powers', and Campbell noted that the play's trial scene gave 'great scope to Mrs. Siddons's acting'.[105] The *Morning Herald* further stated that 'the performance of this Drama seemed the result of many close rehearsals'.[106] That this aspect was deemed worthy of comment suggests that Siddons's and Kemble's attention to preparing for these new roles was innovative and unusual.

Kemble also tried his hand at playwriting in order to create roles for himself and his sister. One of his earliest alterations of a pre-existing text was his version of Philip Massinger's Renaissance tragicomedy *The Maid of Honour*, which debuted on 27 January 1785. Appearing soon after *The Carmelite*, it may also be seen as a response to that play in that Campbell claimed Kemble wrote this adaptation in order to rectify the 'modern poverty of the national drama' (of which Cumberland's play presumably was symptomatic) by 'turning back upon its ancient resources'.[107] The *London Magazine* found Camiola, the lead role played by Siddons, 'too declamatory . . . to suit her *forte*', though in some places 'it furnished her with opportunities to display with effect the powers of which she is mistress'.[108] Boaden highlighted, for example, Camiola's response to 'an unworthy accusation' from the King when she vows to '*rise up* / In my defence', a moment reminiscent of the pride and majesty that Siddons displayed as Constance in *King John*.[109] Kemble's performance of Adorni (a follower of Camiola's father) was subjected to a critique that was by now becoming familiar: 'It appeared to have been studied with attention, and his delineation of it was accurate; but more *spirit* would have improved the part.'[110] Kemble was praised for his alterations, in particular for fixing 'the singularity of the plot' and remedying 'the want of poetical moral in the catastrophe'.[111] But *The Maid of Honour* 'was by no means a successful revival' and 'the joint powers of Mrs. Siddons and her brother prolonged the reception of this play only for three nights'.[112] It then sank without a trace and was never published. However, its failure may have been a result of the staging, rather than Siddons's and Kemble's acting: after the impressive scenery of *The Carmelite*, which had been 'brought forth . . . with great splendor', *The Maid of Honour* seemed lacklustre as its 'dresses and decorations discovered too much *frugality*'.[113]

In general, the siblings were more successful in already established plays than in dramas that were newly created for them. *Venice Preserved* is a case in point. Siddons had played Belvidera since her earliest days on the provincial stage and acted the role from her first season in London onwards. Kemble noted the role of Pierre in the play as one of his favourites when he applied to Wilkinson, though he later played Jaffier under the manager in Yorkshire. The siblings first appeared together in *Venice Preserved* in London on 11 February 1786 with Siddons as Belvidera and Kemble as Jaffier (a role he could now assume following the departure of Brereton), and they continued to act alongside one another in these roles for the next twenty years. Siddons later described the intensity that she was able to achieve when acting with Kemble: 'In one of the scenes with my brother John who was the Jaffier . . . the real tears coursed one another down my innocent nose so abundantly that my handkerchief was quite wet with them when I got off the stage. I felt every word as if I were the real person, and not the representative.'[114] But at the same time, Siddons acknowledged that Kemble was not necessarily her ideal Jaffier:

> I do not like to play Belvidera to John's Jaffier, so well as I shall when Charles has the part. John is too cold, too formal, and does not seem to put himself into the character. His sensibilities are not as acute as they ought to be for the part of a lover. Charles, in other characters far inferior to John, will play better in Jaffier, – I mean to my liking. We have rehearsed it.[115]

From 7 November 1805, Charles took over Jaffier and Kemble began to play Pierre before eventually relinquishing the part to Cooke. According to Percy Fitzgerald, the character of Pierre, 'where a sort of dissolute indifference was assumed to hide ferocious designs . . . suited Kemble's own manner'.[116] It was in this part that Kemble appeared alongside Siddons when she acted Belvidera in her retirement season.

Both Kemble and Siddons played multiple characters in the highly popular *Jane Shore*. They first acted in it together in London on 13 March 1788, with Siddons in the title role and Kemble as Hastings, and it became a staple of their repertoire. Boaden questioned whether 'the dignified expression of Mrs. Siddons' was well suited to representing a character who 'had melted before the ardour of a royal suitor', implying that the actress was too noble and too virtuous to play Jane Shore.[117] Her decision to act Alicia (a part that had been played by her sister, Frances Kemble, at Drury Lane from 1783 to 1786), as she did for two performances in 1787, attracted even more incredulity. Campbell wondered why Siddons would take on the part of the 'guilty wretch' who betrays Jane Shore and concluded that the 'impassioned' nature of the character and the performer's desire to respond to the audience's 'craving' for novelty must be the reasons.[118] Although Siddons's early regional repertoire had included both Jane Shore and Alicia, and, indeed, she indicated that she preferred the latter part, she subsequently returned to the title role.

While Siddons had first acted Jane Shore in 1782 (as we have seen), Kemble could assume the character of Hastings only following Smith's retirement. He acted it for his benefit in 1788 alongside his sister, surprising the audience 'with the unaccustomed powers of the part!'[119] In 1805, Kemble tackled the role of Gloster (a part owned for many years by James Aickin at Drury Lane while Kemble was in the company there) as a subtle way of reminding the audience of his claim to one of his great Shakespearean roles, Richard III, which Cooke had begun to usurp. As both characters are based on the same historical figure, this deliberate move allowed Kemble to demonstrate to the audience 'how boldly he could both conceive and execute the character of the son of York'.[120] Boaden saw Rowe's emulation of Shakespeare as particularly successful in the character of Gloster, whose 'diction is often not only similar but *identical*' to his Shakespearean counterpart, and identifies this as a factor in Kemble's success in this role.[121] Boaden noted the 'electrical' effect that Kemble produced in delivering what he considered a particularly Shakespearean speech ('Behold my arm, thus *blasted*, *dry*, and *wither'd*, / Shrunk like a foul abortion, and decay'd / Like some *untimely product* of the seasons'), praising 'the way he *rush'd* upon the table, the sudden *baring* and *display* of his arm, and the overwhelming *energy* of the accusation'.[122]

The interactions between Jane Shore and Gloster were recognized as highlights of Siddons's performances of the role. Their scene together at the start of Act IV was the point at which 'the part ascended to the level of Mrs. Siddons's powers' and 'her voice took a richness beyond the wailing of penitence, and her cheek a nobler glow than the blush of shame'.[123] Boaden wondered 'what Gloster could appear otherwise than insignificant by the side of Mrs. Siddons'?[124] But Kemble's electrifying effect in the part must have been heightened with his sister opposite him on stage. Ultimately, however, the play belonged to the actress playing Jane Shore. Boaden recounted how in the scene at Alicia's door, Siddons used the theatre's architecture to enhance the pathos of the situation:

> There was, in my early days, such a permanent property as a *stage-door* in our theatres, and the proscenium beyond it; so that when Shore was pushed from the door, she was turned round and staggered till supported by the firm projection behind her. Here was a terrific picture full in the eye of the pit, and this most picturesque of women knew the amazing value of it.[125]

Siddons's performance of Jane Shore's death scene was also praised for its transitions: 'Her eagle eye, obedient to her will, at times parted with its lustre, and, though open, looked sightless and bewildered; but resumed its fire as wonderfully, when, "*with life's last spark that flattered and expired,*" she turned to her husband and uttered the heart-piercing words, "Forgive me! – but forgive me!"'[126]

* * *

Though Kemble's London debut made less of a splash than his sister's, audiences were keen to see him act alongside her in order to augment her already considerable popular and artistic appeal. This strategy was clearly one that the siblings accepted and adopted as a way of bolstering their ever-growing fame. Although they faced constraints in the form of the theatrical convention of actors' ownership over parts, the number of plays in which Siddons and Kemble appeared together is considerable, and the 1780s saw them experimenting with a wide range of roles alongside each other (see the Appendix), some of which would become important and regular features of their repertoires and some of which were quickly set aside. Acting together, then, was something of a marketing gimmick rather than an artistic imperative. Their greatest success together in Shakespearean drama at this time was in plays that contained significant roles for each actor, but which did not necessarily require them to interact all that much, notably *King John* and to a lesser extent *King Lear*. In established works from the Restoration and eighteenth-century repertoire such as *Venice Preserved* and *Jane Shore*, Siddons achieved success first in the lead female roles and was subsequently joined on stage by her brother, who often had to wait for parts to become available from other actors. New plays such as Cumberland's *The Carmelite* and Kemble's *The Maid of Honour* focused on creating significant roles for Siddons, with Kemble tackling supporting characters. Kemble would come to shine when he began to stage Roman plays, casting himself in the lead role and often drawing on the support of Siddons. Although Siddons was by and large the star of the partnership, performing with her brother did give her some advantages as it 'allowed a freer course to the feelings of the actress. There is always some reserve in a woman of delicacy towards a mere representative relation'.[127]

The freedom of emotion generated by their sibling bond enabled Siddons and Kemble to play a wide variety of relationships, including parent and child as well as lovers. Rarely, however, did they act sister and brother, although they did later play sibling roles in revivals of two earlier tragedies and in two original dramas. They acted Horatia and Publius in William Whitehead's *The Roman Father* (1750), based on Corneille's *Horace*, on 15 November 1794, and Palmyra and Zaphna in James Miller's *Mahomet the Imposter* (1744), adapted from Voltaire's *Mahomet*, on 27 April 1795. Their roles in *The Roman Father* were considered 'very well fitted' for the actors' talents: Horatia allowed Siddons to deliver a passionate speech in Act V casting opprobrium on her brother, the effect of which was 'electric', and in Publius Kemble could 'display the stoic grandeur of those Romans', as he loved to do.[128] But the plot was pronounced 'revolting' (the play ended with Publius stabbing and killing his sister) and the drama was deemed inferior to Shakespeare.[129] As Boaden put it, 'this brutal instance of Roman patriotism' did little for the actors and *The Roman Father* ran for only three nights.[130] *Mahomet the Imposter* was acted for Siddons's benefit on 27 April 1795 and the receipts were a very healthy £569 8s. 6d. Like Horatia, Palmyra was a role Siddons had played in the provinces early in her career, between her first and second London debuts, but after this performance 'she never repeated the character'.[131] In this play, Palmyra and Zaphna, held captive by Mahomet, discover that they are sister and brother after developing a strong affection for one another. Both end up stabbing themselves when they learn how Mahomet has deceived them. Like *The Roman Father*, this drama was deemed inhumane and its incestuous undertones may have become more unsettling for the audience with real-life siblings in the lead roles.

When *De Montfort*, Joanna Baillie's tragedy on hatred, was first performed on 29 April 1800, the *Sun* noted the strength of the actors' performances and the suitability of their roles: 'The acting of KEMBLE and Mrs. SIDDONS was perfect in its kind. The Characters they supported seemed expressly to have been written for them, and certainly could not be better adapted to draw forth their respective powers.'[132] But the *Star* raised doubts about the play's dramatic merit: 'Take Mr. KEMBLE and Mrs. SIDDONS from the two principal characters, and we believe that it would become too languid for the stage.'[133] After murdering Rezenvelt, De Montfort (Kemble) dies 'the victim of penitential agony', but the drama was somewhat kinder to its female lead than Whitehead's and Miller's works, dispatching Jane De Montfort (Siddons) to a convent after her brother's death.[134]

The fate of Helena, Siddons's role in William Godwin's *Antonio*, however, was much more disturbing. The titular character (played by Kemble) murders his sister when he discovers she has married Don Gusman and not Antonio's friend, Roderigo. Parallels were drawn with *The Roman Father*, but Godwin's drama was pronounced 'still more outrageous to the feelings' because unlike Publius, who stabs Horatia offstage, '*Antonio*'s cruel murder of his amiable and affectionate sister, is committed in the sight of the audience'.[135] One review recorded that when playgoers 'witnessed a catastrophe so brutal, and unnatural, a general disapprobation burst forth, and a cry of *off! off!* pervaded the whole house; nor would the audience suffer it to be announced for a second representation'.[136] Spectators were accustomed to seeing Siddons and Kemble die on stage and even praised their death scenes (as we shall see in the next chapter), but the murder of a sister by her brother, whether on stage or off, was too much for the audience to bear and the play had only a single performance.

These four tragedies offered Siddons and Kemble the somewhat rare opportunity of performing sibling roles. But despite their powerful acting, the plays were apparently not strong enough to establish themselves in the actors' repertoires. The works were critiqued as declamatory and languid, and all but *De Montfort* were considered excessively violent. Boaden's comment that *The Roman Father* was revived in order 'that Mr. Kemble and Mrs. Siddons might perform the Publius and Horatia' suggests a desire to see them act as sister and brother rather than an interest in the play itself.[137] But Siddons's and Kemble's ongoing popularity in performing marital, filial and parental relationships demonstrates that the real drive was to see the actors on stage in the same play rather than performing any version of their sibling relationship.

2

Producing Shakespeare at Drury Lane (1788–96, 1800–2)

On 23 September 1788, Kemble wrote in his diary, 'this Day I undertook the Management of D. L Theatre', further strengthening the stage partnership of the siblings.[1] As acting or stage manager, Kemble could now exert greater influence over which plays were produced and how they were performed, but he ultimately had to answer to Sheridan as proprietor and patent holder. Although David Francis Taylor has dispelled the myth that Sheridan's work as a Member of Parliament kept him away from the day-to-day running of Drury Lane, he also acknowledges that Kemble had 'significant freedom . . . in matters of casting, rehearsal, and the production of stock plays'.[2] The one aspect of management that Kemble eschewed completely was that of reading and approving new play scripts, which he left entirely to Sheridan. Kemble preferred engaging with dead authors over dealing with living ones and chose to focus on staging classic plays, placing Shakespeare as a 'dramatic sun' at the centre of the Drury Lane theatrical system.[3]

In the early years of his management, Kemble directed his energies, and the theatre's finances, which were rather perilous as a result of Sheridan's mismanagement, to improving the staging of the traditional repertoire through judicious alteration of the texts, consideration of casting, careful research and attention to 'the dresses, the properties, and the scenery of his revivals'.[4] This emphasis on the classics allowed the new manager to privilege his own acting (including roles he had played in the provinces but not yet in London) and also to foreground that of his sister, and often to showcase their joint performances.[5] Kemble's inaugural season would see him stage two important Shakespeare revivals in which he appeared with Siddons, one which displayed her acting talents (*Henry VIII*, in which she played Queen Katharine) and one that allowed him to shine (*Coriolanus*). As 'the first great "producer" of Shakespeare on the English stage', Kemble's productions 'aided the impression even of Mrs. Siddons herself' while the manager benefited from having 'the finest tragic actress in the world' in his company.[6]

Henry VIII

Kemble's revival of *Henry VIII*, which debuted on 25 November 1788 billed as 'not acted these 20 years', was the first of these spectacular Shakespeare revivals.[7] Kemble may have been inspired to tackle this play by Francis Gentleman's assessment that its 'success in representation . . . depends chiefly on decoration, and splendor of show' while also containing several 'nervous and pathetic scenes'.[8] The new manager realized that *Henry VIII* would provide a vehicle both for spectacle and for Siddons's acting. In particular, Kemble indulged his 'natural turn for magnificence' with the play's processions, which were staged 'with punctilious exactness', employing research into 'ancient habits and manners' and careful thought about the placement of actors on stage in a way that became foundational to his Shakespearean production style.[9] The revival, advertised as featuring 'new Scenes, Dresses, and Decorations' including 'in Act I a *Grand Banquet*. In Act II the *Trial of Queen Katharine*. In V a *Procession to the Christening of Princess*

Elizabeth', was successful, achieving twelve performances that season and receiving the approval of the press for the fact that the key scenes 'were all highly magnificent and conducted with suitable decorum' in a manner that was 'historically exact'.[10]

As Herschel Baker notes, the audience was 'awed by Siddons as much as the scenery' and the actress's performance of Queen Katharine was a major factor in the production's success.[11] In his diary comments on the first performance, Kemble noted that his sister was 'supremely pathetick' in the role and on watching the actress later in her career, Hunt proclaimed that 'it was in *Queen Katharine* that [Siddons's] dignity was seen in all its perfection'.[12] Thus both pathos and majesty were key to her interpretation of the character. Siddons's power in the part is suggested by an anecdote about a performance in Edinburgh. The actor who played the Surveyor came offstage 'perspiring with agitation', having been rebuked by Siddons in the character of Queen Katharine for delivering his accusations of treason against Buckingham.[13] When asked what the matter was, the actor replied, 'that woman plays as if the thing were in earnest. She looked on me so through and through with her black eyes, that I would not for the world meet her on the stage again'.[14]

Siddons's acting in the trial scene (2.4) drew particular praise. For example, in the speech in which Queen Katharine proclaims her royal status, Siddons effectively blended both pathos and majesty. The actor Daniel Terry noted that Siddons expressed the passage's 'mingled feelings' with 'their natural gradations' and 'quick and violent transitions', resulting in a powerful effect:

> There were none who did not feel the agonies of sympathy when they saw her efforts to suppress the grief to which her woman's nature was yielding, – who did not acknowledge, in her manner, the truth of her assertion of Royalty, and who did not experience a portion of that awe which *Wolsey* might be supposed to feel when her 'sparks of fire' darted through her 'drops of tears.'[15]

In the remainder of the scene, Siddons evinced 'such true grandeur' that on her exit it seemed 'quite time to break up the council' as the King and Wolsey held little further interest for the audience.[16]

Terry also noted an important touch of nature that Siddons brought to the portrayal of Queen Katharine's decline and death: instead of acting sickness with the usual 'motionless languor, and monotonous imbecility of action and countenance', Siddons 'displayed through her feeble and falling frame, and death-stricken expression of features, that morbid fretfulness of look, that restless desire of changing place and position, which frequently attends our last decay'.[17] More specifically, 'she sought relief from the irritability of illness by the often shifting of her situation in her chair', by having the pillows 'removed and adjusted', and by playing with the drapery 'with restless and uneasy fingers'.[18] This byplay allowed Siddons to render 'a most beautiful as well as most affecting portraiture of nature fast approaching to its exit'.[19] Siddons showed how Katharine's strength was 'made gradually to decay from the beginning to the end of the scene' and so 'acted this display of languor that never wearied, with inimitable majesty'.[20]

In the 1788 revival of *Henry VIII*, Kemble played the part of Cromwell (which subsumed the minor character of Griffith, Queen Katharine's usher), leaving Wolsey to Robert Bensley, who had previously acted the role at Covent Garden in the 1770s. By choosing a less significant character, Kemble was able to focus on bringing his research to life on stage in the production. Kemble nevertheless gave Cromwell careful attention as an actor and made him 'an enchanting exhibition of humility, affection, and reverence'.[21] Boaden pronounced that 'neither Wolsey would have been so striking, nor Katharine so affecting, without the "well-played passion" of Cromwell'.[22] The press's evaluation was less effusive but still positive: Kemble's Cromwell was deemed to have been 'performed . . . with great propriety', though 'somewhat too creeping and servile'.[23] Other reviewers expressed a desire to see Kemble as Wolsey: 'We really think Kemble too modest in choosing the part of Cromwell – he should have played Wolsey, and in our opinion would have played it to advantage.'[24] This in fact came to pass later in the season, when Kemble took over as Wolsey for two performances while Bensley was absent for health reasons. He spoke to Boaden of 'the *rawness* of his first performance' in the part but when he revived *Henry VIII* as manager of Covent Garden in 1806, he played Wolsey again and continued to play this character until the end of his career, having left the part of Cromwell to his brother Charles some years earlier.[25] The press pronounced that as Wolsey he 'tower[ed] above all rivalry'.[26]

Key to Kemble's success in the role was acting alongside Siddons as Queen Katharine. In the trial scene, each showed touches of genius that helped elevate the other's performance. Writing of Siddons, Terry emphasized 'one of those unequalled pieces of acting by which she assists the barrenness of the text, and fills up the meaning of the scene'.[27] As Queen Katharine speaks the words 'Lord Cardinal', intended for Wolsey, Campeius 'imagines it addressed to him, and comes forward as if to answer'.[28] G. J. Bell recorded what follows: 'When Campeius comes to her she turns from him impatiently; then makes a sweet bow of apology, but dignified. Then to Wolsey, turned and looking *from* him, with her hand pointing back to him, in a voice of thunder, "to *you* I speak."'[29] At this point, having reassumed 'the fulness of majesty' and 'glowing with scorn, contempt, anger, and the terrific pride of innocence', when she addresses Wolsey 'her form seems to expand, and her eye to burn with a fire beyond human'.[30] Queen Katharine then denies Wolsey's authority as a judge of her situation and accuses him of having a 'heart / . . . cramm'd with arrogancy, spleen, and pride'.[31] According to the manuscript stage directions in Kemble's 1806 promptbook, Wolsey, who had advanced towards Katharine as she addressed him, now retreats and 'returns to his seat'.[32] Walter Scott praised Kemble's brilliant rendition of the beginning of Wolsey's demise as he responded to Siddons's acting: 'You saw the full-blown dignity of the ambitious statesman sink at once before the regal frown, and you felt at the same moment that he had received the death wound.'[33] Acting together, Siddons and Kemble achieved 'complete personifications' of Wolsey and Queen Katharine.[34]

Following Siddons's retirement from the stage in 1812, Kemble played Wolsey less often, but he acted the part annually and did so three times at the end of his final season (1816–17).[35] In March 1817, just before leaving the London stage, Kemble gave a series of twelve farewell performances in Edinburgh, including one as Wolsey. A lengthy review appeared in the Edinburgh press, offering perhaps the most detailed account of Kemble's interpretation of this character. The critic deemed Wolsey one of Kemble's 'very best' roles: 'Indeed it is doubtful whether, in the whole range of dramatic history, a picture has been presented, of more force yet of greater delicacy, so bold in its colouring yet so nice in its tints, so finished by art yet so faithful to nature.'[36] The reviewer noted that the spectator's attention 'is first caught by the grandeur of his fine figure, venerable in the gorgeous vestments of priestly splendour; and the lofty scorn which alternately rides in the commanding aspect, or scowls from the lurking eye'.[37] Kemble's majestic appearance and haughty countenance as Wolsey were thus reminiscent of his characterization of Coriolanus, as we shall see.

The review concentrates on Wolsey's appearance in Act 3, perhaps because without Siddons opposite him, the scenes with Queen Katharine were now deemed less important.[38] The first speech demonstrated his 'vexation and ire' at the King's desire to marry Anne Bullen combined with 'the tone of the overbearing politician' whose plans are being thwarted, 'a fine and just colouring, in which the skill of the actor powerfully illuminated the genius of the poet'.[39] In Wolsey's soliloquy following the exit of the King '*frowning upon*' him, as the nobles who are plotting against him follow the monarch '*whispering and smiling*', Kemble introduced a novelty in the delivery that was 'so palpably just that one wonders it could ever be overlooked': as Wolsey's mind searches for hope in the midst of fear, Kemble spoke 'with a resumption of exultation so striking, as to indicate at once the pride of successful artifice, anticipated triumph over his enemies, and recovered ascendancy with his King'.[40] Then, as Wolsey realizes that the paper he has been given is his own letter to the Pope advising him to refuse Henry's divorce from Katharine, 'the sudden overthrow of these bright images ... was delineated with equal strength and felicity'.[41]

When Norfolk, Suffolk and Surrey re-enter to announce Wolsey's arrest, Kemble maintained 'the same exquisite tone of vigour and truth'.[42] Wolsey's soliloquy following the departure of his accusers ('Farewell, a long farewell, to all my greatness!') 'was resistlessly affecting', causing even audience members who usually remained dry-eyed to shed tears in 'sympathy with the mournful self-pity of the fallen statesman'.[43] The scene, and Wolsey's part in the play, ends as he learns of Henry's secret marriage to Anne Bullen and comes to understand his fall from grace: Kemble delivered the lines 'all my glories / In that one woman I have lost for ever' with 'a burst of the most piteous affliction'.[44] The analysis of Kemble's Wolsey concludes by comparing this character with the actor's other major roles: 'Without boasting the glare and blaze of many of his other performances, we are inclined to rank this almost at the head of the whole; for it exhibits all the highest powers of intellect, in the most ample and admirable manner, while it brings them to bear as powerfully as possible upon all the feelings of the heart.'[45] Pathos was thus a feature of Kemble's Wolsey just as it was of Siddons's Queen Katharine.

Like her brother, Siddons acted in *Henry VIII* during her retirement season (1811–12), appearing alongside Kemble several times. A few months earlier, Siddons had given a round of performances in Edinburgh that were announced 'as of a farewell nature', just as her brother later did.[46] Her final appearance was a benefit performance of Queen Katharine on 13 March 1812, after which she spoke a farewell address. The *Caledonian Mercury* reported a 'dreadful crush' as spectators crowded into the theatre 'to witness the last exhibition of this great performer'.[47] But this was not to be the last time that

Siddons acted in Edinburgh or the last time she played Queen Katharine there. In 1815, the actress came out of retirement to give a series of performances for the benefit of her daughter-in-law, Harriet, and her children, following the death of Siddons's son, Henry, who had managed the Edinburgh playhouse. Queen Katharine was one of the roles chosen. There was 'scarcely any falling off in her powers' and she managed to sustain even 'the most exacting characters', despite 'her advanced time of life' (she was sixty years old).[48] She acted in *Henry VIII* on 21 November 1815 opposite Terry as Wolsey, the actor who would later provide such detailed recollections of her performance. The *Caledonian Mercury* remarked on the usual high points for Queen Katharine in the play, the trial scene and her death scene, and also commented on Siddons's ability to interpret Shakespeare:

> There is, in the exquisite and sublime simplicity of Shakespeare's thoughts and expressions, ample scope for the powers of Mrs. Siddons; while, at the same time, the genius of this great performer aids the conceptions of the poet, and gives to his portraits both a higher finish and a richer colouring. This was strikingly exemplified in her performance of the character of Queen Katharine.[49]

Not only did Shakespeare's drama offer Siddons an opportunity to demonstrate her talents as an actress, but she was also able to enrich Shakespeare's plays through her exceptional performances.

Fitzgerald considered Siddons's characters 'of Shakspearian grandeur and dignity' such as Lady Macbeth, Queen Katharine, Constance and Volumnia as the most significant parts in her repertoire.[50] Some critics thought Siddons's Queen Katharine equal to her Lady Macbeth (which came to be her most famous role) and Fitzgerald claimed that the actress was able to portray 'the sustained majesty and pathos of the part' as a result of her acting process.[51] Siddons made sure she was 'penetrated with the character', that is, she acted it consistently from beginning to end rather than springing into action at particular moments (what Fitzgerald calls 'conventional bursts and claptrap'), employing the same method she had used as Constance (keeping her dressing-room door open to stay engaged with the part).[52] In his obituary of Kemble, Hazlitt declared that 'in the melancholy pride and rooted sentiments' of Wolsey, Kemble 'had no equal'.[53] Siddons and Kemble were depicted together in the play alongside their brothers, Charles as Cromwell and Stephen as Henry VIII, in *The Court for the Trial of Queen Katharine*, painted by George Henry Harlow in 1817 (Figure 3).[54] Like many such images, the painting is unlikely to reflect stage practice with complete accuracy. But it offers a sense of the siblings' powerful acting in these roles and the intricate staging of Kemble's spectacular revival of *Henry VIII*.

FIGURE 3 *John Sartain after George Henry Harlow,* Trial of Queen Katharine *(nineteenth century). ART File S528k4 no.70 (size M), image 29115. Used by permission of the Folger Shakespeare Library.*

Coriolanus

Kemble's next major production as manager was *Coriolanus*, which debuted on 7 February 1789. This play provided a major lead role for Kemble and an important part for Siddons, who acted Volumnia. As with *Henry VIII*, Kemble introduced several spectacular elements: the play was billed as featuring 'in Act II an Ovation, or Entry of *Coriolanus* into Rome. In Act V a Procession of *Roman Matrons* to the Volscian Camp'.[55] This marked a new approach to *Coriolanus*, realizing the drama's 'classical effect' through a 'visual rhetoric' rather than an oratorical one.[56] Press reviews of the opening night recognized Kemble's achievement with this production and the strength of the siblings' performance. The *World* pronounced that 'the revival of this Tragedy, is a credit to the skill which manages the Theatre: for there is much preparation, and all of it classical at once and dramatic. The costume is exact! There is much knowledge and accomplishment of effect!'[57] And the *Times* reported that 'to *Coriolanus* we are much indebted for *Kemble* and Mrs. *Siddons* in two new characters, perfectly adapted to, and worthy of their talents'.[58]

Kemble's innovations to the play consisted in the elaborate staging and spectacle, particularly in his handling of processions and crowd scenes, but his text was not wholly original: his version contained a mixture of Shakespeare (fairly heavily cut), elements of earlier adaptations of *Coriolanus* by James Thomson and Thomas Sheridan and some additions by Kemble himself.[59] The use of Thomson notably allowed Kemble 'to strengthen the dramatic impact of Volumnia'.[60] Kemble kept Thomson's revision of the pleading scene in which Volumnia tries to persuade her son by threatening to stab herself. This moment was criticized by some (the *Examiner*, for example, called it a 'despicable stage-expedient'), but other critics lauded Siddons's performance (the *Oracle and Public Advertiser* agreed with Coriolanus's assessment of Volumnia in pronouncing Siddons the 'most noble mother in the world').[61] Kemble's rearrangement of the text and his attention to the visual dimension of staging 'focussed attention on himself as Coriolanus and on Mrs. Siddons as Volumnia' and the siblings were particularly suited to these classical roles because 'as performers, the brother and sister were perfect samples of the heroic form and of the heroic action'.[62] Jane Moody nuances this assessment by explaining how 'Kemble's stiff, patrician Caius Martius perfectly complemented Siddons's towering maternity in the part of Volumnia'.[63] Kemble was considered physically and temperamentally well suited to delivering a portrayal of Coriolanus as a haughty Roman: 'The Roman energy of his deportment, the seraphic grace of his gesture and the movements of his perfect self-possession, displayed the great mind, daring to command, and disdaining to solicit, admiration.'[64] Siddons employed the majestic dimension of her acting so that she 'towered above her sex, and seemed worthy to bear about her the destinies of imperial Rome'.[65] Indeed, she was 'the only contemporary performer who could match [the] hauteur' of Kemble's Coriolanus.[66] Kemble wrote of their joint success on opening night in his diary: 'This Play was very splendidly ornamented – M^{rs}. Siddons was prodigiously admired, and it was said that I never acted better. The whole Play was greatly applauded.'[67]

Although the play relied on both Siddons and Kemble for its success, it was Kemble who became particularly identified with it, to the extent that it was 'impossible to think of either the character or the man, without reference to each other'.[68] Scott extended this identification to encompass all classical roles, pronouncing Kemble 'a complete model . . . of the Roman'.[69] The production was also a huge financial success, securing considerable earnings for the actor: Jonathan Sachs notes that 'when Kemble played Coriolanus, his receipts were routinely the highest of the week'.[70] The importance of the part to Kemble's career can be gauged by the fact that he chose this role for his final appearance when he left the stage in 1817 (a performance which I will discuss in the book's Conclusion). However, Siddons's engagement with the play was also lengthy and sustained: one of her earliest performances as Volumnia was at Manchester on 10 February 1777 and she also appeared in *Coriolanus* several times during her final season.[71] Both actors honed their performances 'by a course of peculiar study' into antiquity.[72] In Siddons's case this research in part took the form of learning sculpture, inspired by her friend Anne Damer, for as Boaden said, 'the application to statuary is always the study of the antique' and allowed Siddons to develop acting which 'reminded the spectator of classic models'.[73]

In his memoirs of the actor, John Ambrose Williams offered a detailed physical description of Kemble as Coriolanus which emphasized his classical appearance and called to mind the kind of sculpture with which Siddons had been engaged:

> In his first encounter with the rabble, it is impossible not to admire the noble proportions and majestic *contour* of his figure; the expression of his face, naturally of the Roman character; his right arm erected in conscious authority; his chest thrown forward, and his head slightly back; his right leg fearlessly advanced, and firmness in all his attitude, together with the exact adjustment and tasteful folds of the classical drapery with which his person is invested, compose a most superb and commanding *tout ensemble* of the human form.[74]

Kemble therefore expressed Coriolanus's disdain for the people through his pose and through costuming.

Kemble's *Coriolanus* contained three key scenes, all of which married an impressive visual dimension with strong acting and two of which relied on Siddons's Volumnia as well as Kemble's Coriolanus for their effect. Firstly, the Order of the Ovation (2.2), was a 'highly complex' stage moment which demonstrated Kemble's 'experienced skill in planning how to handle large numbers of extras, and his willingness to introduce subsidiary processions and eye-catching tableaux crowded with military and political figures'.[75] This moment had actually been created by Sheridan but Kemble greatly expanded it in order to provide a striking celebration of Coriolanus's victory at Corioli.[76] An account of this scene based on Charles Mayne Young's copy of the play and his recollections of its performance (he was an actor at Covent Garden) attests that 'no fewer than 240 persons marched, in stately procession across the stage' in addition to the 35 cast members.[77] The stage was thus filled with 'vestals, and lictors with their fasces, and soldiers with the spolia opima, and sword-bearers, and standard-bearers, and cup-bearers, and senators, and silver eagle-bearers, with the S.P.Q.R. upon them, and trumpeters, and drummers, and priests, and dancing-girls, &c., &c'.[78] The scene was designed to mark Coriolanus's triumphant return to Rome and therefore formed part of the trend in Kemble's adaptation of putting himself at the centre of the action. This was achieved visually both by the impressive procession and by Kemble striking a statuesque pose amidst the scenery: 'The spoils, the captives, the soldiers, the citizens had passed over, and there, *alone*, beneath the triumphal arch, stood the hero, in his simple, graceful, crimson robe, with his black head uncovered, and his attitude dictated by the very spirit of classic taste!'[79]

Young's account, perhaps the most detailed description of Siddons's Volumnia, and certainly the most frequently quoted, makes clear the importance of the actress in creating this scene's effect. He writes that in the procession she 'forgot her own identity' and fully became the character she portrayed: 'She was no longer Sarah Siddons, tied down to the directions of the prompter's book; she broke through old traditions; she recollected that, for the nonce, she was Volumnia, the proud mother of a proud son, and conquering hero.'[80] Instead of 'march[ing] across the stage, from right to left, with the solemn, stately, almost funeral, step conventional', her character's pride in her son's triumph meant that the actress 'towered above all round her, and rolled, and almost, reeled across the stage; her very soul as it were, dilating, and rioting in its exultation; until her action lost all grace, and, yet, became so true to nature, so picturesque, and so descriptive, that, pit and gallery sprang to their feet, electrified by the transcendent execution of the conception'.[81] Siddons's depiction of burgeoning maternal pride (she had her 'hands pressed firmly on her bosom, as if to repress by manual force its triumphant swellings') was a highlight of the ovation procession, itself a key element of Kemble's production.[82]

The Intercession scene (5.1 in Kemble's version), in which the Roman women, headed by Volumnia, beg Coriolanus to make peace, was another high point of the play and similarly depended on Siddons for its effect. The scene also used 'solemn procession', this time joined with 'mourning costume, and dagger'.[83] This was the famous moment, derived from Thomson, in which Volumnia threatened to stab herself while taunting her son: 'Tread on the bleeding breast of her, to whom / Thou ow'st thy life! – Lo, thy first victim.'[84] Siddons here maintained her majestic character as 'she was ardent in her solicitude to rescue her country from impending desolation, yet she would not even do so much by means which were incompatible with her honor'.[85] Like Coriolanus, she was 'firm and ... eloquent in her expression of dignity' but 'her loftiness of soul was sweetened by morality'.[86] Another critic noted that Siddons's Volumnia entreated her son with 'irresistible tenderness, maternal dignity, and female patriotism'.[87] Kemble responded powerfully to Siddons's acting in this scene, appearing particularly striking 'when Nature finally overcomes; and, bending on the neck of his mother, he exclaims, "Rome is saved, but thy son is lost"'.[88] David Rostron elucidates the movement incorporated in performance beyond that stipulated in the play text, pointing out that this scene contains 'Kemble's most detailed notes' about the actions of the characters in his promptbook of 1806.[89] Kemble has Volumnia advance before Virgilia as she demands respect from Coriolanus and notes that Coriolanus rises from his seat in response to this speech. Thus we see the relationship between the characters thought out on the level of physicality, which enhanced the emotional effect of their lines.

The third key moment was the assassination of Coriolanus at the very end of the play, in which Kemble shone. Scott praised the actor's performance for having 'the most striking resemblance to actual and instant death we ever witnessed' and for avoiding overacting ('all that rolling, gasping and groaning, which generally takes place in our theatres').[90] The hero's death was so realistic that, Scott claimed, women in the audience screamed out loud as Coriolanus/Kemble 'dropped as dead and as flat on the stage as if the swords had really met within his body'.[91] This pantomimic action demonstrated Kemble's superior 'command of muscle and limb' and his 'ability to express character and emotion' with his body.[92] It also showcased the same skill in performing death scenes as Siddons had demonstrated with Queen Katharine, when she was similarly praised for the 'excellence' of her 'pantomime'.[93]

In the moments leading up to the assassination, Kemble again used elements of Thomson and Sheridan's texts as Coriolanus 'redeemed his venal past in patriotic reaffirmation', pronouncing that there was 'more virtue in one single year / Of Roman story, than your Volscian annals / Can boast'.[94] The most striking change that Kemble made to the play's climax was to have Coriolanus murdered by the Volscian officers, rather than a group of anonymous conspirators as in Shakespeare. The Volscian assassins do not call for the hero's death nor remind the audience of Coriolanus's crimes and there are no Lords to upbraid Aufidius, who pronounces his final lines more or less as they appear in Shakespeare. The focus, then, is squarely on Coriolanus. Kemble's annotations show that trumpets and muffled drum rolls were heard as the ensigns and arms were lowered, augmenting the effect of the denouement leading up to the '*dead March*' at the play's conclusion.[95]

While Kemble's ending followed Thomson and Sheridan in effacing civil unrest in favour of asserting a nationalistic agenda, he restored the mutinous citizens to the opening of the play in order to foreground Coriolanus as early as possible in the action. As the events of the French Revolution unfolded, audiences inevitably began to draw parallels between the drama and contemporary politics: as Jonathan Bate points out, 'a play which began with an assemblage of citizens – the word resonant of the French revolutionary "citoyens" – . . . was potentially explosive'.[96] Kemble therefore employed strategies to quash the radical potential of the play. Sachs notes that Kemble's removal of 'all reference to the grounds of the dispute between the patricians and the plebeians' made their protest appear 'ridiculous and possibly despicable'.[97] Ripley describes how Kemble made the plebeians 'little more than a group voice', an interpretation that in later productions was 'underlined by dressing them all identically in the toga alba'.[98] This lack of individualization sought to limit the audience's sympathy for the citizens. Kemble's production satisfied his desire for visual effect that could be created with crowd scenes (with his character at the centre) but also enabled him to stage the containment of the political potential the plebeians represented: 'Kemble's firm handling' of the mob 'served as an image of control, a proclamation that London would not go the way of Paris'.[99]

The fluctuating political situation over the course of Kemble's career naturally had an effect on the play's production history. His *Coriolanus* was sometimes suspended for political reasons, but when it resumed, Kemble's tendency was to make the play increasingly reactionary. Inchbald explained how the manager's bias against the lower classes affected audience response to *Coriolanus*: 'When the lower order of people are in good plight, they will bear contempt with cheerfulness, and even with mirth; but poverty puts them out of humour at the slightest disrespect.'[100] Thus while Kemble made use of 'the distancing effects provided by antiquity' in order 'to stage volatile political issues . . . by displacing these concerns into a Roman setting', playgoers were not always willing to be distracted from contemporary parallels.[101] By and large, Siddons shared her brother's politics and by acting in his Shakespeare productions she supported his agenda. The siblings' conservatism would lead them into trouble with audiences, notably during the Old Price Riots of 1809 (explored in Chapter 4).

The influence of Kemble's *Coriolanus* was profound. During his career, Kemble's interpretation reached far beyond the London stage as the actor performed the role in

Edinburgh, Liverpool, Bath, Bristol, Dublin and Glasgow and Kemble's text was staged, though with other actors in the lead, in Manchester, Edinburgh, Liverpool and Bristol.[102] David George claims that 'only since the 1990s has the Shakespearean text caught up with Kemble's in number of performances'.[103] The endurance of this interpretation is in part because in preparing to leave the stage, Kemble employed a series of surrogates, actors who performed the role with Kemble's text and in his style. These surrogates included Young and William Augustus Conway, both of whom played Coriolanus at Covent Garden in 1813, while Kemble was absent from the theatre. But when the manager returned in 1814, these actors might even have been interchangeable with Kemble himself: John Genest's record of a performance on 15 May 1815 states that Kemble 'was seized with the gout, and Conway acted the part'.[104] Conway continued to play the role until 1817 in England (that is, at the same time as Kemble) and then in America from 1824 to 1827, popularizing Kemble's Coriolanus across the Atlantic, while Young acted Coriolanus in the provinces until 1824.[105] George notes that overall there are '94 known performances by Kemble and at least 38 by his surrogates'.[106] While one critic pronounced that the character 'would lose much of its interest in any other hands' so that Coriolanus 'could not outlive' Kemble, in training these substitutes the actor-manager ensured that it would in fact do so.[107]

Siddons's Volumnia, however, was not so easily replicable or replaceable. Charles Shattuck points out that it was not just the political climate of 1789 that kept *Coriolanus* off the stage but also Siddons's absence from the theatre in the second season of Kemble's management that prevented the play from establishing itself firmly in the repertoire at that time.[108] Ripley notes that following Siddons's retirement, the actresses who succeeded her as Volumnia, Eliza O'Neill and Harriet Faucit, although regarded as great performers, turned out to be 'inadequate matrons' who 'failed dismally', thus emphasizing 'the uniqueness of [Siddons's] achievement'.[109] Kemble was depicted several times as Coriolanus, often alone, as in Thomas

FIGURE 4 *Richard Westall*, Volumnia Pleading with Coriolanus *(c. 1800). FPa33, image 3130. Used by permission of the Folger Shakespeare Library.*

Lawrence's famous painting. But one striking image depicts him alongside Siddons in a visualization of the play. *Volumnia Pleading with Coriolanus* (Figure 4), painted around 1800 and attributed to Richard Westall, may not proclaim itself as an image of Siddons and Kemble but the faces of Volumnia and Coriolanus in the painting bear a striking resemblance to the siblings.[110] Like Harlow's depiction of *Henry VIII*, this image demonstrates the influence of Kemble and Siddons acting together on the perception of Coriolanus and Volumnia in the public imagination.

From Kemble to Sheridan and back again

Kemble recorded the challenges he faced in his first season as manager: 'The Theatre laboured under great Disadvantages from frequent Indispositions of the Performers, from the uncommon Severity of the Winter, from the Concern all People took in his Majesty's Indisposition and from their loyal Joy for his Recovery.'[111] Given that Siddons's acting was crucial to Kemble's success as manager, it was a blow to him when she withdrew for the 1789–90 season suffering from ill health but also fed up with the continual failure of Sheridan, who still controlled the theatre's purse strings, to pay her. Although Siddons did subsequently return to Drury Lane, the financial problems persisted. In May 1796, Siddons wrote to a friend from 'a little wretched inn, in a little poking village' en route to stints in Manchester, Liverpool, York and Leeds.[112] She explained that whether or not she would return to Drury Lane in the autumn depended entirely on Sheridan, whom she described as 'uncertainty personified' as the proceeds from her last benefit, 'a very great one' had been 'swept into his treasury' without her seeing a shilling.[113] Thus her intensive provincial tours were necessitated by Sheridan's financial negligence. The star actress was not the only member of the company that Sheridan overlooked; he also failed to pay his manager and other actors and personnel.[114] Kemble, as manager, often gave his word to actors or suppliers that they would be paid but when this led to a situation in which he 'had the mortification to be arrested', his frustration with Sheridan's business practices led him to resign from management at the end of the 1795–6 season.[115]

Other factors also played into Kemble's decision to step down, including the staging of the faux-Shakespearean play, *Vortigern* (as we shall see in the next chapter). Furthermore, a critical commonplace has suggested that Kemble was also unsettled by the changes to performance practice necessitated by the rebuilt and enlarged Drury Lane, which had opened in 1794.[116] Siddons described the new theatre as 'a wilderness of a place'; it accommodated considerably more spectators and its size meant that more elaborate visual effects were required in order to engage the audience.[117] But Kemble's stagings of Shakespeare had been paving the way for this kind of spectacle, which was further emphasized in his inaugural production at the new theatre. In a letter, Siddons described the splendour of both the new playhouse and the new show: 'Our new theatre is the most beautiful that imagination can paint. We open it with "Macbeth," on Easter Monday. I am told that the banquet is a thing to go and see of itself. The scenes and dresses all new, and as superb and characteristic as it is possible to make them.'[118]

Later that season, Kemble debuted *Lodoiska*, a new operatic afterpiece he had adapted from French sources, as a way to delight the audience with spectacular entertainment suitable for the size of the new Drury Lane. The *Courier* pronounced that 'the Scenery was, beyond description, beautiful, and the decorations, unprecedentedly, magnificent and appropriate'.[119] The music (by Stephen Storace) was also crucial to the production, particularly as in a large theatre some audience members may have had difficulty in hearing dialogue. Thus neither Siddons nor Kemble acted in the play, instead leaving the main roles to professional singers Anna Maria Crouch and Michael Kelly. Critics have sneered at *Lodoiska* as 'full of Gothic nonsense' that 'pander[ed] to popular taste' and have rather grudgingly acknowledged its success: it ran for twenty nights from its debut on 9 June until the end of the season, moving to the mainpiece slot for its last few performances, had thirty-four performances in 1794–5 and became a staple of the repertoire.[120] It also had a profound influence on later drama, including the popular *Timour the Tartar* (1811): as Boaden put it, *Lodoiska* was 'the model of all the fortresses subsequently stormed'.[121]

Yet to be noted is the influence *Lodoiska* had on *Pizarro*, the smash hit play produced by Sheridan in 1799 once Kemble was no longer serving as manager but was still acting in the company. *Lodoiska*'s climax featured a castle stormed by Tartars and the dramatic rescue of the heroine, Lodoiska, from a burning tower, by her lover, Floreski. A manuscript containing designs for the play's scenery features an image showing Lodoiska's tower on a high terrace within the castle and also includes a note pronouncing this scene design 'a Relic of the Old School' and attesting to the complexity of the staging: 'very heavy set & always took (including striking the 1st scene) 20 minutes. it was very effective'.[122] Kelly, who acted Floreski, recounted what happened in performance when the flames came too close to Crouch, who was playing Lodoiska:

> Seeing her in such peril I ran up the bridge, which was at a great height from the ground, towards the tower, in order to rescue her; just as I was quitting the platform, a carpenter, prematurely, took out one of its supporters, down I fell; and at the same moment, the fiery tower, in which was Mrs. Crouch, sank down in a blaze, with a violent crash; she uttered a scream of terror. Providentially I was not hurt by the fall, and catching her in my arms, scarcely knowing what I was doing, I carried her to the front of the stage, a considerable distance from the place where we fell. The applause was loud and continued.[123]

Indeed, the effect was so splendid that Kelly and Crouch repeated it in all subsequent performances. This powerful moment showcased both spectacular scenery and exciting action. When Sheridan produced his *Pizarro* in 1799, he may have recalled *Lodoiska*'s dramatic rescue on the bridge. A key scene of the later drama involved Kemble as Rolla snatching a baby from its captors and escaping across a bridge, which he then collapsed so the villains could not give chase. Campbell described the moment as 'a strikingly improving touch' on Sheridan's source text, August von Kotzebue's *Die Spanier in Peru*, and Boaden claimed the scene 'excited a sensation of alarm and agony beyond any thing perhaps that the stage has exhibited'.[124] Thus Sheridan's spectacular drama did not replace Kemble's Shakespearean stagings but was influenced by them and by his own experiments with spectacle.

In addition to the importance of Kemble's acting as Rolla, *Pizarro* also relied heavily on Siddons's performance as Elvira. Many spectators deemed this character a morally dubious one (Elvira leaves her lover Pizarro, the leader of the Spaniards, in favour of the Peruvian general, Alonzo) and so Elvira seemed rather at odds with Siddons's usual roles, which were majestic or pathetic but almost always virtuous. Thus her achievement in popularizing the part was deemed all the more significant. When Boaden praised Kemble's Rolla, the actor replied, 'NAY, nay, I have every thing to aid me; it *is* a noble character. Carry your wonder to Mrs. Siddons; she has made a heroine of a soldier's *trull*'.[125] Critics have noted that *Pizarro* was recognizable to its audiences as a 'reworking' (or even 'rehashing') of Sheridan's parliamentary rhetoric, particularly in Kemble's speeches as Rolla and most famously in the lines in which Rolla characterizes the support offered by the Spaniards to the Peruvians as 'such protection as vultures give to lambs', the same trope Sheridan had employed to critique the East India Company during the trial of Warren Hastings.[126] Selena Couture demonstrates how Sheridan adapted Kotzebue's play specifically for Siddons's acting style and celebrity, expanding the role of Elvira and giving her a final speech that 'functions as a companion' to Rolla's highly rhetorical lines containing the vulture–lamb metaphor.[127] Furthermore, Elvira's costume in the final scene (a nun's habit) would have recalled the 'flowing white gown and headdress' Siddons wore in the sleepwalking scene as Lady Macbeth and would therefore have 'lent even greater power to Elvira's final speech'.[128]

Sheridan also invoked the siblings' earlier joint Shakespearean triumphs in *Pizarro*. One image of the play depicts the moment when Elvira brandishes a dagger as Rolla looks on (Figure 5), recalling Volumnia's threat to harm herself in front of Coriolanus. Elvira subsequently gives Rolla the dagger to murder the sleeping Pizarro but the would-be assassin hesitates, leaving Elvira to regret 'that I trusted to thy weakness, and did not strike the blow myself' in a situation highly reminiscent of *Macbeth*, the most celebrated work in

FIGURE 5 *Joseph Stadler after Joseph Barrow,* Pizarro Act 4 Scene 1 *(1800). E.2-1939. © Victoria and Albert Museum, London.*

which the actors appeared together (explored in Chapter 4).[129] The success of *Pizarro* therefore derived from the fact that Sheridan created roles for both Kemble and Siddons and harnessed the power of their joint acting.

Pizarro was acted thirty-one times in a row at the end of the 1798–9 season, 'brought at least fifteen thousand pounds into the theatre in its first season' and remained in the theatrical repertoire for many years to come.[130] When Kemble took over the management of Covent Garden in 1803, he produced his own version of *Pizarro* there and the revisions and careful staging annotations in his promptbook show the manager putting his own political spin on the play. Taylor notes that Kemble staged the 'scenes of Peruvian pageantry' in such a way as to amount to '*Coriolanus* redux'.[131] For example, in Sheridan's already elaborate Temple of the Sun ceremony (2.2), the movement and music of the '*solemn Procession*' of priests and virgins is mapped out in precise detail.[132] Thus Kemble's *Pizarro* transformed Sheridan's play 'into a loyalist extravaganza that revelled in spectacular exhibitions of carefully choreographed and manifestly hierarchical ceremony', offering 'reassuring order'.[133] Images of Kemble as Rolla portray him wearing 'a knee-length, white Roman tunic with gold trim' and sandals, though occasionally with costume elements designed to suggest Rolla's Indigenous Peruvian identity, such as the 'gold headdress with white, feathered plumes' depicted by Robert Dighton.[134] Siddons's Elvira in Dighton's companion portrait was similarly classically attired. Such classical costumes, which can also be seen in the image of Elvira wielding the dagger (Figure 5), would have further called to mind Kemble's *Coriolanus*. *Pizarro* remained an important play for Siddons and Kemble but was also linked with some of Covent Garden's misfortunes: when the theatre was destroyed by fire in 1808, the press speculated that the blaze might have been caused by 'the wadding of the gun fired during the performance of *Pizarro*' becoming 'lodged in one of the scenes'.[135] Boaden went so far as to conclude that as Siddons and Kemble 'were the positive causes of Pizarro's being acted at Covent Garden Theatre ... the KEMBLES were the *cause* of this conflagration'.[136]

In 1800, Kemble returned to management, enticed by the prospect of acquiring a one-quarter share of the theatre, which would make him both manager and proprietor and give him greater control at Drury Lane.[137] Kemble continued to emphasize Shakespeare in the repertoire, including a revival of *The Winter's Tale* in 1802 in which Siddons played what was to be her last new role, Hermione. In this character, Siddons again employed her study of antiquity and in the final scene she appeared as 'one of the noblest statues, that even Grecian taste ever invented'.[138] Kemble as Leontes was 'every thing that either feeling or taste could require'.[139] The manager noted that the play was 'very greatly applauded'.[140] But a note from Kemble to the theatre's treasurer, Richard Peake, highlights the ongoing financial difficulties involved in his productions, including his stagings of Shakespeare: 'Let me remind you, that you are to send me FIFTY pounds for Mrs. Siddons today, or we shall have no *King John* on Saturday. . . . They are standing still in Greenwood's room, for want of a little canvas. Unless you help us there, we can have no Cymbeline, nor no pantomime at Christmas.'[141] Ultimately, Kemble's lawyer was unable to establish Sheridan's title to the property and so the negotiations to buy into the theatre patent fell through. Furthermore, Siddons's and Kemble's continual inability to extract money from the theatre in payment of their salaries led them to leave Drury Lane at the end of the 1801–2 season and subsequently to defect to Covent Garden.

3

Vortigern (1796)

'A most audacious impostor'

The one and only performance of *Vortigern* on 2 April 1796 was a curious episode in the theatrical careers of Siddons and Kemble. The staging of this drama demonstrates that not everything with which the siblings were involved that purported to be Shakespearean was actually by Shakespeare and reinforces that new drama produced during this period was often heavily influenced by the actors, with lead roles written with their talents in mind and productions drawing on elements of Kemble's famously spectacular stagings. *Vortigern* was billed simply as 'a new Play in 5 acts', featuring 'new Scenes, Dresses, and Decorations' (Figure 6). Although the playbill did not advertise *Vortigern*'s supposed connection with Shakespeare, many playgoers would have been aware that this new drama was part of the Shakespeare Papers, a cache of documents allegedly by, or related to, Shakespeare that the Ireland family claimed to have newly uncovered. The Shakespeare Papers were being hotly debated in London cultural circles at this time and the performance of

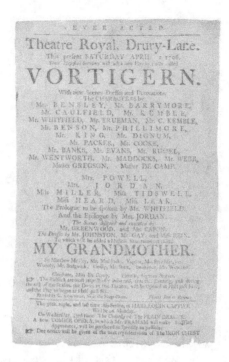

FIGURE 6 *Playbill for the production of* Vortigern *at the Theatre Royal Drury Lane (2 April 1796). 8MWEZ+n.c. 918, https://digitalcollections.nypl.org/items/9c08fa90-6be5-5163-e040-e00a180601b9. Billy Rose Theatre Division, New York Public Library.*

Vortigern would come to represent the public trial of this new bardolatrous discovery.

The history of *Vortigern*

In December 1794, a young man named William Henry Ireland produced a hitherto unknown document bearing Shakespeare's signature, much to the delight of his father Samuel, who was both an antiquarian and a bardolator.[1] It was, of course, a fake. More manuscripts followed and ten days after the first document had been revealed, William Henry announced to his father that among the cache of materials he had uncovered was an unknown play of Shakespeare's entitled *Vortigern*, a five-act historical tragedy on the theme of the ancient Briton who had betrayed his country by murdering King Constantius and inviting in the Saxons, Hengist and Horsus.[2] William Henry also produced a series of letters between Shakespeare and a printer named William Holmes negotiating payment for the play's production, with Shakespeare professing this to be one of his best works and refusing to settle for less than he thought it deserved.[3] This correspondence both authenticated the play and asserted its status as the best drama in Shakespeare's repertoire. *Vortigern* was delivered to Samuel in instalments of a few pages each time because William Henry claimed he was making a copy of the original manuscript, which its present owner would not relinquish, though in reality he was writing the play from scratch, aided by his father's copy of Holinshed's *Chronicles*.[4] Both Covent Garden and Drury Lane showed considerable interest in the drama since regardless of whether the play was authentically Shakespearean or had aesthetic merit, it would bring in playgoers and make money for the theatre at which it was staged. William Henry later claimed that Thomas Harris (the Covent Garden manager) offered '*carte blanche*' to Samuel to declare his terms for *Vortigern*'s staging.[5] But as we shall see, the play was created very much with the Drury Lane company in mind and Samuel chose that theatre for its premiere, taking a keen interest in plans for the play's production. Throughout, Samuel negotiated on behalf of his son, who at nineteen was still legally a minor.[6]

By March 1795, the manuscript of *Vortigern* was put on display with the Shakespeare Papers (which consisted of various other falsified documents, included legal records, Shakespeare's correspondence, annotated books from the playwright's library and the original manuscript of *King Lear*) at the Ireland home in Norfolk Street upon payment of an entrance fee of two guineas. The documents were published at Samuel's behest as

Miscellaneous Papers and Legal Instruments Under the Hand and Seal of William Shakespeare on 24 December 1795, but *Vortigern* was not included in the collection. Publishing the play separately would allow Samuel to make more money and withholding it from readers until performance would maintain an element of mystery about it. Although *Vortigern* was just one element of the Shakespeare Papers, through its performance in one of the capital's two patent theatres in a production featuring the country's leading Shakespearean actors, playgoers were encouraged to pronounce judgement on both the play and the broader set of documents. Furthermore, public performance opened up access to *Vortigern* to a broader cross-section of society. The invitation to view the documents was addressed only to 'Gentlemen' and numbers were obviously limited in the Irelands' home; thus, a production of *Vortigern* at Drury Lane represented a way for many more people to engage with the discussions surrounding the Papers. Adding further to the sense of debate was the fact that leading Shakespeare scholar (and friend of Kemble) Edmond Malone published his demolition of the Ireland Shakespeare materials, *An Inquiry into the Authenticity of Certain Miscellaneous Papers and Legal Instruments*, just two days before the performance (selling 500 copies before the curtain went up).[7]

It is important to understand why there was so much ado about Shakespeare in the 1790s, when *Vortigern* was performed. As we have seen, Shakespeare occupied a pre-eminent position in the theatrical repertory at this time. Following the bardolatry that had grown over the course of the eighteenth century, culminating, it is often said, with David Garrick's Shakespeare Jubilee of 1769, Shakespeare was at the forefront of literature and culture as well as theatre. This intense interest in Shakespeare grew alongside an artistic culture that prized antiquarianism and therefore occasioned a quest for documentary traces of the dramatist's life and works. The desire expressed by Samuel for an authentic Shakespearean signature and his pursuit of such a document on a trip to Stratford-upon-Avon with his son in 1793 should be placed in this context.[8] As Antonia Forster puts it, in an atmosphere of 'ever-increasing devotion to Shakespeare ... People believed in the documents because they wanted them to be real'.[9] William Henry's fabrications simply gave the Shakespeare-loving public what it wanted. Indeed, George Chalmers even blamed Malone for the fraud of the Shakespeare Papers, arguing that his scholarly research 'had encouraged people to believe that Shakespeare documents might be found'.[10] Throughout the century, Shakespeare had been used as a national icon in the face of threatened invasions, both physical and cultural, by foreign powers, notably the French. And in the context of the 1790s, Shakespeare came to represent British culture against the republican sentiments working their way across the channel from France, which were largely considered disturbing. That Shakespeare provided the English with a sense of national identity in troubling times explains why he was both highly prized and hotly contested.

Siddons, Kemble and *Vortigern*

Shakespeare's theatrical and cultural pre-eminence was due in no small part to Siddons and Kemble. Kemble's focus on producing Shakespeare popularized the works and by linking themselves with Shakespeare through their choice of roles, Siddons and Kemble enhanced their reputations as actors. Bardolatry was therefore a two-way street for the siblings. Furthermore, given their reputations as Shakespeareans, the public looked to Siddons and Kemble for guidance as to how to evaluate and respond to this new Shakespearean work, taking their cues from the actors' handling of *Vortigern*. While *Vortigern* contained many echoes of Shakespeare's drama (from the opening scene in which Constantius divides his kingdom like *King Lear* onwards), William Henry's imitation of Shakespeare focused particularly on emulating roles in the canon in which Siddons and Kemble had been especially popular and successful. Kemble played the tragic hero Vortigern, a role that called to mind some of the Shakespearean protagonists that the actor had made famous: Vortigern's murder of King Constantius recalls Macbeth's regicide and his identification of the King's sons as further obstacles to his power evokes Richard III. The part of Edmunda, Vortigern's wife, which was created for Siddons, has shades of Queen Katharine, Lady Macbeth and Constance in her nobility, madness and grief. Indeed, William Henry later explicitly noted that 'every leading character' in the play 'was positively written for some certain performer'; that is, he tailored the roles in *Vortigern* to the most popular actors on the London stage at the time.[11] In addition to writing for Siddons and Kemble, William Henry created the part of Flavia (daughter of Vortigern and Edmunda) for the star actress Dorothy Jordan. Flavia, the play's romantic heroine, is exiled from her father's court and pursues her lover (one of Constantius's sons) dressed as a boy. Jordan had been particularly popular in breeches roles, including Rosalind in *As You Like It*. Flavia's exile from the court is reminiscent of Rosalind's cross-dressed sojourn in the Forest of Arden. William Henry's imitation of Shakespeare therefore relied heavily on the plays performed in the theatre of the period rather than on those that were most valued as literary texts.[12]

While William Henry was obviously enthusiastic about the possibility of Siddons and Kemble participating in *Vortigern* when it was staged, the feeling was not reciprocated. The manager allegedly originally pushed for the play to have its premiere on April Fool's Day and though this idea was vetoed and *Vortigern* was staged on the following night, the new play was paired with the musical farce *My Grandmother*, a piece which featured a gullible art collector, presumably with Kemble's approval, or perhaps even at his suggestion.[13] Michael Dobson points out that the actor-manager found himself in an impossible situation: as a friend of Malone's, Kemble 'can't have thought the play genuine for a moment' but as an employee of Sheridan's, he 'could neither refuse the part nor damage the play's profitability by openly declaring it to be fraudulent'.[14] Dobson concludes that 'being obliged to play the leading role in a manifestly forged play was clearly a deeply humiliating position for Kemble, calculated to undermine his authority as a learned and discriminating Shakespearean actor'.[15] Although as manager Kemble had a great deal of power over what was staged and how it was produced, Sheridan remained in overall charge at Drury Lane. While for Kemble staging Shakespeare was an artistic and intellectual pursuit, for Sheridan the works were simply good box office. It was for this reason that the latter agreed to produce *Vortigern*: the play's authenticity was beside the point and its significance was not artistic or cultural but financial.[16]

Kemble might have been obliged to star in *Vortigern*, but he did not have to like it and according to William Henry, the actor deliberately sabotaged the performance. Kemble allegedly purposefully stressed and repeated a line ('And when this solemn mockery is o'er') in Vortigern's key speech on life and death, which elicited a 'most discordant howl' from the pit.[17] Critics have read the actor's emphasis on these words as Kemble's pronouncement of his own derogatory judgement of the play: Bernard Grebanier, for example, claims that Kemble contrived to make the line 'sound like a résumé of the whole evening'.[18] But although the anecdote has been frequently repeated, it was not widely reported in the press at the time. The *Times*, though, noted that some members of the audience 'became seriously angry' when Kemble reiterated the line (rendered 'I wou'd this solemn mockery were over' in this report) so that unrest continued 'for several minutes' until Kemble was able to address the audience to remind them 'that the title to authenticity which this Play lays claim to, depends on your giving it a fair and full hearing'.[19] Further evidence of Kemble's hostility to *Vortigern* can be found in two accounts by Joseph Farington: in late 1795, he recorded that 'Kemble told Boaden that He had read the play of Vortigern, and that it was wretched stuff' and he later reported that immediately after the performance, Kemble socialized with a group of men which included Malone.[20] One can well imagine them dissecting the performance in the same way that Malone had scrutinized and lambasted the Shakespeare Papers in his *Inquiry*. Kemble later offered an assessment of the play in which he described how 'Mr. Malone, in a few minutes conversation, convinced [him] that [the Shakespeare Papers] were spurious'.[21] He further noted that he was accused of pronouncing the words 'solemn mockery' 'with a malicious emphasis, to assist the downfal [*sic*] of the piece' but claims that 'the allusion was too obvious not to be caught in a moment by an audience wearied to death with what they had already gone through', and thus, 'at this line, the most overwhelming sounds of mingled groan and laughter ran through the house'.[22] However, the multiple inaccuracies in Kemble's account, produced many years after the event, cast doubt on its validity and suggest that it was written with the benefit of the knowledge that history would side with him in judging *Vortigern*.[23]

Siddons lacked both the power and obligations that Kemble faced as manager and seems to have had more leeway in refusing the role in *Vortigern* that had been written for her, although she did so in a somewhat disingenuous way. A letter from Siddons to Samuel in March 1796 demonstrates that she used illness as an excuse:

> Mrs. Siddons' compliments to Mr. Ireland; she finds that 'Vortigern' is intended to be performed next Saturday, and begs to assure him that she is very sorry the weak state of her health, after almost six weeks of indisposition, renders her incapable of even going to the necessary rehearsals of the play, much less to act. Had she been fortunately well, she would have done all in her power to justify Mr. Ireland's polite sentiments on the subject, when she had the honour of seeing him on Saturday.[24]

Earlier that month she had told her friend Hester Piozzi that while she was busy learning the role of Edmunda, her part in *Vortigern*, she also had doubts about the play's authenticity: 'All sensible persons are convinced that "Vortigern" is a most audacious impostor. If he be not, I can only say that

Shakespeare's writings are more unequal than those of any other man.'[25] However, it seems that the Irelands and others saw through her excuses. William Henry later wrote that Siddons 'had doubtless a fore knowledge of the Janus like part her brother intended to adopt' and that 'she declined accepting the character under a plea of ill health', adding that she 'was never behind hand in jesuitry', thereby implying that he did not believe her.[26] Another contemporary letter from one T. Nixon, apparently a member of the Ireland circle, described how when Samuel saw Siddons about a week before the performance 'she seem'd perfectly well & said, that though she was afraid she should not be able to play on Saturday, she hoped she should in three or four days afterwards'.[27] The writer went on to say that Kemble 'refused to put [*Vortigern*'s premiere] off a single day, notwithstanding it has been postponed three months beyond the Time stipulated in the agreement', implying that the manager's refusal to delay the play's debut so that it would have to go ahead without Siddons was another of his deliberate attempts to sabotage it.[28]

That the Irelands' perceived of Siddons as central to the play's success is demonstrated by the letters that passed between Samuel and Drury Lane as the production was being prepared. These emphasized that the part of Edmunda was designed for the actress and expressed increasing panic as it became clear that she would not act in the play. As early as December 1795, Samuel insisted to Kemble (repeating a conversation they had held earlier) that 'Mrs Siddons alone can take ye part of Edmunda'.[29] When the play went into rehearsal in March, Samuel wrote to William Powell, the Drury Lane prompter, begging to know whether 'Mrs Siddons has relinquished the Character of Edmunda' or if 'indisposition prevents her appearance on ye 2^d April', following a report that 'she is not to perform in ye play of Vortigern'.[30] A few days later, Samuel hounded Sheridan (having already called on him and sent a note), writing that 'it is highly necessary I sh^d see you in ye Course of this day, in Consequence of a Conv^n I had yesterday with Mrs Siddons', presumably the one referred to in the letter by Nixon, quoted previously.[31]

The question of the actress's participation in *Vortigern* became a matter of public interest. A press report noted that 'Mrs. SIDDONS improves in health, yet her recovery is too tardy to allow her to take a part in *Vortigern*, which comes out on Saturday se'nnight. Mrs. POWEL is studying her part'.[32] Just as with Kemble, playgoers would have read Siddons's involvement as an endorsement of the play's authenticity, hence her failure to appear as Edmunda was a damning blow to *Vortigern*. Piozzi noted that if the play were delayed as a result of Siddons's ill health, the actress could 'save[] Ireland awhile'.[33] Piozzi also expressed her own judgement of the play's authenticity: 'Vortigern will, I trust, be condemned almost without a hearing, so completely does the laugh go against it.'[34]

The 1795–6 season was, indeed, one 'in which [Siddons] suffered recurrent illnesses', so her failure to appear in the play may genuinely have been a result of poor health.[35] However, she had a reputation for using physical infirmity as an excuse to avoid performing when it did not suit her: Thomas Gilliland claimed that during her later career at Covent Garden, Siddons 'more than once, on pretence of a finger ach [*sic*] has caused the alteration of the expected Drama, at *a very late hour* of the day'.[36] Given her ongoing struggles with Sheridan over payment, the actress's refusal to appear in such a high-profile production may have been a calculated strategy to make the theatre proprietor realize her worth and to encourage him to pay her accordingly. But Kemble's (much later, and perhaps unreliable) account seems to confirm the Irelands' suspicions that Siddons's non-appearance was a result of her judgement of the play more than her health. He noted that while he consented to appear in *Vortigern* at Sheridan's request, 'Mrs. Siddons positively refused to enter, as she expressed herself, into so abominable a conspiracy against the memory of Shakspeare'.[37]

The third performer for whom a key part in the play was written, Jordan, was much more enthusiastic about the drama and Boaden praised the actress's handling of *Vortigern*: 'She acted her character of Flavia, *bonâ fide*, with exquisite simplicity; and very properly did not affect to play the *critic*, which is in fact decided treachery, where you have liberty to reject the part you play.'[38] She also secured royal backing for *Vortigern*, encouraging the Duke of Clarence (later King William IV), with whom she was in a long-term relationship, to subscribe for copies of the Shakespeare Papers and to be present in a box for the performance. Jordan's encouragement provided a stark contrast to Siddons and Kemble, who refused to use their acting powers to support the play. But even she found a way to express some reservations about the authenticity of the work: Farington recorded that when she spoke the epilogue, she 'skipped over some lines which claimed the play as Shakespeares'.[39] According to Boaden, other members of the cast knew the manager's opinion of *Vortigern* 'and acted quite up to it'.[40] The Irelands went so far as to accuse Kemble of deliberate miscastings which undermined the play, including John Phillimore as Horsus, whose 'nose was long enough to d—n the finest play Shakspeare ever wrote' and who managed to contrive to make his death scene ridiculous as he 'so placed his unfortunate carcass that on the falling of the drop-curtain he was literally divided between the audience and his brethren of the sock and buskin', and Charles Dignum as the Second Baron, whose 'guttural pronunciation' of the line 'let them bellow on' (when calling for trumpets) 'set the whole house in a convulsive peal of laughter'.[41]

Nick Groom writes of how William Henry 'blended two strains of bardolatry – the ardour of the amateur antiquarian with the fashionable taste of the stage'.[42] In this sense, his sensibilities were not too far from Kemble's, who, as we have seen, used his own antiquarian research to create spectacular popular performances. Thus, in addition to relying on the manager to make appropriate casting choices, the Irelands also hoped that *Vortigern* would be presented in the same impressive fashion as Kemble's other productions (such as those discussed in Chapter 2), both those of Shakespeare and entertainments such as *Lodoiska*. Numerous letters between the Irelands and the theatre in the lead-up to the production emphasize the importance the former placed on '*New Scenery & dresses*' which the Drury Lane management had apparently promised.[43] But although the play was ultimately advertised as being presented with 'new Scenes, Dresses & Decorations' by the theatre's leading painters and costumiers, these production elements could not save *Vortigern*.[44] While Samuel Ireland and even Sheridan prepared for *Vortigern* to have a long run, it achieved only a single performance.[45] When William Barrymore, the actor who played Aurelius, came forward to announce the play again for the following Monday, an uproar ensued that lasted for fifteen minutes until *Vortigern* was replaced by *The School for Scandal* as the next drama to appear on the Drury Lane stage.

Iron chests and other controversies

In addition to catering to the public's interest in Shakespeare through its claim to be an authentic work by the dramatist and its many echoes of Shakespeare's plays, *Vortigern* also responded to the theatrical trends of the late eighteenth century. Shakespeare provided the bulk of the high tragedy produced in the theatres at this time, but critics of the stage repeatedly called for contemporary writers to produce new drama in this vein. When dramatists of the period did write tragedy, they tended to do so in the popular Gothic style, often combining this with Shakespearean influences, as can be seen in the works of Joanna Baillie and Walter Scott. Furthermore, Kemble excelled as an actor in the Gothic mode because 'he was a master in the portrayal of brooding intensity'.[46] Thus William Henry tailored the role of Vortigern both to Kemble's strengths as a Shakespearean and to his popularity in contemporary Gothic characters. *Vortigern* also taps into the genre of Shakespearean Gothic in its choice of subject matter, the dramatization of Britain's national origins, in the tragic mode. Shakespearean

Gothic was a contested form because while Shakespeare was valued, the Gothic was deemed suspicious for its associations with Jacobinism. Taylor notes that *Vortigern*'s 'narrative of conspiracy, espionage, defection, the threat of invasion, and regicide' was, in fact, 'a dramatization of the political landscape in the mid 1790s' and the press worried that the drama was too '*immoral, indecent,* and *Jacobinical*' to receive a licence for performance.[47] The play thus negotiates complex cultural politics through 'its dual position as both new play and historical document', but is also 'buttressed by its unique cultural status' as a play 'supposedly written by Britain's national author'.[48]

One recent example of the Shakespearean Gothic was *The Iron Chest*, which had premiered a few weeks before *Vortigern*'s debut. This drama was George Colman the Younger's adaptation, commissioned by Sheridan, of Godwin's radical novel *Caleb Williams* (1794). Although the playwright claimed to have 'avoided all tendency to that which . . . is termed Politicks', some critics insisted on underlining the play's connection with the novel and 'its moral and political tendency, [which] ought . . . to be consigned to infamy and oblivion by the hands of the common hangman'.[49] Kemble's own conservative views were in opposition to the political outlook expressed in both *The Iron Chest* and *Vortigern* and so it was unsurprising that he at best did not support and at worst actively hindered each play.

The parallels in Kemble's treatment of the two works are instructive. When first performed at Drury Lane on 12 March 1796, *The Iron Chest* 'disappointed the expectations of one of the most crouded audiences of this season'.[50] The play was criticized for its length and lack of dramatic interest, but reviewers also noticed Kemble's lacklustre performance in the lead role of Sir Edward Mortimer. Some critics were sympathetic to the actor's apparent illness: the *Oracle* described how Kemble was 'tormented with an incessant cough' and took upon himself the blame for 'the displeasure of the house', although the audience told him, 'No, no, KEMBLE – it is not your fault'.[51] The playwright, however, was less willing to accept that Kemble's poor performance was a result of illness and publicly attributed it to the actor-manager's desire to sink the play, detailing his accusations at length in the preface to *The Iron Chest* when it was printed. Colman wrote that while the actor might be 'entitled to pity' for his illness, 'for his conduct under it, he, undoubtedly, deserved censure'.[52] Specifically, Colman claimed he 'found Mr. KEMBLE, in his dressing room, a short time before the curtain was drawn up, taking *Opium Pills*' and that he seemed 'very unwell' and extremely drowsy.[53] Kemble was known to be a habitual opium user in order to relieve the persistent cough from which he suffered and with which he was afflicted at the time of this performance. But the opium could affect the actor's performance, the languid effects of the drug rendering his movements even slower and more ponderous than usual. As Colman wrote: 'The great actor was discover'd, as *Sir Edward Mortimer*, in his library. Gloom and desolation sat upon his brow. . . . The picture could not have look'd better – but, in justice to the picture, it must also be added, that, the picture could scarcely have acted worse.'[54] The preface to *The Iron Chest* gives only Colman's side of the story and doubtless Kemble's illness was a significant factor in his behaviour. But the events surrounding this earlier work strongly suggest that Kemble was not above sabotaging plays in performance if he did not approve of them. Although writing with the benefit of hindsight, Fitzgerald claims as much, noting that *The Iron Chest* episode was 'highly characteristic of Kemble, when in that strange and lofty mood which frequently settled on him'.[55] William Henry made the link between *Vortigern* and *The Iron Chest* through what he (like Colman) saw as Kemble's poor behaviour and its subsequent negative influence on the audience. Ireland writes of Kemble's delivery of the 'solemn mockery' line (which provoked laughter and derision from playgoers) as 'uttered in the most sepulchral tone of voice possible, and accompanied with that peculiar emphasis which on a subsequent occasion so justly rendered Mr. Kemble the object of criticism (*viz.*, on the first representation of Mr.

Coleman's Iron Chest)'.[56] Boaden made the same connection: 'While Mr. Kemble thus suffered in the opinion of an *able* man [Colman] from his indisposition, during the first night's performance of the Iron Chest, he was shortly after to bear, from an *impudent* one, the imputation of having played the critic, when he should have acted Vortigern, and by downright treachery producing the damnation of Shakspeare himself.'[57]

In addition to similarities in Kemble's acting in the two plays, there were also parallels in the rehearsal practices he instituted. According to Colman, Kemble's inattention to the script of his play provided further evidence of the manager's sabotage of it, and Samuel's correspondence shows that he was eager to ensure that Kemble took care over the text of *Vortigern* as he readied it for performance to avoid such mishaps. Kemble, who had been absent for much of the rehearsal process of *The Iron Chest* as a result of illness, 'suffered the piece to be produced, *uncut*, ... surcharged with all his own incapacity, and all his opium'.[58] However, Colman deemed this 'a proof of the neglect of those whose business it was to have informed me ... that it appeared in the *last rehearsal*, to want curtailment', placing the blame on Kemble for critiques that the play was too long.[59] In the preface to *Vortigern*, Samuel explained that after being accepted at Drury Lane, 'some alterations were deemed necessary to fit it for representation', including reducing its unwieldy length.[60] The excessive length of the play is confirmed by William Henry's later comment that it contained over 2,800 lines (considerably more than the average of 1,400), leading Sheridan to quip that *Vortigern* was a bargain 'as there were two plays and a half, instead of one'.[61] When the revised manuscript was submitted, 'it was delivered to the Theatre, with a request, or rather *intreaty*, that all further alteration, deemed necessary, should be made by the acting manager, or any other person competent to the business' and presumably this included any further cuts that might need to be made to reduce its running time.[62] However, Kemble responded '"that the play would be acted faithfully from the copy sent to the theatre"; and it was accordingly acted, literally from the Manuscript delivered to the house'.[63] Samuel argued that this behaviour was 'unprecedented in the management of a Theatre', but that was not quite the case, as Colman's preface to *The Iron Chest* demonstrates.[64] In invoking the play's length as a drawback to its success, Samuel may have been trying to connect *Vortigern* with *The Iron Chest* and to mobilize those that had backed Colman over Kemble to support him in his dispute with the manager as well.

There was also an intriguing thematic link between the title of Colman's play and the cultural understanding of the circumstances in which literary documents, largely spurious, were being discovered in the period. Some years earlier, Thomas Chatterton, William Henry's idol and inspiration, claimed at a similarly youthful age to have found literary works in chests that his father (an amateur antiquarian like Samuel Ireland) had acquired from the muniment room of a local church.[65] William Henry did not claim to have uncovered his Shakespearean manuscripts in a trunk but, rather, among 'a vast collection of old deeds and papers tied up in bundles' shown to him by the mysterious 'Mr. H.'.[66] But the cultural imagination made the link between the discovery of such spurious documents and the presence of a chest or trunk. The graphic satire *The Oaken Chest or the Gold Mines of Ireland a Farce* depicts the entire Ireland family – Samuel, William Henry, Jane and Anna Maria (William Henry's sisters), and Mrs Freeman (born Anna Maria de Burgh Coppinger, thought to be the Irelands' housekeeper but in fact Samuel's romantic partner and the mother of his children) – and prominently features a large chest full of manuscripts.[67] The verse underneath the image begins by highlighting the trunk: 'In A musty Old garret some where or another, / This Chest has been found by some person or other.'[68] The poem continues to enumerate the treasures unearthed from the chest and closes with the crowning glory of the discoveries: 'Hark great Vortigern comes now ye criticks be dumb; / This is Shakspeares I'll swear: if 'tis not 'tis a Hum.'[69] The satirist's point is, of course, that the Shakespeare Papers, including *Vortigern*, were obvious forgeries and that the entire Ireland family was actively involved in their creation.[70] The inclusion of the chest so prominently in the image and its accompanying text would have recalled Chatterton's fraudulent discoveries, thus further suggesting that *Vortigern* and the Shakespeare Papers were also fakes. The proliferation of such supposedly literary findings caused one writer to joke that 'many old Ladies are now at work in searching their *old trunks*, in hopes of finding a few Comedies from the pens of *Congreve* or *Vanbrugh*'.[71] The print's title, *The Oaken Chest*, would also have evoked Colman's play *The Iron Chest* (in which the chest arouses the curiosity of Wilford, Mortimer's secretary, and is subsequently revealed to contain evidence of Mortimer's guilt for a murder) and Kemble's lacklustre and, indeed, sabotaging performance in the drama, in order to foreground in the public imagination the idea of the great Shakespearean's animosity towards the play.[72]

Public discourse at the time did not make the connection between *Vortigern* and an earlier spurious Shakespearean drama, *Double Falsehood*, but it is a link worth drawing, particularly in its bearing on Siddons's relation to Shakespeare. The reception of the play (now fairly widely accepted as an adaptation of *Cardenio*, the lost work by Shakespeare and Fletcher), which was first performed in 1727, was more positive than that of *Vortigern* seventy years later. Brean Hammond attributes this to the fact that by the end of the century, questions of materiality and provenance had become central to any discovery related to Shakespeare, and Jack Lynch identifies a shift from a cultural understanding of Shakespeare's 'universality' to a celebration of his 'eccentricity', which was felt to make his work readily identifiable for its unique qualities.[73] *Double Falsehood* had 'a long and successful life in print and on stage': its last eighteenth-century performance had taken place on 6 June 1791 at Covent Garden, when (unlike *Vortigern*) it did not attract undue attention.[74] Although prior to this performance it had not been acted since the 1770s, perhaps *Double Falsehood*'s connection with Shakespeare had come to be accepted and did not need to be challenged. It was also a much less contentious play in the political climate of the 1790s. Finally, it was a single work and not connected with a broader set of documents that threatened to upend the public's understanding of Shakespeare. But what of the Siddons connection? The actress in fact appeared as Leonora in *Double Falsehood* at Bath in the early 1780s.[75] Siddons may have been more flexible with her repertoire at this early stage of her career or she may not have found the play troubling because it was already accepted as Shakespearean. But the contrast with her subsequent reaction to *Vortigern* is striking.

Like Kemble in *The Iron Chest*, Siddons had had her own recent brush with the failure of a new tragedy. Frances D'Arblay (née Burney)'s *Edwy and Elgiva* premiered on 21 March 1795 with Siddons and Kemble in the lead roles. The play, based on the history of ancient Britain, like *Vortigern*, was deemed nothing more than a 'beautiful Poem' which failed 'to excite emotions' as a tragedy should.[76] While Kemble's character gave him 'many opportunities to display his excellent powers, of which he amply availed himself', the part played by Siddons 'was unworthy her abilities'.[77] As one critic put it, 'it was kindness in Mrs. SIDDONS to lend her person and voice to character undiscriminated, and dialogue unimpassioned'.[78] Furthermore, Siddons was subjected to ridicule as she 'for once in her life, died a stage-death amidst general laughter' when her character was brought out from behind a hedge on her deathbed and then rapidly concealed behind the foliage once more after she had expired.[79] Even Siddons could not save this moment from ridicule: 'The laughter which this scene occasioned, although supported by the dying words of Mrs. SIDDONS, was inconceivable.'[80] The play was announced for the next night but withdrawn after resistance from the audience. Unlike her brother's performance in *The Iron Chest*, Siddons seems to have done her best with the material she was given and did not attempt to sabotage the play. However, her embarrassment at being implicated in the failure of *Edwy and Elgiva* may have led her to be cautious about getting involved in other new tragedies like *Vortigern* lest she should once more fall prey to derision.

Dobson underlines the connection between *Vortigern* and an earlier scandal in which Kemble's offstage life became 'every bit as Gothic as his roles onstage': his attempted rape of an actress in the Drury Lane company during the previous season.[81] The woman in question was Maria Theresa De Camp, who was subsequently to marry Kemble and Siddons's brother, Charles, in 1806, although only after much opposition from her assailant. Unsurprisingly, few biographies of Kemble discuss this scandal other than to reproduce the public apology Kemble eventually issued. Williams's account is the most direct: 'While Miss DE CAMP was dressing or undressing herself at the theatre, Mr. KEMBLE . . . forced open the door to her apartment, and proceeded to take some very abrupt liberties with her person.'[82] The actress 'firmly resisted his assaults till more effectual assistance could be procured to her aid', presumably from other theatre personnel.[83] Kemble subsequently apologized in the press for his 'very improper and unjustifiable behaviour'.[84] However, we should note the problematic language of his apology, which emphasizes that De Camp's 'conduct and character' in no way 'authorized' his assault, the implication being that the rights and wrongs of the situation might have been more ambiguous had the woman displayed other types of behaviour or personality.[85] Even more recent sources such as the *Biographical Dictionary* have continued to portray the incident in dubious terms: the entry on Kemble describes his 'drunken assault on the enticing actress' and that on De Camp again emphasizes Kemble's inebriation and De Camp's beauty as extenuating circumstances (he was 'so overcome by her attractions that . . . he made a drunken assault on her').[86] Although the apology would have been positively received by many of Kemble's contemporaries, there is no doubt that damage was done to his reputation: Williams terms this 'an affair which more seriously affected Mr. KEMBLE's honour than any other part of his conduct that we are acquainted with through life'.[87] Scandals such as this one, as well as Colman's critique of Kemble's behaviour surrounding *The Iron Chest*, would have made the actor more aware than ever of the need to preserve his public reputation; hence, any involvement with a spurious work such as *Vortigern* was dangerous. His assault on De Camp had tarnished Kemble's personal reputation, and his behaviour in *The Iron Chest* had cast doubt on his skill as an actor. Taking the lead role in *Vortigern* risked damaging his standing as a Shakespearean, a position that Kemble took very seriously and valued extremely highly.

Given the number of problematic events experienced or perpetrated by Kemble at this time, this seems to have been a particularly challenging moment in his career. Indeed, soon after these incidents took place, Kemble resigned from the management of Drury Lane. Both Siddons and Kemble did remain at the theatre as performers, but the circumstances in which they appeared were somewhat different under the new acting manager, Richard Wroughton, whose 'stage-creed' was that 'the public might be entertained much more effectively on comedy than on the costlier pomp of tragedy'.[88] That tragedies were expected to have elaborate (and therefore costly) scenery and costumes is borne out by Samuel Ireland's insistence, outlined earlier, on *Vortigern* being staged in spectacular fashion. Thus Wroughton's privileging of comedy over tragedy was a sensible move, given the parlous finances of the theatre at this time, though it risked sidelining Siddons and Kemble to some degree. As previously noted, Kemble briefly resumed the Drury Lane management in 1800 and began privileging Shakespeare in the repertoire again, before ultimately moving to Covent Garden to continue his work as manager at that theatre.

The aftermath of *Vortigern*

The next chapter will discuss in more detail events in the careers of Siddons and Kemble after *Vortigern*. Before leaving the story of the play it is worth noting that William Henry Ireland did not give up his dramatic aspirations following its failure. As part of the Shakespeare Papers, William Henry had produced another play, *Henry II*, which was published along with *Vortigern* in 1799. Given that Shakespeare was famed for his cycle of English history plays, it was not implausible that a work dealing with a monarch that the dramatist had not previously been known to have explored might be uncovered. Indeed, William Henry had grand plans to write 'a series of Plays to make up with Shakspeares a compleat history of the Kings of England'.[89] *Henry II* was never performed, though it was apparently offered to Harris at Covent Garden. William Henry's playwriting continued with the blank verse drama *Mutius Scævola*, which he completed in 1801. This too was offered to, and refused by, Covent Garden. More surprisingly, William Henry sent the script to Kemble, now manager again at Drury Lane, 'having never spoken to him since the fatal Shakspberian business' and unsure as to 'how he might relish my application'.[90] Even more unexpected was Kemble's response: he noted that he had 'nothing to do myself with the acceptance or refusal of pieces offered to the Theatre' but claimed that 'all prejudice is so far from my Mind & I think so stupid in itself' that he offered to present the play 'to the Gentlemen who have undertaken to read all Productions presented to the Proprietors of Drury Lane Theatre', concluding that 'I very heartily hope that their answer will be exactly what you wish it'.[91] William Henry was gratified by this 'very liberal answer' but ventured further in asking Kemble to read the script and specifically to comment on the potential for staging, since 'no one can be so capable . . . as to its scenic effects &c. as yourself'.[92] William Henry evidently hoped to take advantage of the manager's famous skills in planning spectacular productions, just as Samuel had hoped to do with *Vortigern*. Though *Mutius Scævola* was then apparently rejected by Drury Lane and returned to its author, Kemble offered William Henry further assistance: 'If it should be in my Power to do you any Service on this Occasion, I assure you you may freely command me.'[93] Though never staged, the play was published with a preface that explained the drama's historical source and pointed out its morals.

Grebanier describes *Mutius Scævola* as presenting 'an eighteenth-century version of ancient Rome'.[94] This is certainly true, but more importantly, it was a contemporary image of Rome directly influenced by Kemble's staging of the Roman plays (such as his *Coriolanus*, discussed in the previous chapter). The dramatis personae calls for many supernumeraries ('Officers, Guards, Chorus Singers, &c.').[95] Furthermore, the stage directions for the last two scenes evoke Kemble's spectacular productions with their careful arrangement of these extras and use of scenic elements to provide a focal point. The last Act opens with an *'inside view of Porsenna's Tent – who is seated on an elevated throne; numerous Guards, &c. ranged round, and a large tripod before the king in the centre of the stage, in which is placed a blazing fire'* (this fire is central to the action as Mutius plunges his hand into it in an act of stoicism).[96] The play's final scene consists of a pageant of numerous characters: '*Enter in procession through the gates. Valerius and Lucretius, Senators, Clelia bearing a wreath of oak, Vestal Virgins, Patricians, Soldiers, Plebeians, &c. From the side of the stage, enter Guards, followed by Porsenna, Mutius, Manlius, Silvia, Servius, &c. grand march playing while arranging round the stage. Mutius' arm in a sling.*'[97] Even if Kemble did not oblige him with comments on staging possibilities for the play, William Henry took inspiration from the manager in attempting to create the kind of Roman spectacle that would certainly have been appealing to a contemporary audience.

But what of *Vortigern*? Many reasons have been posited for the play's failure, including the actors' sabotaging of the work through their performances (or in Siddons's case, her refusal to appear) and the devastating timing of the publication of Malone's *Inquiry*. Others contend simply that the play was bad and in no way worthy of Shakespeare. As the *Observer* asserted on 3 April 1796:

> Whatever might have been the previous opinion respecting the author of this play, we are persuaded, that all those

who witnessed its performance last night, will exhonerate [*sic*] the memory of Shakespeare from the obloquy which the imputation of this combination of absurdity and bombast would cast upon it. Throughout the Piece, we could not discover a single thought or expression which might denote the mighty master's mind: for the energetic dignity conspicuous in his writing, was substituted the most incoherent rhapsodies.[98]

By the end of the eighteenth century, Shakespeare was supposed to function as a unifying national symbol but, as Lynch has argued, William Henry's play failed to synthesize the disparate elements of Britishness to provide 'a coherent national identity'.[99] I would argue that *Vortigern* failed because of the controversy surrounding it and the Shakespeare Papers, more broadly. The play spread a sense of division as critics, actors and audience argued over the ends to which Shakespeare should be put and who had the right to use the bard.

Kemble's possessiveness over Shakespeare, on display during his time as manager of Drury Lane in his sabotage of a play, *Vortigern*, which he deemed unworthy of the dramatist's name, was later even more seriously challenged during his managerial tenure at Covent Garden. If Kemble did deliberately incite public unrest when *Vortigern* was staged, he would have regretted this in 1809 when the Old Price Riots broke out during a performance of *Macbeth* in response to the changes in theatre layout and pricing that he had instituted when Covent Garden was rebuilt after a devastating fire. At stake in both *Vortigern* and the Old Price Riots was the public's perception of its right to assert ownership over Shakespeare in performance. Playgoers who attended *Vortigern* did so as a way to pronounce judgement on the authenticity of the play (and of the Shakespeare Papers, more broadly). Indeed, by producing and selling the Shakespeare Papers, the Irelands contributed to the public's sense of Shakespeare as a commodity that could be owned. As we shall see in the next chapter, the OP Rioters resented the increase in ticket prices imposed by

Kemble because it curtailed their access to the works of the national poet in performance. Similar issues were at stake over *Vortigern*. Malone's efforts to debunk the play and the other Ireland forgeries were perceived by some critics as 'an attempt to stifle free speech and public debate' about Shakespeare.[100] In his 1797 pamphlet, Chalmers proclaimed himself uninterested in 'the genuineness of those Shakspeariana' and challenged Malone on the grounds that the common people (those 'who read Shakspeare, as a relaxation of life') had just as much right to the dramatist as the eminent scholar ('whose days and nights have been occupied about Shakspeare, during thirty years').[101] The motives of the OP Rioters were similar as they sought to reclaim Shakespeare in performance for all. Kemble as actor-manager and Siddons as star performer had to negotiate the public's sense of ownership over Shakespeare as they asserted their own title to the bard.

4

Macbeth and unrest

Covent Garden management (1803–12) and the OP Riots (1809)

The palace of Shakespeare

When Kemble's negotiations with Sheridan to buy into Drury Lane fell through, he turned his attention to the rival theatre, Covent Garden. Kemble's friend Elizabeth Inchbald, a successful dramatist at that theatre, conducted the negotiations with the proprietor, Harris, on his behalf. By borrowing heavily, Kemble was finally able to realize his dream of part ownership of one of the patent houses by acquiring a one-sixth share of Covent Garden in 1803. He was to be paid £200 per year for managing the theatre and £37 16s. per week for acting on three nights, with £12 8s. for each additional performance.[1] According to Fitzgerald, 'in those days of patent theatres, it was wise policy for a great actor to hold a share in the house in addition to his salary; for he thus enjoyed a portion of the profits his own talents were bringing to the theatre'.[2] Although still answerable to Harris and his son Henry, the major shareholders at Covent Garden, partial proprietorship gave Kemble greater artistic freedom than he had enjoyed at Drury Lane under Sheridan. In writing of Kemble's attempts to obtain a share of Drury Lane, Boaden claimed that William Siddons 'was not disinclined to embark a considerable sum with [Kemble] in the concern'.[3] The money involved would, of course, have been generated by Siddons. In fact, William had previously used his wife's money to buy into the management of Sadler's Wells theatre.[4] Management of the patent London theatres was not generally open to women and Siddons's desire to avoid animosity from the public may have led her to leave such endeavours to her brother. While no funds were forthcoming from Siddons for Kemble's share in Covent Garden, 'her presence there was vitally important to him' in order for the theatre to succeed.[5] The actress wrote to a friend at this time that 'nothing but my BROTHER could have induced me to appear again in public, but HIS interest and honour must always be most dear to ME'.[6] Siddons acted sixty nights at Covent Garden in her first season there and somewhat more sporadically afterwards, receiving large sums of money for doing so.[7] Though she assumed no new roles, she remained at that theatre alongside her brother until her retirement in 1812.

Kemble aimed to make Covent Garden 'the palace of Shakspeare', transferring his innovations in production (such as elaborate crowd scenes, spectacular scenery and historical accuracy in costuming) from Drury Lane and expanding them in his new theatrical home.[8] Harris, however, favoured 'the two principles of *variety* and *novelty*', staging popular entertainments that were commercially successful.[9] One such novelty was thirteen-year-old William Henry West Betty, who acted at Covent Garden in the 1804–5 and 1805–6 seasons. Betty had been inspired to take to the stage after seeing Siddons act Elvira in *Pizarro* at Belfast in 1802. During the height of Bettymania, crowds flocked to the theatre to watch the boy's performances, including in Kemble's roles such as Hamlet and Rolla. But the siblings wisely chose to distance themselves until the fuss died down.[10] In 1805, Thomas Holcroft lamented 'the deep wounds which the sound understanding has received from the vapid attempts of children' and praised in contrast 'the high satisfaction and delight' derived from 'three such extraordinary performers' as Kemble, Siddons and Cooke in *Othello*.[11] He further praised Kemble 'for the correct and classical manner in which many pieces', especially tragedies such as *Othello*, 'have been performed under his management, and with the addition of his great abilities'.[12] The new manager's other major Shakespeare productions at Covent Garden included *Henry VIII* in April 1806, in which Kemble took over the role of Wolsey, and 'an ostentatious revival' of *The Tempest* in December 1806, in which he played Prospero.[13] Kemble's production of *Coriolanus* at Covent Garden in November 1806, 'revived with prodigious pomp and expence', cemented the return of the siblings' Shakespeare to the stage after the Betty affair.[14] During a performance of this play, Siddons and Kemble experienced a taste of the audience dissatisfaction that was to mar later seasons when 'an *apple* was thrown upon the stage' and landed between them, causing the manager to petition the spectators for protection and to assert that 'nothing shall induce me to suffer insult'.[15] At the start of the 1808 season, the siblings were very much in favour again, drawing an 'audience piled to the roof' which 'attested the attraction of Shakspeare and themselves'.[16]

Fire and riot

On 20 September 1808, Kemble suffered enormous damage to his theatrical investment when Covent Garden was destroyed by fire. Siddons wrote to a friend of the losses her family sustained and the challenges they faced: 'I have lost every article of Stage Ornament that I had in the world, and my poor Brother almost <u>all he possessd</u> – and he has nearly to begin in the world again.'[17] The company spent the ensuing season performing at the King's theatre and at the Haymarket but Covent Garden was quickly rebuilt to a Greek revivalist design by Robert Smirke, intended 'to represent Kemble's classical taste' and to reinforce his link with Shakespeare.[18] The exterior of the theatre was 'decorated by basso-relievo representations of the Drama, antient and modern', with Greek poets and muses representing the former and Shakespeare the latter.[19] The Shakespeare section included 'Lady Macbeth, with the daggers; and Macbeth, turning with horror from the dead body of Duncan', which would have reminded playgoers of Siddons and Kemble by depicting characters in which they were highly successful.[20] The conjunction of ancient and modern continued inside, with a grand staircase 'ornamented by pilasters of porphyry' and 'a large statue of Shakspeare . . . in yellow marble'.[21] Hunt pronounced the theatre 'classical and magnificent throughout' and the entrances as 'worthy of introducing you to a stage over which SHAKSPEARE presides'.[22] Covent Garden's grand reopening took place on 18 September 1809 with a performance of *Macbeth*, Kemble and Siddons, of course, taking the lead roles. From its opening night, the rebuilt theatre was therefore deeply connected with Shakespeare in the choice of a favourite Shakespeare play and two wildly popular Shakespearean actors to inaugurate the new venue, as well as the inclusion of Shakespeare in the decor.

However, triumph did not rise from the tragedy of the fire. In fact, calamity continued in the new theatre. In order to finance the rebuilding, the Covent Garden management had made several changes to the seating arrangements and ticket prices that proved radically unpopular with playgoers and in fact led to the outbreak of a riot. The third tier of dress boxes had been replaced with twenty-six private boxes that were to be rented for the season. The upper gallery, the cheapest area of the auditorium, was now even higher and the rake so steep that it was difficult to see more of the stage than the performers' legs from these seats. Admission to the regular boxes increased from 6s to 7s and tickets for the pit were raised from 3s and 6d to 4s. Playgoers interpreted these changes as 'a realignment of social relationships', privileging the rich and squeezing out the less well-off members of the audience.[23] The private boxes were a particular bone of contention because they afforded more privilege to the rich at the expense of the comfort and sightlines of those who occupied the cheaper seats. Indeed, with their anterooms and private entrances, they were seen as offering a way for the nobility to purchase (by a subscription of £300 for the entire season), their separation 'from the public at large'.[24] The changes to Covent Garden were so unpopular that on opening night a riot broke out that was to persist for three months. The Old Price (or OP) Riots (named after the rioters' demands to reinstate the old admission prices to the theatre) became the longest-running disturbance in English theatre history.[25]

Kemble tried various tactics to try to quell the disorder. On the second night he scheduled *The Beggar's Opera*, for reasons he explained in 1791: 'Whenever there is Danger of a Riot, always act an Opera; for Musick drowns the noise of opposition.'[26] This strategy was unsuccessful, however, as 'not a word or note was heard'.[27] Before the season began, Kemble had engaged the Italian soprano Angelica Catalani to perform for the large sum of £75 per night, but this was another major source of discontent for the rioters, who objected to her exorbitant salary and felt that her presence signalled a turn away from English drama towards Italian opera and 'the exclusion of native talents of the highest excellence'.[28] Kemble subsequently hired pugilists to control the disturbances in the pit: a handbill distributed in the theatre on 10 October claimed that 'Daniel Mendoza, the fighting Jew' and '*Dutch Sam*' (Samuel Elias) had been 'engage[d] to assault every person who had the courage to express their disapprobation of the managers' attempt to ram down the new prices', a 'shameful abuse' of the audience.[29] As with Catalani, the antipathy towards Mendoza and Elias was doubtless exacerbated by their perceived foreignness.

Gillian Russell contends that 'the O. P. riots were not exceptional in theatre history but were in fact the culmination of a traditional form of eighteenth-century theatre politics

– the theatre riot'.[30] The OPs built on previous patterns of behaviour but also developed new methods, and as the disturbances continued for sixty-seven nights, these strategies evolved. The various tactics the OPs employed are detailed by John Joseph Stockdale in his *Covent Garden Journal*, which offers a night-by-night account of events. The rioters in the pit began by turning their backs to the actors and 'through the whole play they kept a standing position on the benches, with their hats on'.[31] They subsequently invented dances, in one of which 'a violent stamp with the right foot, was accompanied by the exclamation of O, while the left beat the benches to the sound of P' and in another 'the pit danced to the music of their OP, forming a long vacancy, up and down which they footed it in couples'.[32] The OPs frequently sang patriotic songs, often 'in concert with ... rattles and French horns'.[33] Many placards were displayed in order that the OPs' concerns, which risked being lost in the noise and confusion, were communicated within the auditorium and 'to ensure the newspapers reported the arguments of the rioters as well as noticing the general level of fracas'.[34] These are detailed by Stockdale (with an emphasis on wit and novelty as new slogans were developed) and several are quoted in this chapter. The letters OP 'surmounted by a crown, cast in silver' or pewter also became an insignia that could be worn by playgoers.[35] Some of these tactics encouraged the spread of OP behaviour, or the reporting of it, beyond Covent Garden and in society more broadly; thus the OP conflict and its rituals were 'marketed for the general public which became an audience of an audience, extending further the dimensions of social theatricality involved in the event'.[36]

On 23 September, Kemble proposed 'that a committee of the most respectable gentlemen may be appointed to inspect the state of the concern; and, from the profits thence derived, to say whether the advance is necessary or otherwise'.[37] The theatre remained closed until the committee's work was completed, reopening on 4 October. The report was found in favour of the proprietors and did little to quell the OPs' opposition.[38] Kemble and his fellow proprietors were eventually forced to capitulate to the demands of the rioters. Terms were agreed at a dinner at the Crown and Anchor tavern on 14 December as follows: that at the end of the season the number of private boxes be returned to what it was when Kemble took over as manager in 1803; that the old price of admission to the pit should be reinstated (though the price of admission to the boxes could remain raised); that an apology be made to the public and James Brandon (Covent Garden's box office keeper, thought to have been overzealous in his prosecution of the OPs) be dismissed; and that all legal action be dropped.[39] Eventually, placards were hoisted in the pit stating 'We are satisfied' and the riots came to a close.[40] However, Scott noted that the OP Riots affected Kemble deeply: 'His favourite art lost some of its attractions when he experienced to what unjust humiliation it subjected him.'[41] And Siddons described her agitation at the events to a friend: 'What a time it has been with us all, beginning with fire, and continued with fury!'[42]

The Kemble 'family party'

Kemble bore the brunt of the OPs' animosity because in his role as both actor and manager he was more visible than Harris and his son: an observer commented that 'the disapprobation . . . abated when he left the stage, and increased to a furious height on his re-entrance'.[43] Furthermore, the OPs used the play in question, *Macbeth*, in which Kemble, of course, played the lead role, to harass the actor: 'When Macbeth appeared with his crown on his head, the ingenuity of the oppositionists was racked to invent discordant sounds; some imitated the squalling of infants, others the barking of dogs, others the mewing of cats, and others the screams of women in hysterics.'[44] Then, in the banquet scene:

> A sham or real fight, now took place in the pit, succeeded by cries of *a ghost! a ghost!* and when Banquo's embodied spirit appeared, several persons exclaimed – '*Well done,*

bravo, John Kemble! You never played that scene so well before – you are really frightened now!' When the weird sisters struck up, 'We fly by night', the audience thundered out the rolling chorus –

'While the stormy winds do blow;'
and sarcastically repeated –
'Bubble, bubble,
Toil and trouble,
When shall we
Three meet again.'[45]

While the opposition made sure the play was not heard, they certainly paid attention to which play was being performed and engaged carefully with the entirety of the performance.

The choice of *Macbeth* to open the new theatre was a calculated one. If Kemble had wanted to showcase only himself, he would probably have chosen *Hamlet*, as he did in his first performance at Covent Garden after becoming a proprietor on 24 September 1803. But *Macbeth* was a play which relied on both Kemble and Siddons. Thus, although she had no official involvement in management, Siddons was foundational to the success of the theatre. Perhaps Kemble even hoped to soften criticism of himself by staging a production in which his sister would also star. Siddons's appearance alongside Kemble on opening night in *Macbeth* bolstered the appeal of that play. However, she was also affected by the vehement expressions of displeasure from the audience, though through some combination of her powerful acting, the audience's respect for her and her supreme professionalism, Siddons had greater success in making herself heard: 'The play proceeded in pantomime; not a word was heard, save now and then the deeply modulated tones of the bewitching Siddons. On her entrance she seemed disturbed by the clamour; but in the progressive stages of her action, she went through her part with wonderful composure.'[46] Although she was not the main target (the OPs' disapprobation began before she appeared on stage and was not primarily directed at her), Siddons subsequently refused to perform while the unrest persisted. The siblings did not appear on the second night; thus Kemble's choice of *The Beggar's Opera* that evening can be construed not just as an attempt to use music to drown out the sounds of audience disturbance but also as a way to remove himself and his sister from the unrest as this was not a play in which they acted. This is confirmed in a letter from Thomas Lawrence to Farington: 'To-night they act the Beggar's Opera. Neither Kemble nor Mrs. Siddons chusing to be again insulted, nor indeed would it be wise to *throw away* her Talents and attractions in this her last Season.'[47] His comments reflect the widely held belief that Siddons was on the cusp of retirement.[48] Boaden claimed that the audience paid 'respectful attention to Mrs. Siddons during this whole business . . . they did not desire her to *act* where she could not be heard; and being out of their sight, the rioters had nothing to remind *them* of her existence'.[49] Siddons wrote to her daughter-in-law Harriet some weeks later: 'I think it very likely that I shall not appear any more this Season, for nothing shall induce me to place myself again in so painful & degrading a Situation.'[50] And indeed, she was absent from the London stage for seven months, not reappearing until well after the OP Riots had been resolved.[51]

Although her performance in *Macbeth* on opening night may not have attracted disruption to the same extent her brother's did, Siddons was still the object of critique in the press. A report in the *Times* asserted that 'it was a noble sight to see so much just indignation in the public mind, and we could not help thinking, as Mr. Kemble and Mrs. Siddons stood on the stage, carrying each £500 in clothes upon their backs, that it was to feed this vanity, and to pay an Italian singer, that the public were screwed'.[52] Fitzgerald quoted from a handbill entitled 'The Necessity of the Advance in Prices' which critiqued the 'family party' (that is, the Kemble clan and their seeming monopoly over performance) and outlined the salaries and benefits of Kemble, Siddons, Charles Kemble and his wife and Catalani, with a total of £25,175.[53] Here, Catalani becomes an honorary member of the Kemble family and in addition to Kemble and Siddons, their brother Charles and his wife (formerly the Miss De Camp whose assault by Kemble is discussed in the previous chapter and now acting under the name Mrs C. Kemble), also become objects of the OPs' hostility. As Stockdale put it: 'The whole family of the Kembles now came under public displeasure, and no greater sin was requisite, for the damnation of a performer, than an alliance with this obnoxious family.'[54] This was echoed in the visual response to the disturbances: James Gillray's *Theatrical Mendicants, Relieved* (Figure 7), for example, shows Kemble, Siddons and Charles going cap in hand to the Duke of Northumberland (who in fact gave Kemble a loan of £10,000 to rebuild Covent Garden, which he later converted to a gift), casting an ironic light on their high salaries at the theatre.

During the opening night performance, Charles was cheered when as Macduff he vanquished his brother as Macbeth:

FIGURE 7 *James Gillray,* Theatrical Mendicants, Relieved *(1809). ART File S568 no.62 (size M), image 28941. Used by permission of the Folger Shakespeare Library.*

'Many cried out, "Well done, kill him, Charley," and exulted in the ideal pangs of the dying Macbeth.'[55] But subsequently, the audience's hostility was directed towards him, probably because although Kemble sometimes appeared on stage to address the audience, he did not act again until 15 December when terms had been agreed to end the unrest. Thus other targets were needed for the OPs' animosity. Stockdale offers numerous examples of the disruptions faced by Charles, who apparently 'never opened his mouth without receiving manifest signs of an illiberal personal attack, for his crime of consanguinity'.[56] Lawrence interpreted the hostility towards Charles as a sign that the audience 'would have torn Kemble himself in Pieces' had he appeared.[57] Maria Theresa Kemble, Charles's wife, also attracted hostile behaviour: on one night, she 'escaped, narrowly, being struck by an apple, thrown by some unknown ruffian. On another she was taunted for her family-appearance'[58] While Kemble's wife Priscilla did not appear on stage (she had retired in 1796), she was targeted by the OPs' visits to her home. In early December Siddons wrote in a letter that she was anxious for her brother's personal safety, 'such were the outrages committed on his house' and expressed empathy for Priscilla's suffering, 'she, poor soul, living with ladders at her windows, in order to make her escape through the garden, in case of an attack'.[59] Inchbald, who lived nearby and was friendly with the Kembles, also expressed sympathy: 'Poor Mrs. Kemble, I am told, and no wonder, is nearly dead with terror.'[60] Sean McEvoy highlights the potential for the storming of Kemble's house to be read as 'a theatrical fall of the Bastille', an attempt to overturn an authority deemed dictatorial.[61] Hence, the police presence on the streets was increased to deter such violence.

Shakespeare and nationalism

While Kemble did not appear on stage in Shakespearean or any other roles during the disturbances, he was still closely connected with Shakespeare in the placards, caricatures and other discourse surrounding the OP Riots. These paratexts identified the actor with his most famous, and not uncoincidentally most autocratic, characters and with roles in which he appeared alongside his sister. Unsurprisingly, given the choice of play for the first night's performance, he was often represented as Macbeth, for example in Isaac Cruikshank's *Is This a Rattle Which I See Before Me?* (Figure 8), which

FIGURE 8 *Isaac Cruikshank,* Is This a Rattle Which I See Before Me? *(1809). PC 1-11422 (A size) [P&P]. From Library of Congress, Prints and Photographs Division, Cartoon Prints, British.*

replaced the famous dagger with a type of noise-making instrument used by the rioters.[62]

He was also depicted as King John. On the night of 16 October a placard in the theatre audience read:

> King John of old, by sturdy barons aw'd,
>   Our British rights in Magna Charta sign'd;
> To stage crown'd John, in insolence and fraud,
>   Shall our dramatic rights be now resign'd?
> From British favour has they pseudo king
>   His fame, his wealth, his impudence, deriv'd;
> By British spirit let this empty thing
>   Of all his borrow'd feathers be deprived.[63]

The placard urged audience members to act in the national interest in reclaiming what was rightfully theirs from the pseudo king and manager, Kemble. Cruikshank's *King John and John Bull* visually pitted the Covent Garden manager against the quintessential Englishman: a defiant King John Kemble is shown asking John Bull 'What is it you want?' while the latter waves a sign that reads 'OLD PRICES No Italian private Boxes No Pigeon Holes NO CATALANI'. Kemble had been excoriated when in his address on 20 September he told the audience, 'Ladies and gentleman, *I wait to know what you want*', which was deemed 'a ridiculous and insulting affectation'.[64] Marc Baer pinpoints this incident as the beginning of the identification of Kemble with King John as the historical figure 'had asked his rebellious barons the same evasive question'.[65]

Kemble's apparently insulting query was also the basis for a piece that appeared in the *Morning Chronicle* which excerpted speeches from *Coriolanus* in which the protagonist addresses the plebeians. Lines such as '*What's the matter*, you dissentious rogues' and '*What would ye have*, curs?' are taken directly from the play, with the implication that Kemble had addressed the Covent Garden audience in similarly autocratic and condescending tones.[66] Other commentators cast Kemble as Cardinal Wolsey. Another placard on 16 October read:

> Kemble remember how Wolsey was proud
> Of his *patent right* and very high station,
> But how lowly was Wolsey when the king and the crowd
> Bore him down to the language of humiliation.[67]

This was clearly intended as a warning to the manager and, indeed, turned out to be prophetic as Kemble was ultimately forced to apologize to the public from the stage and to capitulate to the OP supporters' demands. As we have seen in previous chapters, these characters were some of the most popular in Kemble's Shakespearean repertoire. Furthermore, all of these figures can be perceived as acting against the state: Macbeth is a regicide, King John incites civil war, Coriolanus is accused of treason by the people and Cardinal Wolsey betrays Henry VIII.[68] Hence the OP Rioters chose to link Kemble specifically with these roles in order to claim that the changes made to the Covent Garden theatre ran counter to the best interests of the nation.

Significantly, these four Shakespeare plays were all ones in which Siddons had appeared alongside Kemble (as Lady Macbeth, Constance, Volumnia and Queen Katharine) to great acclaim. As I argue in this book, a great deal of the siblings' success came from performing together in the same Shakespeare plays. In Chapter 1, I discussed how *King John* was selected early in the siblings' careers as a vehicle to showcase them both as Shakespearean actors. By 1809, the play was a staple in each of their repertoires. Siddons's success as Lady Macbeth was augmented when her brother began to act Macbeth alongside her regularly. As explored in Chapter 2, Kemble's Coriolanus gained considerably from Siddons's casting as Volumnia. Siddons triumphed as Queen Katharine from Kemble's first production of *Henry VIII* but the play received even greater critical acclaim when Kemble switched from the part of Cromwell to that of Wolsey. Thus the Shakespearean characters with whom Kemble was particularly identified during the OP Riots were also closely connected with Siddons. The actress was therefore crucial to the Shakespearean dimension of this important theatrical disturbance.

Shakespeare continued to be performed during the OP Riots, albeit without Siddons and Kemble in their leading roles. But these performances were also disrupted by the rioters, especially when Charles Kemble played supporting parts. On 16 October, 'a roar, that almost shook the house, burst forth when Charles Kemble appeared in the character of *Richmond* [in *Richard III*], and continued during his presence to the end of the tragedy'; on 19 October, his 'appearance as Bassanio [in *The Merchant of Venice*] was the prompter's bell that summoned the exertions of that extraordinary vocal overture exhibited this season in the front of the house'; and on 21 October, his Cassio in *Othello* was received approvingly by some of the audience, which 'provoked from the Anti-Kemble party a violent hiss'.[69] As these examples demonstrate, the audience faced considerable difficulty in hearing and seeing the play as a result of the disturbances in the auditorium. Indeed, the behaviour of playgoers became the focus of attention and chief form of entertainment, rather than what was happening on stage: as the anonymous biographer of Kemble wrote, 'the scenes in the audience part of the house were so much more novel and curious than those transacting on the stage, that the audience turned their backs to the latter, where the performers "Fretted and strutted their hour" for *their own* amusement'.[70] The rhetoric connecting Kemble with Shakespeare found in placards, press reports, graphic satires and so on not only strongly evoked his absent sister but also allowed Shakespeare, Siddons and Kemble to live on as entertainment outside the theatre. Russell writes of how during the OP Riots, 'the London public could . . . keep up with the conflict in the windows of the print shops, where a succession of satires on the riots, often directed against Kemble, formed a kind of newsreel of events'.[71] With the impossibility of seeing and hearing plays in the theatre and the absence of Siddons and Kemble from the stage, London audiences got their fix of Shakespeare and their favourite performers from other media outside the theatre.

The identification of Kemble as an enemy of the state through the evocation of particular Shakespearean characters demonstrates one aspect of the nationalistic dimension of the OP Riots. As in Cruikshank's *King John* image, Kemble was frequently depicted in opposition to John Bull, the down-to-earth representative of the English people who was coming to be seen as an anti-establishment, anti-corruption figure. John Bull's denunciation of Catalani in the Cruikshank satire explicitly identified the Italian singer as at odds with true Britishness, a trope common across OP discourse. For example, Henry Redhead Yorke, a staunch opponent of the Covent Garden proprietors, criticized Catalani's Italian nationality and French husband and claimed that 'the attempt to force this foreigner upon the people was a specimen of audacity for which *alone*, the proprietors ought to forfeit their monopoly'.[72] Virulent anti-Semitism was another significant component of the nationalistic language of the OPs. The pugilists employed by the Covent Garden management to control the crowds in the pit included Jewish prize fighters Elias and Mendoza. Thus placards appeared proclaiming, for example, 'oppose Shylock and the whole tribe of Israel' and 'who support the managers? Profligate Jews, hired ruffians'.[73] Nationalism was also evident in the patriotic songs, including 'God Save the King' and 'Rule Britannia', that could frequently be heard in the theatre auditorium, which became part of the alternative performance offered in the playhouse by the rioters. For example, on 20 October 'during each of the songs in the opera, (the Duenna,) the pit united in a grand chorus of "God Save the King"', drowning out the voices of the professional singers on stage.[74] Thus the rioters turned on its head Kemble's strategy of staging musical entertainment to hide the sounds of discord by overwhelming this performance of Sheridan's short comic opera with their noise. Placards included slogans such as 'King George for ever, / The managers never'.[75] In an attempt to pander to the OPs' patriotism, on 25 October the Covent Garden managers used the occasion of George III's golden jubilee to stage a spectacular afterpiece, the final scene of which featured a warship firing a royal salute and 'a procession of soldiers and sailors, bearing inscriptions, which designated all the victories and important acquisitions of the present reign'.[76] Audience unrest made the play inaudible, although the pit did join in with the patriotic songs and dance at the end. The piece was repeated a handful of times but did not become as popular as the smash hit of the other *Jubilee*, Garrick's afterpiece in praise of Shakespeare.

Given that Shakespeare had by this time become a symbol of the English nation, it is perhaps surprising that he did not much feature in this way in the rhetoric of the OPs. Because Shakespeare was so closely connected with Siddons and Kemble through their performances of major roles in his canon, the dramatist was identified with the Covent Garden establishment and not with the opposition. Bate reads the OP Riots as 'a battle for the possession of Shakespeare', but this is not entirely correct.[77] The OPs did not necessarily wish to wrest control over Shakespeare from Siddons and Kemble. Rather, they wanted to continue to enjoy Shakespeare in performance without the innovations of the new Covent Garden theatre (raised prices and private boxes). But the Shakespeare they desired was Shakespeare as performed by Siddons and Kemble. One commentator remarked of the new theatre that the rake of the gallery now made it impossible 'to see more than the legs of those in the beautiful Bridge Scene in *Macbeth*'.[78] This scene (1.3), in which Macbeth, Banquo and the army enter by crossing a bridge and meet the witches for the first time, was apparently a key part of Kemble's production of the play: his promptbook shows the movement and arrangement of actors planned out carefully.[79] Ironically, however, the actions of the OPs meant that even when Shakespeare was staged, very little of it could be heard.

On 15 December, Kemble appeared as the disaffected Penruddock in Richard Cumberland's comedy *The Wheel of Fortune* (1795) in a performance that was supposed to mark the end of the disturbances. Despite this being a favourite role, the applause he was met with at first soon gave way to displeasure at the fact that Brandon had not been dismissed. Kemble subsequently announced that Brandon had resigned and the performance continued.[80] Thus the OP Riots drew to an end. As Thomas Tegg described it in his long poem about the events:

> In every wish th' O. P.'s were gratified.
> And so, for the succeeding days,
> In quietness went on the plays;
> And Mr. Kemble deem'd it right
> To come forth every second night.
> He did successively appear
> In Hamlet, Zanga, and King Lear.[81]

Kemble's choice of repertoire immediately following the OP Riots shows his desire to please the audience by appearing in his most popular roles, both Shakespearean (Hamlet and King Lear) and non-Shakespearean (Penruddock and the Othello-like Zanga in Edward Young's 1721 tragedy *The Revenge*). However, even if these characters were less tyrannical than the Shakespearean ones with which Kemble had been identified during the riots, choosing such parts was no guarantee against criticism: during a performance as Hamlet, 'Kemble was hissed, on his appearance on the stage, and when he spoke the lines – "The times are out of joint – Oh, cursed spite! / That ever I was born to *set them right!*" – there was an universal shout of derision'.[82] That theatregoers continued to want to see Kemble in Shakespeare and to want to challenge him in these roles, often simultaneously, demonstrates the complex part Shakespeare played in the events of the OP Riots.

Macbeth

If the Covent Garden audience had had no cause to riot on 18 September 1809 and if spectators had remained calm and attentive (or at least as attentive as playgoers of the period usually were in an era when audience members were much less passive than they are today), what would they have seen? Boaden described the collaboration of Siddons and Kemble in *Macbeth* as 'the utmost perfection of the art'.[83] This was a key work for the siblings across both of their careers. While we cannot be sure when they first appeared in *Macbeth* and if they ever acted it together before coming to London, we know that Kemble had played the lead role in Hull in 1778 (his engagement there was 'the first appearance of any consequence', according to Boaden) and Siddons had performed Lady Macbeth in Bath in 1779, though apparently she had first learned the role at the age of twenty (in 1775).[84] Siddons acted Lady Macbeth in London regularly from 1785 and Kemble took over the role of Macbeth as soon as possible after Smith's retirement in 1788, having previously played Macduff. Siddons performed Lady Macbeth nine times during her last season (1811–12) and, indeed, made her official farewell performance in the part, as we shall see. Kemble included Macbeth in the selection of major characters that he performed in the season leading up to his retirement (1816–17). Siddons occasionally even came out of retirement to act Lady Macbeth, often with her brother, and the actors made their last joint appearance in the play on 5 June 1817. Thus we see the centrality and longevity of this play to the siblings. Reiko Oya claims that in the late eighteenth century, *Macbeth* 'was often labelled a second-rate tragedy' because 'its impressive array of intrigues, murders, and supernatural apparitions overwhelm[ed] genuinely tragic characterisation'.[85] Siddons's and Kemble's careful engagement with the play helped elevate its status in the repertoire.

Both actors wrote about their interpretations of the text: Siddons's 'Remarks on the Character of Lady Macbeth' were printed in Campbell's biography and Kemble's *Macbeth Reconsidered* was published in 1786 and revised in 1817.[86] However, these texts are somewhat at odds with playgoers' accounts of the actors' performances in this play. While Fanny Kemble (daughter of Charles) claimed that Siddons's

Lady Macbeth 'was to be found *alone* in her representation of it' and that the essay gave 'not the faintest idea' of the 'magnificence' of her performance, this seems unjust.[87] More helpfully, Joseph Donohue has argued that Siddons's Remarks describe 'a private image helpful in creating her role', rather than a definitive interpretation of the character.[88] Dennis Bartholomeusz claims that in his writings about *Macbeth*, Kemble was 'more concerned with contesting other views than with his own interpretation of the character on the stage' and that the essay is therefore 'less subtle than his actual performance'.[89] When writing about the siblings in *Macbeth* it is also important to remember that the first-hand descriptions of their performances derive from a number of different points in their long careers and that some commentators may be remembering one or several performances from many years earlier. While certain elements of their interpretations remained the same, doubtless the actors also experimented with innovations that may (or may not) have become part of their established portrayals of the roles. Furthermore, specific circumstances (personal and political) at any given time would also have influenced their performances and the reception of them.[90] What follows is an exploration of Siddons and Kemble in *Macbeth* gleaned from various accounts over many years that focuses on the scenes in the play in which they appeared together in order to understand the significance of their joint performance.

Donohue's analysis of the siblings' acting in this play casts it as a 'cooperative approach' through which they developed an 'extremely sympathetic portrayal' of the main characters.[91] Shaughnessy similarly sees the result of this collaborative interpretation as suggesting that 'the Macbeths' criminal acts were the perverse consequence of a profound marital love and loyalty'.[92] While the actors did maintain elements of the 'dead butcher, and his fiend-like Queen', the sympathy evoked in the audience complicated the moral message of the play as a warning against murder and, more specifically (particularly crucial in the period of the French Revolution), against regicide.[93] In his notes written around 1809, Bell recognized the importance of the collaboration between Siddons and Kemble from their first scene together (1.5). In particular, he commented on how Siddons as Lady Macbeth had to observe the impact of her words on Kemble's Macbeth: 'Much of the effect depends on the fire which she strikes into him, and which the player must make out.'[94] Boaden praised Kemble's ability to 'respond to the alarming incentives of the lady': in delivering the line 'To-morrow – as he *purposes*', the actor 'appeared to shrink from the quick glance which his sister turned upon him. – Though his hopes had depraved his imagination, he seemed unprepared then for the . . . instant determination' in her line 'O never shall sun *that* morrow see'.[95] In fact, Siddons seems to have inserted an additional 'never' in the line for emphasis: after the first 'never', she made 'a long pause' and then 'turned from him, her eye steadfast' before continuing.[96] Bell claimed that in Siddons's delivery of these words, 'her self-collected solemn energy, her fixed posture, her determined eye and full deep voice of fixed resolve never should be forgot, cannot be conceived nor described'.[97] As Lady Macbeth continues her speech ('Your face, my thane, is as a book where men / May read strange matters'), Bell recorded Siddons again 'observing the effect of what she has said on him, now first turning her eye upon his face' and another observer noted that in response, Kemble 'hung his head as if he could not withstand her penetrating gaze or the language which interpreted aright the ambitious whisperings of his own heart'.[98] Siddons's steely resolve and Kemble's shrinking responses in this scene were part of the conception of the characters and their relationship that the siblings had worked out together.

In their next scene together (1.7), Siddons further demonstrated her skill in responding to her stage partner. Lady Macbeth's reaction to her husband's pronouncement 'We will proceed no further in this business' demonstrated a 'sudden change from animated hope and surprise to disappointment, depression, contempt, and rekindling resentments'.[99] Lady Macbeth's response was delivered in a manner 'very cold, distant, and contemptuous' and with a 'determined air and voice'.[100] Halfway through the speech, Siddons, who had 'been at a distant part of the stage' came close to Kemble and her manner changed completely.[101] She 'look[ed] for some time in his face' before speaking the 'I have given suck' lines.[102] Then, still close to him, Siddons spoke 'in a low earnest whisper of discovery' to disclose Lady Macbeth's plan for the murder, pausing occasionally to gauge the effect of her words.[103] Bell noted of the scene overall that throughout, 'she feels her way, observes the wavering of his mind; suits her earnestness and whole manner to it'.[104] Kemble's response was to show Macbeth's hesitancy while simultaneously revealing that his ambition was still present: 'With what a trembling hand, confessing irresolution of purpose, did he grasp his contemptuous wife, and decline to proceed "further in this business," while his eye yet seemed to gloat and glisten at the visionary crown which was leading him to *Duncan's* chamber!'[105]

While Macbeth goes off to commit the murder, Lady Macbeth must await his return. J. H. Stocqueler described this moment in an account of watching a performance from the wings:

> The sepulchral tone in which John Kemble bade Duncan not to hear the bell which summoned him to the world of shades, rings in my ears at this moment. They (the ears) were not more than a foot distant from the mighty tragedian when he uttered the lines. But the horror produced by the apostrophe was dissipated when the Thane of Cawdor, brushing past me, received the requisite hand-daubing [of stage blood] from his dresser. I was examining the process when the whispered words, 'he is about it,' drew my attention to the half-opened door, and recalled me to the scene. The words, of course, came from Mrs. Siddons, who was bending towards the door in the act of listening – her ear so close that I could absolutely feel her breath. The words, I have said, were whispered – but what a whisper

was hers! Distinctly audible in every part of the house, it served the purpose of the loudest tones.[106]

Of interest here (and not noted by other critics) is the light this account sheds on Siddons's performance process. As she describes elsewhere, for example, in the case of *King John* explored in Chapter 1, she remained in character even when offstage by listening to the ongoing events of the play. In *Macbeth* she deepened her characterization while on stage by looking through the partially open stage door to watch Kemble's hands become saturated with blood. Kemble's promptbook notes that 'the door must be kept a little open, till Macbeth comes out', evidently in order to support Siddons's artistic process.[107] Suspense was created by Siddons's portrayal of Lady Macbeth's uncertainty that her husband would be able to do the deed. Her initial response to Macbeth's account of the murder is horror: 'As if her inhuman strength of spirit overcome by the contagion of his remorse and terror. Her arms about her neck and bosom, shuddering.'[108] But this soon changes to 'agony and alarm at his derangement'.[109] Then, 'calling up the resources of her spirit', Lady Macbeth approaches her husband.[110] Bell noted that at this point Siddons 'speaks forcibly into his ear, looks at him steadfastly' with 'fine remonstrance, tone fit to work on his mind'.[111] Siddons then seized the daggers 'very contemptuously', as can be seen in an early visual representation of the siblings in these roles, painted by Thomas Beach.[112]

The actress's portrayal of Lady Macbeth's anxiety and contempt continue as she accuses Macbeth of cowardice. Bell noted that

> Kemble plays well here; stands motionless; his bloody hands near his face; his eye fixed, agony in his brow; quite rooted to the spot. She at first directs him with an assured and confident air. Then alarm steals on her, increasing to agony lest his reason be quite gone and discovery be inevitable. Strikes him on the shoulder, pulls him from his fixed posture, forces him away, he talking as he goes.[113]

Donohue argues that the end of this scene 'fully exemplifies the cooperative playing which has marked Kemble's and Mrs. Siddons's efforts throughout this sequence'.[114] Since Lady Macbeth has to react to what Macbeth does in order to drive the plot forward, Siddons's responsiveness to her stage partner was a major strength of her interpretation of this role. Kemble's Macbeth did not shy away from indecision and inaction (unlike his predecessor, Smith, whose approach to playing tragic heroes seems to have emphasized bravado). The collaboration of Siddons and Kemble thus brought a fresh interpretation to *Macbeth*.

The characters' final appearance together in the play is the banquet scene (3.4). Here Siddons showed Lady Macbeth's unease reaching fever pitch, particularly as Macbeth sees the ghost of Banquo, in a manner that was deeply affecting: 'Her anxiety makes you creep with apprehension: uncertain how to act. Her emotion keeps you breathless.'[115] Siddons's skill at moving between different emotions or, indeed, playing them simultaneously is evident again here. In the scene following the murder of Duncan (2.2) she had performed both anxiety and strength of purpose, here 'her secret agony again agitates her' but in addressing the guests she 'speaks sweetly'.[116] Kemble achieved a similar contrast by first of all appearing 'tame and kingly' but subsequently bringing a 'brief touch[] of feeling in the language of everyday life' as 'the trembling usurper falters out to his approaching queen – "If I stand here, I saw him"' as the ghost vanishes.[117] Thus the intense energy was mingled with a solemn sense of impending doom. On the line 'Hence, horrible shadow!' Kemble's Macbeth 'chid and scolded the ghost out! and rose in vehemence and courage as he went on'.[118] Siddons's Lady Macbeth in dismissing the guests 'descends in great eagerness; voice almost choked with anxiety to prevent their questioning; alarm, hurry, rapid and convulsive, as if afraid he should tell of the murder of Duncan'.[119] At the end of the scene, Siddons became 'very sorrowful. Quite exhausted' and 'feeble', which Bell saw as preparation for the sleepwalking scene and Lady Macbeth's 'final doom'.[120] Donohue notes that this 'split' between 'Macbeth's rising courage and Lady Macbeth's disintegration' was echoed in the staging as Kemble crossed to the right of the stage, leaving Siddons alone in the centre.[121]

Both Siddons and Kemble made striking innovations in their interpretations of their roles in *Macbeth*. From her first London performance, Siddons famously put down the candle in the sleepwalking scene in order to be able to mime the hand washing called for in the text. Kemble's major change came in the banquet scene, when in his 1794 production he banished the ghost of Banquo from the stage and instead 'let it be expressed by Macbeth as the image of His disturbed imagination'.[122] But eventually some playgoers called for Banquo's ghost to appear again and Kemble was 'obliged to comply contrary to His judgment'.[123] At the start of the 1811 season, the *Times* objected to this reinstatement as 'a mere trick for the galleries', an attempt to placate unruly groups in the theatre, some of whom had caused the previous year's disturbances.[124] Thus Dobson reads this moment in the context of the OP Riots as an example of how Kemble ultimately had to capitulate to all sections of his audience, being 'forced to accept that the drama's laws would henceforth be given by all of the drama's patrons', not only the wealthy.[125] The OPs ultimately won out over the Covent Garden management in terms of the specifics of the way in which *Macbeth* was performed as well as the broader issues around access to dramatic representation that the riots brought to light. While Kemble's new interpretation of the banquet scene attracted some criticism, Siddons's change to the sleepwalking scene was 'received with approbation'.[126] However, her innovations were not always so readily accepted, as we shall see in the next chapter's discussion of her Hamlet.

5

Sibling *Hamlet*

As we saw in the Introduction to this book, Kemble made his Drury Lane debut as Hamlet in 1783 and it became one of his most celebrated characters. As Shattuck writes, 'Hamlet may not have been Kemble's best role, but it was the role he played most constantly' in almost every one of his London seasons.[1] Although he did not pick Hamlet for his farewell appearance in 1817 (choosing instead, as we shall see, Coriolanus, which was probably his most successful role), he played it three times in his round of retirement performances. Kemble also played Hamlet many times in the provinces throughout his career. But what is less well known is that his sister played the role before he did and came back to it later in her career at the height of her fame.

Siddons's Hamlet

When Bate evaluated Siddons in Cheltenham in 1775 on behalf of Garrick, part of his assessment was to note 'the great number of characters she plays', including a role that was perhaps surprising for the young actress to have tackled: 'She plays Hamlet to the satisfaction of the Worcestershire Critics.'[2] This remark might also be construed as a snide comment about the tastes of the provincial audience, who Bate suggested were unsophisticated in being satisfied with a female Hamlet.

But as Amy Muse notes, Siddons's success as Hamlet 'likely contributed to her invitation to come to London' to act at Drury Lane.[3] Hamlet was, then, an important and successful early role for the actress. Siddons acted with Joseph Younger's company in 1775 and they had performed at Worcester in March; thus, we have a likely rough date for Siddons's first known performance as Hamlet.[4] The *Manchester Mercury* announced Siddons as Hamlet for 19 March 1777, 'her second Appearance in that Character'.[5] Notable about this performance is that the actor playing Laertes to Siddons's Hamlet was her brother, John. As Shaughnessy points out, this is 'a piece of casting which gives a good indication of where her reputation stood in relation to his' at this time.[6] Like Siddons, Kemble had performed with their father's company as a child. He made his adult acting debut in Wolverhampton on 8 January 1776, several months after his sister had appeared as Hamlet in Worcester.[7] Siddons was therefore the first of the siblings to tackle the role. The Manchester performance was a benefit for Kemble and William Siddons, who played Horatio. As well as Siddons as Hamlet, the performance also featured Elizabeth Inchbald and her husband Joseph (who were to become friends of both Kemble and Siddons) as Gertrude and Claudius, Elizabeth Farren (who would make her London debut later that year) as Ophelia and the manager, Younger, as the Ghost.[8] Between these two performances in Worcester and Manchester, Siddons had made her first debut at Drury Lane, before going back to the provinces.

Siddons next appeared as Hamlet at Liverpool on 3 December 1777.[9] This time, the performance was for Siddons's own benefit night, though she shared it with William Barry, the theatre's treasurer. Siddons wrote to Inchbald: 'I played Hamlet in Liverpool to near an hundred pounds, and wish I had taken it to myself.'[10] Her letter then goes on to describe how the managers 'have determined to employ no more exotics', by which she means star London performers, citing the recent appearance of Elizabeth Younge as having 'rather hurt than done them service; so that Liverpool must from this time forth be content with such homely fare as we *small folks* can furnish to its delicate senses'.[11] These comments are ironic in light of the fact that Siddons would subsequently become the 'exotic' who toured the regions, appearing in Liverpool again in 1783 after she had made her second, successful London debut and returning there many times throughout her career.[12] Even if Siddons received only half of the benefit profits, £50 was still a large sum. Kemble had been hired at a salary of £1 per week, but Siddons, 'an actress of some standing and renown in the provinces', was probably earning more.[13] Siddons played Hamlet for a second time in Liverpool on 2 October 1778 for her husband's benefit.[14] Both Liverpool performances again featured Kemble as Laertes and William Siddons as Horatio.

When a few weeks later Siddons moved to the Bath and Bristol theatres (like the Liverpool and Manchester playhouses they were linked, with the same company acting in both venues), she was employed at a salary of £3 per week (presumably more than she was paid by Younger or by Tate Wilkinson when she acted on his Yorkshire circuit in the spring of 1777). Genest recorded Siddons performing Hamlet at Bristol on 27 June 1781 'for that night only'.[15] It was again a benefit performance, this time for William Siddons and Frances Kemble, a younger sister of Sarah's and John's.[16] William played Guildenstern this time and Frances the Queen, a role that Siddons herself had previously acted. *Felix Farley's Bristol Journal* reported that Siddons 'went thro'' the character to the entire approbation of a numerous and polite audience'.[17]

Scholars have noted that Siddons's performances of Hamlet were for benefit nights, which could introduce novelty and aimed at drawing in large audiences. Muse notes that the recurrent 'pattern of playing Hamlet once in each city for benefit performances' indicates the success of the endeavour: audiences were keen to seize this rare opportunity to see Siddons in an unusual role.[18] Playgoers may also have heard about Siddons's Hamlet from those who had seen it elsewhere. Indeed, this was the strategy employed to evoke curiosity for

Siddons's Bristol appearance by *Felix Farley's Bristol Journal*, which puffed her performance in advance:

> The lovers of dramatic exhibition may be congratulated on the nouvelle entertainment they are going to receive at our Theatre on Wednesday next, when Mrs. Siddons is to play the part of Hamlet. The Writer of the paragraph confesses himself an admirer of that Lady's performances in general, but was never better pleased than by seeing her in this arduous task, which he had the good fortune to do in two capital Theatres – and can confirm, that tho' numbers might go merely out of curiosity, yet never were audiences more agreeably disappointed, or better satisfied, with an attempt of that nature.[19]

It is remarkable that news of Siddons's performances was circulating around the country, even at this early stage of her career, before her second London debut. The report both emphasizes the novelty of the performance and demonstrates that audiences were impressed with Siddons's acting of this role, even if they had expected to be dissatisfied.

This scholarly focus on benefit performances further underlines the unusual status of Siddons's appearances as Hamlet. As Celestine Woo argues, even if these performances were rare, 'for an actress of such stature to have played a role so central to the Shakespeare canon, so pivotal in Romantic thought, and so invested with cultural capital then and now' (and, I would add, so closely identified with the leading actor of the previous generation, Garrick) is surely significant.[20] Woo also rightly argues that Siddons's Hamlet has been 'relegated to a footnote' because she never performed it on the London stage and cautions us not to dismiss it on these grounds.[21] As we have seen throughout this study, regional performance was central to the careers of both Siddons and Kemble and to most actors of the time. They honed their craft and developed their reputations in the regions before transitioning to the London stage and made frequent appearances across Britain, Scotland

and Ireland throughout their working lives as a way to earn additional income and to propagate their fame. Muse posits that the actress's appearances as Hamlet 'planted in viewers' minds the idea that the young Sarah Siddons was fit to be the tragic hero(ine) of the age'.[22]

But what remains so far underexplored about these early benefits is that they were most often benefit performances not for Siddons herself but for her family, most frequently her husband but also her brother and sister. While we do not necessarily have to read this as corroborating the idea that Siddons was in some way reticent or diffident about this part, this fact does suggest that for her own benefits, Siddons preferred to focus on the roles with which she was more readily associated and in which she would make her name. For example, while in Liverpool Siddons played Hamlet for her (shared) benefit on 3 December 1777, in Manchester on 16 March 1778 she chose the part of Isabella instead.[23] This pathetic role was, of course, the one in which she made her famous return to London in 1782. Siddons played the lead role in *Jane Shore*, one of her most famous affective parts, on 17 February 1781 in Bath, taking £124.[24] Then, shortly after performing Hamlet for the benefit of her husband and sister, she experimented with sentimental comedy, acting Lady Brumpton in Richard Steele's *The Funeral* (1701) for her Bristol benefit on 9 July, taking £100.[25]

There are no records of Siddons performing Hamlet after 1781 and before the end of the century and she never acted the role on the London stage. Her only subsequent appearances as Hamlet were in Dublin in 1802. After that, she again seems to have dropped the role, though she did give readings of the play. Muse posits two reasons for Siddons abandoning Hamlet: firstly, 'that the provincial theatres allowed for more experimentation than the London stages did' and secondly, 'that Siddons did not want to compete with her brother'.[26] Indeed, rather than being unsophisticated (as Bate implied), regional audiences might in fact have been more receptive to innovation than their counterparts in the capital. Kemble began acting Hamlet in Dublin in 1781 and news of his performances eventually reached London and led to his engagement at Drury Lane, in the same way that Muse claims was the case for Siddons. Thus, if Siddons had continued to perform the role or had done so in London, an element of competition would have been unavoidable.

As others have noted, Siddons was not the first woman Hamlet. Charlotte Charke claims to have played the role in her memoirs and the first actress in the theatrical record to have tackled the part was Elizabeth 'Fanny' Furnival on 28 April 1741 'by special desire' and for her benefit.[27] In his book on women as Hamlet, Tony Howard notes an intriguing connection between Furnival and Siddons: according to Charles Lee Lewes, Siddons's father, Roger, had been trained by Furnival and they were also romantically involved.[28] When they met in William Smith's company at Canterbury, 'she flattered him with the promise of making an actor of him, and no woman on the British stage was better qualified for giving instructions in theatricals, at that time'.[29] Apparently Kemble needed the help as 'Fanny was full seven weeks in driving the part of Serjeant Kite [the role in which Roger was to make his debut in George Farquhar's 1706 comedy *The Recruiting Officer*] into his head'.[30] They eventually separated and Kemble went on to marry Sarah Ward, Siddons's mother. Perhaps Siddons heard stories about Furnival's Hamlet from her father and remembered this intriguing performance when she began to establish her own repertoire in the early days of her career.

She might also have recalled Furnival when she proposed acting Hamlet in Dublin, which she did at the Crow Street theatre on 27 and 29 July 1802, the only known occasions on which she played the part after she had made her name in London.[31] Just as her father had been coached by Furnival, Siddons also received training for these performances, although not for acting but for sword fighting. An observer described the effect of this coaching: 'Galindo who is a master of the art, was put into the character of Laertes purposely for an exhibition &

Mrs. Siddons had practiced with him so successfully that she astonished the cognoscenti of the audience.'[32] Judith Pascoe highlights how 'inordinately exciting' and, indeed, liberating the prospect of learning fencing must have been to 'a middle-aged woman whose physical assets were shrinking'.[33] However, Siddons would, of course, have performed the fencing scene during her previous appearances in the part, though perhaps without so much attention to detail. It is clear that her early-nineteenth-century performances of Hamlet were of a different order to those at the beginning of her career and may have had different motivations. We might even speculate that in reprising this role, Siddons wanted to recapture her youth. Furthermore, Muse notes that by 1802, Siddons was 'personally distraught, as she was nearly estranged from her husband'.[34] And following her training sessions with Galindo, she was subsequently accused of an adulterous affair with him.

Catherine Galindo claimed that Siddons proposed the *Hamlet* performance to her husband 'for no other purpose than to be taught *fencing* by Mr. G. for by so doing you had an excuse to have him constantly with you, to the exclusion of my company, as you said you could not be instructed while any person looked on'.[35] Catherine also reprints a letter from Siddons to Galindo in which the actress reminisces about their rehearsals together: 'About this time last summer, we used to be practising the noble science of *defence*, it served the purpose of the moment well, very well indeed.'[36] Probably written in the wake of the death of her daughter, Sally, in 1803, Siddons wishes 'for the friend who knew so well how to keep me "up up up"'.[37] Catherine glosses the words in quotation marks as a phrase of her husband's, presumably used in fencing instruction, but here referring to his ability to lift Siddons's spirits. The letter attests to their intimacy and Catherine clearly believed that Siddons's claim that rehearsing with Galindo 'served the purpose of the moment well' was suggestive. A caricature that appeared in the *Dublin Satirist* shows Galindo and Siddons rehearsing as Catherine looks on from the doorway, urging her husband to exercise judgement. As Charlotte Boatner-Doane notes, the unflattering depiction of Siddons (who is shown from the rear in breeches, her size no doubt exaggerated), rich with innuendo, demonstrates that 'even an actress as revered as Siddons could face ridicule and sexual suspicion, especially when performing more daring and gender-defying roles'.[38]

The observer quoted previously who described Siddons's fencing in fact provides the only substantial account of the actress's interpretation of Hamlet. Robert Rainey attended several of Siddons's appearances in 1802 and commented in his diary on her performances and more generally on the frenzy of excitement that surrounded her visit to Ireland. On the occasion of her appearance as Hamlet on 27 July 1802, he wrote of how 'the House groaned under the weight of Spectators' who had thronged to watch Siddons act this iconic role, by now so unusual in her repertoire, and who 'were rapt in admiration of her excellence' during the performance.[39] Rainey particularly appreciated the moment in the second scene 'where the secret of the Ghosts appearance is disclosed to Hamlet' by his companions.[40] Garrick had been praised for his reaction to the ghost of his father (apparently aided by the wig he commissioned that allowed his hair to stand on end 'Like quills upon the fearful porpentine'), but what struck Rainey about Siddons was not just the fear she expressed when she saw the Ghost but also the transitions that followed: 'After the first expression of astonishment at the relation, He remained lost in thought; you might trace in imagination the progress of his wonder & his half formed suspicions, till roused from his reverie by the sudden idea of personally communicating with the Spectre he declares his purpose to his companions.'[41] Siddons's Hamlet transitioned through emotional states, reacting with appropriate horror to the apparition, visibly pondering the implications of what he had seen, and then deciding to take action. Rainey also pinpointed other key moments in the play in which Siddons excelled: 'The Interview with the Queen, with Ophelia, & the scene in w. she watches the emotions raised in the King by the representation of the players, & Stings his conscience by her sneering observation, were inimitable pieces of acting – The Fencing scene in the last Act was capital.'[42]

Much critical attention has been paid to Siddons's costume for her 1802 performance of Hamlet, which Rainey described as 'a kind of black scarf which was very nearly equivalent to a petticoat'.[43] The garment can be seen in Mary Sackville Hamilton's sketch of Siddons (Figure 9), which bears the same date as the performance Rainey saw. Scholars have described

FIGURE 9 *Mary Sackville Hamilton*, Mrs. Siddons's Dress as Hamlet. Act I Scene II. 'Aye Madam, it is common . . .' *(27 July 1802)*. *1876,0510.816-896. © The Trustees of the British Museum.*

this costume as androgynous, positing that it offered Siddons a means of moving away from the typical sexualized breeches role. In this way, the actress's attire as Hamlet was similar to the costumes she wore as Rosalind and Imogen early in her career which, as we saw in Chapter 1, revealed Siddons's ambivalence about cross-dressing on stage. Woo importantly draws a distinction between breeches roles, in which female characters don male disguise as part of the plot of the play (such as Rosalind and Imogen), and cross-gendered roles, in which the actor decides to perform a character of the opposite sex (as with Siddons's Hamlet). The cross-gendered role is 'generally more difficult and demanding than a breeches role, since the player would need to sustain the illusion more thoroughly and for the whole duration of the play', rather than featuring cross-dressing as only 'a portion of the storyline' which in part rests on 'the character's imperfect success at representing the opposite sex'.[44] Siddons may have chosen to pursue the cross-gendered role of Hamlet in order to avoid the sexualization inherent in breeches parts, roles which she abandoned fairly early on in her career as she apparently found them problematic. However, it seems unlikely that Siddons wore the carefully constructed outfit depicted by Hamilton and described by Rainey for her early performances of Hamlet, and it is possible that in these appearances she wore a more conventional breeches costume. If Bate could write of her Rosalind in 1775 that she was 'a very good breeches figure', this suggests that no attempt at concealing the body was made in Siddons's cross-dressed performances at the beginning of her career.[45]

Howard argues that Siddons eventually tried to develop a model of tragic cross-dressing, which demonstrated 'an androgyny not of the eroticised body but of the mind' and 'aspired to make gender irrelevant, not the point of the game'.[46] But the critical response to Siddons's Hamlet suggests that the actress's awkward costume only succeeded in drawing attention to her body and her sex, not obscuring it from the observer. Rainey noted that on her first entrance, Siddons 'seemed oppressed with the novelty of her appearance' to the point that he 'expected a very indifferent performance of the character'.[47] Although Siddons overcame these apparent inhibitions about her costume, according to Rainey the effect of her fine acting 'was considerably injured by the awkwardness of the dress & the feminine gait, which was sometimes ludicrous'.[48] Rainey posited that 'if Mrs. Siddons could correct these, she would be an unrivalled Hamlet'.[49] However, despite his reservations, in his discussion of Siddons's acting in the play, Rainey generally referred to the character of Hamlet with male pronouns ('He remained lost in thought', 'the progress of his wonder', etc.). Thus Siddons was clearly able to play the male role convincingly. Furthermore, Rainey's account suggests that these issues are correctible, rather than implying that they are a fault intrinsic to the performance of a male role by a woman.

Kemble's Hamlet

While accounts of Siddons's Hamlet are limited, much more detailed commentary exists on how Kemble conceptualized the part. Kemble took a scholarly approach to the character and offered several new readings of the text in performance. These innovations, detailed in a lengthy article in the *Public Advertiser* of 7 October 1783 following his London stage debut which had taken place a few days earlier, were sometimes controversial. While Shakespeare editor George Steevens criticized Kemble's shift in emphasis in the line to Horatio about the Ghost, 'Did YOU not speak to it?', arguing that the stress should fall on 'speak', Boaden praised this change as Kemble's stress meant the line was 'personally put to Horatio' and therefore underlined the 'peculiar intimacy' between them.[50] Kemble was also noted for toning down some of the sensationalism of his most famous predecessor, Garrick, whose 'start of terror, and near collapse' in the Ghost scene, for example, 'were still remembered and admired in 1783'.[51]

Kemble made two innovations in responding to the Ghost. Firstly, whereas having drawn his sword on the friends that tried to prevent him from following the apparition, Garrick pursued the Ghost with the point of the sword towards it, Kemble 'drooped the weapon after him'.[52] Boaden approved of this change: 'As a defence against such a being it was ridiculous to present the point. – To retain it unconsciously showed how completely he was absorbed by the dreadful mystery he was exploring.'[53] Secondly, in his encounter with the Ghost (1.5), Kemble knelt to it, which 'suitably mark'd the filial reverence of Hamlet, and the solemnity of the engagement he had contracted'.[54] Kemble's scholarly consideration of the text and his less sensational acting style were hallmarks of his interpretation of Hamlet.

Commentary on Kemble's Hamlet largely focuses on his London performances of the part. Here I will consider an 1811 pamphlet entitled *Critical Observations on Mr. Kemble's Performances at the Theatre Royal, Liverpool*, and an unpublished essay by Inchbald on Kemble's Hamlet in order to parallel the sources used in my discussion of Siddons (which necessarily focused on performance outside London and which included a manuscript account) and to offer some lesser-known perspectives on the actor's interpretation of this role. Inchbald's essay is apparently a draft for the prefaces she contributed to the plays in *The British Theatre*, a twenty-five-volume collection published by Longman between 1806 and 1809. These introductory remarks often included notes on contemporary stage practice, but in her published preface to *Hamlet*, Inchbald shied away from commenting on the play because a 'work of such intellectual magnitude' is 'too well known' and turned to biography, instead, since 'the celebrity of a work naturally excites contemplation on its author'.[55] In the unpublished essay she expressed herself equally unwilling to comment on 'a work of such intellectual magnitude that it has employed in comments, the pen of men not far subordinate in genius to the author himself'.[56] But instead of biography, she 'steals abashed from Hamlet, to his attendants – the Players'

– and the bulk of the preface is focused on Kemble, the most celebrated performer of the role at the time.[57] Inchbald's text begins by highlighting Kemble's suitability for the character: he is 'tall, graceful, & dignified', which allows him to represent 'the Heir-apparent of a throne' realistically.[58] She went on to explain how 'the solemn sadness of his features on his first appearance fixes at once every thought of the audience upon his sense of sorrow' and also praised the way in which Kemble's 'varied countenance' powerfully portrays 'the whole catalogue of passions' that Hamlet experiences.[59]

Like other commentators, Inchbald was particularly impressed with Kemble's performance of the scenes with the Ghost in the first Act, including 'his eager attention whilst he listens to the information of Horatio, Barnardo & Marcellus that – "his father's spirit Walks". His determination to search the truth of such intelligence. His tenderness & care; terror and bravery when the revered phantom appears'.[60] These comments give a sense of some of the varied passions that Kemble was able to convey in the role. She also discussed the third act, praising 'his rebukes yet pathos with his mother' in the closet scene and 'the wondrous and instantaneous effect he produces on his hearers, when having slain Polonius he exclaims in a kind of frantic joy, "is it the King"?'[61] While these may be considered 'bold proofs of the actor's art, which elevate him to the summit of his profession', Inchbald expressed some concern at the brilliance of Kemble's performance: 'A peculiar instance of Kemble's powers in this character is – he forces his spectators to forget all Hamlet's failings. This artificial grace may have an immoral tendency.'[62] For example, we should not overlook Hamlet's slaying of Polonius because although it was accidental, Hamlet expresses no remorse. Other commentators also noticed the 'frantic joy' identified by Inchbald: the reviewer for the *Morning Chronicle* called it a '*smile of exultation*' and the *Public Advertiser* thought the smile was more like a grin, which 'may set on some Quantity of *barren Spectators* to exult – yet cannot but make the *Judicious* grieve'.[63] Some of these published reviews imply reservations about Kemble's approach to the line but Inchbald was more explicit as to why she considered this delivery problematic.

An 1811 account of the actor's performances in Liverpool gives us a regional perspective on Kemble's Hamlet.[64] Kemble's interpretation was pronounced a 'masterly performance' but the writer noted that the 'dazzling splendour' of Kemble's acting could obscure some 'defects'.[65] This evaluation chimes with Inchbald's concerns about Kemble's brilliance concealing less desirable aspects of the character. One of Kemble's performance choices singled out by this writer for criticism is another of the actor's innovations in the part, the introduction of two miniatures in the closet scene instead of the wall portraits of Claudius and Old Hamlet. The Liverpool writer argued that as Hamlet discusses the murder of his father, his eyes should fall on the portraits on the wall and then 'burst[] out in that fine apostrophe, "Look here, upon this picture!"'.[66] But by 'producing the picture-cases from his pocket, and examining them first', Kemble 'cooled the fire that he had kindled'.[67] Boaden's account suggests that the portraits were handled somewhat differently on the London stage, with Old Hamlet appearing as a half-length painting on the wall and Claudius as 'a miniature worn by her majesty as a bracelet'.[68] Boaden disliked this staging, arguing that 'the two pictures should be *whole* lengths, the constant furniture of royal apartments, and thus incidentally supplying to Hamlet a powerful, obvious, and undeniable illustration'.[69] The two miniatures were probably a more portable option for props when Kemble toured outside London but it seems uncharacteristic of Kemble to forego the opportunity for grand spectacle which addressing a full-length portrait would have afforded. The differences between Boaden's account and the Liverpool writer's in their discussion of this scene remind us not only that Kemble's Hamlet evolved over the course of his career but also that it must have been played differently in different theatres.

Scholars have noted the centrality of Hamlet to Kemble's London acting career but not yet to his work in the regions. But like Siddons, Kemble played the part before making his debut on the London stage: at Leeds (1779), Edinburgh (1781), Dublin (1781) and Cork (1782).[70] A letter to the *Gentleman's Magazine* from Dublin in April 1783 gives a detailed account of this new performer, as yet unknown in the capital but recently engaged to perform at Drury Lane for the following season. Kemble is declared 'a phænomenon in the theatrical world' and his Hamlet is pronounced 'a most masterly performance' and placed at the top of the list of his best characters.[71] Just as Hamlet consistently remained an important part of Kemble's London repertoire, the same was true in the regions, as his 1811 Liverpool performance demonstrates.[72] Whenever Kemble toured, he would naturally be expected to perform his most famous characters. So just as Kemble's successors on the London stage needed to reckon with his interpretation of Hamlet, so too did actors in the regions. At a meeting of the Sheffield Shakespeare Club on 30 November 1825, an actor named Salter recounted an anecdote from his time working at the theatre in Dover a few years previously. He explained that as he was about to begin his performance of Hamlet, 'the manager came round to inform him that the great Kemble was in the house'.[73] Kemble had stopped at Dover on his way to Lausanne at the end of his final visit to England. Salter, of course, 'was naturally agitated; he feared to meet the gaze and judgment of so great a master'.[74] Kemble watched the entire play and Salter was encouraged to visit him the next morning. When he did so, just as Kemble was about to board his boat to the continent, the actor 'received him with kindness, and encouraged him with his praise'.[75] Salter declared his 'melancholy satisfaction' at being 'the last English actor who held converse with him here' and at knowing 'that the tragedy of *Hamlet*, which had contributed so much to his fame, was the last play which the great tragedian witnessed on his native theatre'.[76] Dobson highlights echoes of Hamlet's encounter with his father's spirit in this interaction and describes it as 'a defining moment of professional legitimation' for Salter.[77] Kemble's validation took place in the context of regional performance, demonstrating that the actor's Hamlet provided a crucial model for performers not just on the London stage but across Britain.

Comparisons of the siblings

When Kemble first appeared on the London stage as Hamlet in 1783, the audience immediately commented on the 'very striking resemblance' the actor bore to his sister.[78] This similarity was perceptible to the ear as well as the eye: a commentator in the *Morning Chronicle* claimed that Kemble's voice was 'so like that of his sister, that were a blind person, familiar to the voice of Mrs. Siddons, to hear Mr. Kemble speak, he might mistake the one for the other'.[79] As Boatner-Doane points out, the role of Hamlet presented spectators with a rare chance to consider 'how the two siblings would differ in their interpretation of the same character', an opportunity usually denied them because Siddons otherwise stuck to parts of her own sex.[80] The contrast between Siddons's Hamlet and Kemble's was frequently elucidated with regard to the scenes with the Ghost at the beginning of the play, considered crucial in 'setting the tone for the performance'.[81] Rainey commented that Siddons's 'superiority even to her brother was first discernible where the secret of the Ghost's appearance is disclosed to Hamlet'; thus, he found the actress's ability to show the character's thought process as he moves from astonishment to action (as discussed earlier) more accomplished than Kemble's acting in this scene.[82] The novelist Ann Radcliffe mused on how Siddons would have differed from Kemble and in what sense she would have surpassed him:

> I should suppose she would be the finest Hamlet that ever appeared, excelling even her own brother in that character; she would more fully preserve the tender and refined melancholy, the deep sensibility, which are the peculiar charm of Hamlet, and which appear not only in the ardour, but in the occasional irresolution and weakness

of his character – the secret spring that reconciles all his inconsistencies. A sensibility so profound can with difficulty be justly imagined, and therefore can very rarely be assumed. Her brother's firmness, incapable of being always subdued, does not so fully enhance, as her tenderness would, this part of the character.[83]

Siddons could present not just Hamlet's melancholy (which Kemble was also able to do) but also the softer side of his sorrow, which required flexibility in order to show Hamlet's occasional hesitancy, a flexibility that Kemble was believed not to possess (Hazlitt famously commented that Kemble acted Hamlet 'like a man in armour, with a determined inveteracy of purpose, in one undeviating straight line').[84] Boaden did not witness Siddons's Hamlet but felt himself qualified to speculate on the actress's interpretation of the role in comparison with Kemble's because of his detailed knowledge of her acting. He claimed that Siddons's 'conception would be generally *bolder* and *warmer*, not so elaborate in speech, nor so systematically graceful in action' and that when Horatio and his companions describe the Ghost to Hamlet, Siddons's 'real feminine alarm' would be even more impressive than Kemble's reaction.[85] As Boatner-Doane points out, 'Siddons's gender would elevate her performance above Kemble's in the scenes with the Ghost' in the eyes of audiences of the period because as a woman, she was better able to portray qualities deemed as inherently feminine: the tenderness and sensibility identified by Radcliffe as central to the character of Hamlet and the 'real feminine alarm' that, according to Boaden, would constitute a powerful response to the Ghost.[86]

Siddons was celebrated as 'a brilliantly *reactive* performer and therefore well-matched to the role' of Hamlet.[87] Just as Rainey emphasized the way the spectator could trace Hamlet's astonishment, then rumination, then commitment to action in the way Siddons reacted to the Ghost, Boaden posited that 'her breathless attention to the spirit during his disclosure, . . . benefited by sex itself, would . . . be transcendent'.[88] His comment that 'she heard a narrative at all times better than one was ever told' emphasizes Siddons's skill in responding to words spoken by other characters as she remained silent, a talent which, as we have seen, she used to great effect as Lady Macbeth, when she imagined the murder of Duncan, and as Constance in *King John*, when she kept the door of her dressing room open to hear the events on stage in order to achieve the proper mental state for her subsequent performance.[89] The reactive quality of Siddons's performance was achieved by her voice as well as her action. In contrasting Siddons's and Kemble's delivery of the 'to be or not to be' speech, Boaden wrote that the soliloquy 'from the quality of her organ, would be more like *audible rumination* than Kemble's, who declaimed it in the higher tones of his voice, and lost the cast of *thought*, that the galleries might catch the words he uttered'.[90] Rainey praised Siddons's responsiveness in the Mousetrap scene 'in w[ch]. she watches the emotions raised in the King by the representation of the players, & Stings his conscience by her sneering observation'.[91] An account of Kemble's rendering of this moment in the play is provided by Harriet Martin in a pamphlet which was published in the same year that Rainey saw Siddons's Dublin performance. Martin described how Kemble's Hamlet 'laid himself at her [Ophelia's] feet – he took her fan, and gallanted it with such easy grace; but soon he turned it to use – speaking to her, his eyes were scrutinising the dark soul of his uncle – behind its sticks he sometimes artfully shaded his observation'.[92] This byplay with the fan, which enabled Kemble to emphasize his responses to Claudius's reaction to the play, is reminiscent of Rainey's emphasis on Siddons's 'sneering observation' of the King, though she did not need a prop to convey Hamlet's feelings during this scene.

One of the major similarities between Siddons's and Kemble's Hamlet, at least in 1802 when Rainey and Martin were writing, lies in the way they dressed the role. Siddons's costume as depicted by Hamilton in 1802 is strongly reminiscent of Kemble's as shown in the iconic painting by Thomas Lawrence completed in 1801 (Figure 10). Kemble

FIGURE 10 *Henry Dawe after Thomas Lawrence,* John Philip Kemble as Hamlet *(1827). ART File K31.4 no.53 copy 2 (size M), image 28632. Used by permission of the Folger Shakespeare Library.*

had himself experimented with costume, introducing an outfit 'which was a stage adaptation of the Elizabethan style'.[93] This costume, known as the Vandyke style and considered a break with the tradition of acting the part in modern court dress, consisted of 'a sleeved doublet, trunk hose, tights, and a lace collar, with a baldric to support his sword. To this he added for certain crucial scenes the long, enveloping, dark cloak and the bonnet with its tall black plumes' strikingly depicted by Lawrence.[94] Siddons's Hamlet costume as illustrated by Hamilton contains many elements of the Vandyke dress worn by Kemble, notably the cloak and bonnet. Woo claims that the garment allowed Siddons to conceal her body and thus refuse the sexualization of the cross-dressed role, but more than that, the costume would also have connected her with Kemble's Hamlet in the minds of the audience.[95] While Siddons may not have been able to rival her brother as Hamlet on the London stage, she issued a significant challenge by invoking him in her performances in Dublin and was considered superior to him by critics such as Boaden, Rainey and Radcliffe.

Hamlet beyond the lead role

As we have seen, Kemble began by performing Laertes, not Hamlet. Siddons, on the other hand, may have begun as Hamlet and transitioned to the female roles in the play later in her career. On 15 May 1786, Siddons acted Ophelia for her second benefit that season 'for this night only' with her brother in the lead role.[96] This switch to Ophelia supports the idea that Siddons did not want to compete with Kemble on the London stage, but it can also be read as a tactical move to showcase once more their collaborative acting. As we saw in Chapter 1, during their early years in London, the siblings often chose plays in which they could appear together, particularly to boost their profits on benefit nights (indeed, this performance grossed £326 14s. 6d., second only that season to the benefit for Charles Dignum, a popular singer). A review in the *Public Advertiser* pronounced that the actors 'excel[led] every other effect and attraction. Such was the consequence of Kemble and Mrs. Siddons acting together' in *Hamlet*, emphasizing that the conjunction of the two performers was key to the success of the play.[97] Siddons was praised for developing a new and just interpretation of Ophelia:

> We know not that she ever had a representative worthy of her till Monday night. – Till then there never was, in sensible discrimination, as there ought to be, the real

madness of Ophelia from the feigned distraction of Hamlet. Till then neither the dignity nor the love of the character was discernible. – Till then even the pathos of the part was but poorly, if at all administered.[98]

Perhaps because Siddons had already played Hamlet, she was uniquely positioned to make Ophelia's madness distinct. Boaden particularly praised Siddons's rendering of Ophelia's speech about the death of her father, especially the line 'My BROTHER *shall know of it* – ', which 'as delivered by Mrs. Siddons, was never to be forgotten'.[99] Although Siddons's real-life brother was now playing Hamlet, not Laertes, the audience would surely have made the connection and the pathos of Siddons's delivery would have been heightened by having Kemble appearing in the same play.

Later in his career, critics wrote of Kemble's harsh treatment of Ophelia in the nunnery scene: Holcroft claimed he followed the tradition of appearing 'to persecute, nay to bully, Ophelia'.[100] The pathos would have been increased here if the 'lovely and harmless woman' that Kemble's Hamlet was treating with 'threatening of fists, . . . ferocity of voice, . . . stamping of feet, . . . clattering of doors' had been his sister.[101] However, it is hard to imagine Siddons being beaten down in this scene. Campbell recounts an anecdote about the powerful effect her performance of Ophelia had on others in the cast: 'Her fellow actress, who played the *Queen*, in "Hamlet," was so electrified by the Siddons's looks, when she seized her arm, that she hesitated and forgot her part.'[102]

Siddons subsequently switched her attention to another role in the play, that of Gertrude, again showcasing her cooperative acting with Kemble. Her first London appearance in this part was on 29 April 1796, but she had played the Queen as early as 1777 in Liverpool and had also acted it at Bath in 1778.[103]. Siddons soon gave up Ophelia and Gertrude to other actresses.[104]

Although there are no recorded performances of Siddons as Hamlet after 1802 or ever on the London stage, her engagement with the play continued after her retirement through the readings she gave in 1813, both to the royal family at Windsor Castle and to the public at the Argyll Rooms. When Bell evaluated Siddons's acting in *Macbeth* as superior to Kemble's, he noted that 'Mrs. Siddons in reading "Hamlet" showed how inimitably she could by a mere look, while sitting in a chair, paint to the spectators a horrible shadow in her mind'.[105] Hazlitt was also impressed: 'No scenic representation that I ever witnessed produced the hundredth part of the effect of her reading Hamlet. This tragedy was the triumph of her art.'[106] Siddons's Hamlet lived on beyond the theatre and after her retirement, leaving a profound and lasting impression on those who witnessed her readings.

Conclusion

Retirements (1812, 1817)

Although by the time of her death in 1831 Siddons had not appeared as Hamlet in many years, the actress ended her life playing the part in her private life. Her niece, Fanny Kemble (daughter of Charles and Maria Theresa), wrote of her aunt a few weeks before her death: 'What a price she has paid for her great celebrity! – weariness, vacuity, and utter deadness of spirit. . . . She has stood on a pinnacle till all things have come to look flat and dreary; mere shapeless, colourless, level monotony to her.'[1] Although it would appear that she had longed for retirement for several years, apparently it did not always bring her the peace she had hoped to achieve: Samuel Rogers recalled that

> after she had left the stage, Mrs. Siddons, from the want of excitement, was never happy. When I was sitting with her of an afternoon, she would say, 'Oh, dear! this is the time I used to be thinking of going to the theatre: first came the pleasure of dressing for my part; and then the pleasure of acting it: but that is all over now.'[2]

In contrast, Fanny Kemble remembered her uncle on his visit to London in 1820 more positively with 'his venerable white hair and beautiful face, full of an expression of most benign dignity', though Hazlitt, who met him at the same time, thought him 'bent down, dispirited, and lethargic'.[3] It seems that both of the siblings succumbed to Hamlet's melancholy once they left the stage.

'Those tears shall flow no more'[4]

There are references in Siddons's correspondence to her desire for retirement as early as 1807, when as she prepared to play Belvidera in Leeds she wrote in a letter: 'I am not i' the mood for acting, but I must play yet a little while longer, and then! – how peaceful, how comfortable shall I be, after the storms, the tempests, and afflictions of my laborious life!'[5] It seems that the reason that Siddons continued to perform was economic: Boaden noted that 'she had frequently intimated her intention to withdraw from the scene', especially following the fire and Old Price Riots at Covent Garden, 'but circumstances had induced her to renew her engagements as the interests of the concern might require'.[6] This suggests that she stayed on in order to help the theatre and her own financial situation.[7] On 18 September 1811, Siddons made her first appearance of the season as Lady Macbeth, with the announcements proclaiming this 'the last season of Mrs. Siddons's appearing on the stage'.[8] From June 1812, 'the play-bills now, announcing the character of the night, with melancholy accuracy stated, that it would be the *last time* of her ever appearing in it'.[9] During this season Siddons acted fifty-seven times in fourteen different parts, including her major Shakespearean roles.[10] She was often supported in performance by her brother. In a letter written ten days before her final appearance, Siddons described the prospect of retirement as 'awful and affecting – to know one is doing the most indifferent thing for *the last* time induces a more than common seriousness'.[11] Her comment reveals both a sense of ambivalence about her acting and a great deal of regret and trepidation about her retirement.

Siddons's farewell benefit took place on 29 June 1812 when she acted Lady Macbeth alongside Kemble as Macbeth. Farington's description of the audience's response to Siddons's final performance has become the stuff of legend and testament to the high regard in which she was held: 'When Mrs. Siddons walked off the stage in Her last scene where she appears as walking in Her sleep, there was a long continued burst of applause, which caused Kemble &c. to conclude that it was the wish of the spectators that the Play should there stop.'[12] The curtain was therefore dropped and after some time 'Mrs. Siddons appeared sitting at a table in Her own character' though wearing 'the dress in which she performed the dreaming scene of *Lady Macbeth*', which Farington describes as 'White Sattin' with 'a long vail'.[13] It took some time before 'the clapping & other sounds of approbation' abated enough for the actress to speak but she eventually delivered an eight-minute farewell address written for her by her nephew, Horace Twiss, to 'profound silence' from the audience.[14] Farington described the actress's appearance as 'that of a person distressed & sunk in spirits, but I did not perceive that she shed tears. J. Kemble came on afterwards to ask "Whether the Play shd. go on?" He wiped His eyes and appeared to have been weeping. The Play was not allowed to go on'.[15] Thus as Siddons retired from the stage she swapped roles with her brother, showing the kind of stoic resignation generally ascribed to Kemble and not the pathos in which she usually excelled, while he was the one to shed tears.

Perhaps unsurprisingly, many of Siddons's audience were unwilling to accept her decision to leave the stage. In 1813, a petition to try to entice her to return to the theatre garnered over five hundred signatures, and two years later, a committee from the Drury Lane theatre headed by Lord Byron again attempted to persuade her to resume acting regularly.[16] The actress refused these entreaties but did make occasional appearances after her official retirement from the stage, though always at the request of or in support of others. These performances included benefits for the Theatrical Fund in 1813 and 1816, a series of ten nights in Edinburgh in support of Harriet Siddons (her son Henry's widow) and her children in 1815, benefit performances for her brother Charles and sister-in-law Maria Theresa and appearances at the desire of Princess Charlotte in 1816 (though ironically the Princess was indisposed and unable to attend the performances she had commanded).[17] Siddons's final stage appearance was as Lady Randolph in *Douglas* at Covent Garden on 9 June 1819 for the benefit of Charles and Maria Theresa Kemble. Campbell thought this part 'injudiciously chosen', perhaps in part because it was not a Shakespearean role, but it was well received by the audience.[18]

Siddons occasionally expressed her own reservations about these post-retirement appearances. For example, in a letter of 1815 she felt the need to justify her return to the stage:

> I hope my visit to Edinburgh will be beneficial to my dear son's family. At least it will evince the greatest proof of respect for that public on whom they depend, which it is in my power to give. I have some doubts whether the motives which induce me to return to the public after so long an absence will shield me from the darts of malignity . . . I fear I shall never be able to present myself in Mrs Beverley, who should be not only handsome but young also.[19]

Evidently Siddons was concerned both that she would no longer be able to perform her old roles effectively given her age and that she would be suspected of avarice. Accusations of greed dogged Siddons throughout her career following the incident in Dublin in 1784 (discussed in Chapter 1) and may have been the reason that the actress's later appearances were always benefit performances for others. An Edinburgh theatre critic assuaged fears about the actress ageing: 'Mrs. Siddons not only is, but looks older than when she was last before us. But in this single observation every thing inauspicious to her efforts is included and exhausted.'[20] Hazlitt, however, took issue with Siddons's reappearances. In the famous essay of 1816 in which he claims that 'to have seen Mrs. SIDDONS was an event in every one's life' and writes of the actress as 'tragedy personified' and 'above nature', he also lamented that 'Mrs. SIDDONS retired once from the stage: why should she return to it again? She cannot retire from it twice with dignity; and yet it is to be wished that she should do all things with dignity. Any loss of reputation to her is a loss to the world'.[21] Hazlitt saw these reappearances not as a way to gratify fans and support colleagues (or in this case to pander to royalty as he specifically references the performances for Princess Charlotte) but as mortifying for the actress.

In addition to these performances after her official departure from the stage, Siddons also gave readings to the royal family and to the public in 1813. The latter were, according to Boaden, motivated by 'personal gratification and an important addition to her income' as Kemble revealed to him that, despite the wealth she had apparently accrued, his sister 'was not in that state of affluence, that she could live unemployed, without some diminution of her comforts'.[22] Boaden described the 'simple and yet dignified' style of these readings, which were well received, although the biographer claims that reading Shakespeare's male characters presented some challenges to Siddons in words that echo the critiques of her Hamlet: 'There is ... an almost awkward effort of an elegantly drest female to assume the vehement passions, coarse humours, and often unguarded dialogue of every vanity of manly character.'[23] However, Benjamin Haydon heard Siddons read *Macbeth* in 1821 and recorded that 'she acts Macbeth herself, ... better than either Kemble or Kean', reiterating the favourable comparisons with her brother's Hamlet.[24] Maria Edgeworth powerfully described one of Siddons's private readings at the actress's home, in this case from *Henry VIII*: 'I felt that I had never before fully understood or sufficiently admired Shakespeare, or known the full powers of the human voice and the English language.'[25] Siddons was subsequently invited to give readings at Oxford and Cambridge. Her daughter Cecilia recorded that at the latter, 'she read to almost all the members of the University at present there the trial scene in the *Merchant of Venice*, and more finely she never did it in her life. Every one was, or seemed to be, enchanted and enthusiastic'.[26] These readings therefore allowed Siddons to reprise her most popular parts and to try out new characters, including male roles, continuing the experimentation of her Hamlet.

'All my labours, all my studies'[27]

Peter Thomson suggests that the tears shed by Kemble on the occasion of Siddons's final performance were perhaps 'tinged with envy'.[28] Nevertheless, his career continued for another five years. While Kemble had a 'strong reluctance' to pursue popular entertainments such as Colman's *Blue Beard* (revived on 18 February 1811 'with hitherto unequaled splendour' and sixteen horses), he felt compelled to do so in order to 'compensate in some degree' for the financial losses Covent Garden had sustained after the fire, rebuilding and riots.[29] Following Siddons's retirement and in the knowledge that 'the theatre had got into a steady course of success', Kemble left London for two years to act in Ireland and the provinces and was even offered £5,000 and expenses for eighty performances in America, though he declined.[30] While Siddons risked being denigrated for her provincial performances and accused of avarice, Kemble was lauded for these regional appearances late in his career. Neither did Kemble's ageing body attract the same kind of scrutiny as his sister's. In 1813, Dublin's *Monthly Museum* wrote that in his best roles there, Kemble 'not only stands *unrivalled*, but *alone*', whereas as early as 1805, Washington Irving expressed surprise at Siddons's continued brilliance as a performer, given the changes to her physique: 'I hardly breathe while she is on the stage. She works up my feelings till I am like a mere child. And yet this woman is old, and has lost all elegance of figure.'[31] As Lisa Freeman contends, watching Siddons age and decline was distressing to spectators 'as it not only marked her precarious place in time but also their own'.[32] Later in her career, Siddons served as a highly visible reminder of mortality to her audience.

Kemble made a triumphant return to Covent Garden as Coriolanus on 15 January 1814. He was said to be at the height of his powers and remained extremely popular, despite the sensational debut of Edmund Kean on the Drury Lane stage a few days later. His regional tours continued and the valedictory appearances he made in Edinburgh, culminating in a performance of *Macbeth* on 29 March 1817, provided a rehearsal for his London farewell, as did the address to the audience there which he sobbed his way through.[33] From the end of April 1817, performances at Covent Garden were advertised as 'being the last time he ever will perform that character' and Kemble acted his major roles, both Shakespearean and non-Shakespearean.[34] Some critics noted that his acting had lost some of its impact: Henry Thomson, for example, reported that 'his personal powers are much weakened, and His formal, measured stiffness more expressed than when He was younger'.[35]

Kemble's final performance took place on 23 June 1817 when he appeared, of course, as Coriolanus. The playbill is reproduced in the *Authentic Narrative* of his retirement published later that year, and details an ovation in the second act when the full chorus sang Handel's 'See the Conquering Hero Comes'.[36] Although Dobson comments that Kemble's choice of Coriolanus as his final role could only serve to remind playgoers of 'his defiant assertion of managerial privilege' during the OP Riots, the audience response was enthusiastic, demonstrating a 'zealous and universal testimony of respect and admiration [that] accompanied him throughout his performance, and broke forth on every occasion, in which any passage of the play could be connected with his character and situation'.[37] Hazlitt noted that in general, 'on the last evening, he displayed the same excellences, and gave the same prominence to the very same passages, that he used to do', but expressed some reservations about the reconciliation scene with Volumnia, when he found Kemble 'not equally impressive' as before:

> Mr. KEMBLE's voice seemed to faint and stagger, to be strained and cracked, under the weight of this majestic image [of Volumnia bowing like Olympus to a mole hill]: but, indeed, we know of no tones deep or full enough to bear along the swelling tide of sentiment it conveys; nor can we conceive of any thing in outward form to answer to it, except when Mrs. SIDDONS played the part of *Volumnia*.[38]

Could Kemble have been emotional not because of the challenges of the text but because he was missing the acting support of his sister, who had played Volumnia with him so many times and whose retirement five years before may have been haunting his thoughts as he made his own last appearance?

When the curtain fell, 'the Pit rose up in a body, and continued waving hats and laurels for several minutes' and placards were displayed reading 'No farewell for ever from Kemble'.[39] As Kemble, full of emotion and still costumed as Coriolanus, delivered a valedictory speech, as he had done in Edinburgh, 'he was received with a shout like thunder'.[40] While proclaiming that he felt too agitated to speak eloquently, he gave a brief address referring to his work as both an actor and a manager and singling out his engagement with Shakespeare's drama, claiming that 'all my labours, all my studies, whatever they have been, have been made delightful to me, by the approbation with which you have been pleased constantly to reward them'.[41] Boaden recorded that Kemble's 'voice faltered ... and his tears became visible' when he spoke of 'his efforts for the "divine Shakspeare"'.[42] And thus ended the actor's thirty-four-year career on the London stage.

On 27 June a celebratory banquet was held at the Freemasons' tavern at which 336 people (gentlemen only and solely by invitation) paid two guineas each for a ticket.[43] The large number of speeches, toasts, poetical tributes and songs delivered at the event and the commemorative medal struck for the occasion are all recorded in some detail, like Kemble's final London stage performance, in the *Authentic Narrative*. Lord Holland, who chaired the committee that organized the banquet and presided over the event, gave a speech in which he summed up Kemble's achievements and contributions to the British theatre:

> Mr. Kemble has, by collateral measures, done more for the permanent prosperity of the Stage, and consequently for the fame of its votaries, than any person who has gone before him. For, as long as the British Theatre exists – as long as the plays of Shakspeare shall be represented in this metropolis, the result of his learning and industry will be seen in the propriety of the scenic decorations, in the improvement of the *costume*,

and in many matters apparently of minor consideration; but which, when effected, shew the man of research and ability, and display the mind of the scholar and critic.[44]

Here Holland focused on Kemble's success as manager, underlining how he advanced the presentation of Shakespeare by bringing his scholarship to bear on scenery and costume. Throughout the evening, the link between Kemble and Shakespeare was repeatedly and conspicuously underscored, for example in the décor, which featured 'a Cast of Shakspeare, from the monument in Stratford Church, borrowed from the Proprietors of the Theatre Royal, Covent-Garden for the occasion . . . in honour of so illustrious a votary of its great original'.[45]

No women were present at the event, but Siddons might well have felt ambivalent had she been allowed to participate. Rogers recorded:

When a grand public dinner was given to John Kemble on his quitting the stage, Mrs. Siddons said to me, 'Well, perhaps in the next world women will be more valued than they are in this.' She alluded to the comparatively little sensation which had been produced by her own retirement from the boards: and doubtless she was a far, far greater performer than John Kemble.[46]

The *Biographical Dictionary* describes Siddons's reaction as 'jealousy'.[47] In fact, the actress simply recognized that it was unjust that society publicly celebrated successful men more than successful women. Kemble's retirement occasioned a celebratory banquet, a commemorative medal, a published account of his farewell from the stage and so on, all of which were denied to Siddons. Unlike his sister, Kemble never did any kind of dramatic reading, not even privately: 'Even when attempts were made to get him to read, he would quietly refer his friends to the passage itself.'[48] Like Siddons, Kemble faced appeals for his return to the stage, in this case even at the exact moment he was trying to leave it: at the end of his final performance a petition was presented to him urging him not to retire but 'to consent to perform a few nights each season, so long as your health will admit'.[49] But he never acted again.

'Tragedy personified' and 'Pride of the British Stage'[50]

Siddons's farewell address asked the audience in future years to 'think on HER, whose lips have poured so long / The charmed sorrows of your Shakspeare's song', but Boaden noted that it was not through Shakespeare that 'Siddons established her supremacy', reminding us of the non-Shakespearean drama in which she made her name (roles such as Belvidera, Jane Shore, Calista and Isabella).[51] Although Siddons's Shakespearean characters were 'infinitely more sublime', these pathetic non-Shakespearean roles remained a significant part of the actress's repertoire, even in her final season.[52] Russ McDonald pronounces Siddons 'the first great Shakespearean actress' and suggests that her greatest strength lay in thinking about her roles 'as existing in a network of other persons, actions and words'.[53] Campbell described how Siddons 'threw herself into the assumed character' and praised 'her sustained understanding of her part, her self-devotion to it, and her abstraction from every thing else'.[54] In 1825, *Oxberry's Dramatic Biography* pronounced that 'Mrs. SIDDONS has enjoyed a greater portion of living fame, than any man or woman on record, in any nation, profession, or station', emphasizing the celebrity status and professional respect that the actress had earned.[55]

In her later years, Siddons apparently shed 'tears of joy' on watching her niece, Fanny Kemble, perform.[56] She may have hoped that her legacy would live on in the younger actress, who apparently bore a strong resemblance to her aunt. Indeed, one paper reported that as Fanny acted, 'for the moment Mrs. Siddons seemed to tread the stage'.[57] Fanny first appeared at Covent Garden on 5 October 1829 as Juliet, a role that was not a central part of Siddons's repertoire. But she gradually began to assume many of her aunt's characters in both Shakespearean and non-Shakespearean drama, including Belvidera, Euphrasia, Mrs Beverley, Portia, Isabella, Lady Townly (in John Vanbrugh and Colley Cibber's 1728 comedy *The Provoked Husband*), Mrs Haller (in August von Kotzebue's sentimental tragedy *The Stranger*, translated by Benjamin Thompson), Calista and Constance, all of which she had performed before Siddons's death towards the end of the 1830–1 season.[58] One of her final performances at Covent Garden in 1832 before leaving for America was as Lady Macbeth, Siddons's most famous role, but the *Morning Post* pronounced this 'one of the least fortunate of her undertakings'.[59] Fanny was more successful in giving Shakespearean readings, following the model of her aunt (and her father) and from 1848, she toured Britain and America with her one-woman versions of Shakespeare to great acclaim.

That Siddons's name subsequently came to be synonymous with excellence, even superlativeness, in acting is evident in the 1950 film *All About Eve*, directed by Joseph Mankiewicz and starring Bette Davis and Anne Baxter, which opens with the presentation ceremony of the Sarah Siddons Award for Distinguished Achievement, 'the highest honor our Theatre knows'.[60] The fictitious Sarah Siddons Society responsible for bestowing the prize in the film inspired the creation of a real-life organization of the same name which has conferred the Sarah Siddons Award annually since 1952 to a performer deemed 'most outstanding' in a theatre production.[61] The award is a replica of the statuette of Siddons used in *All About Eve*, which is itself modelled after Joshua Reynolds's famous painting of the actress as the Tragic Muse. As David Román argues, these echoes of Siddons show that 'performance serves as its own archive', enabling past performances and previous actors to be revived.[62] Thus *All About Eve* and the Sarah Siddons Award 'preserved and cultivated' the actress's celebrity many years after her death.[63] A statue of Siddons by Leon Chavalliaud, again modelled after Reynolds's painting, stands on Paddington Green, near Siddons's final resting place (and highly visible next to a major route in and out of London). It was funded by public subscription and unveiled by Henry Irving in 1897. In 1952, Sybil Thorndike successfully campaigned for the statue's restoration and it was repaired again in 2019. This continued interest in Siddons by fellow actors and the general public is testament to her ongoing influence.

Kemble, like his sister, was praised for employing careful attention to detail in his acting in order to create a sustained illusion of character. *Oxberry's Dramatic Biography* reported that 'no man better understood *effect*, and from his attention to even the *minutiæ* of his art, all his personations were like finished pictures; you might gaze at any point, and *discover no deficiency*, – it was perfectly correct'.[64] The careful preparation that went into Kemble's performances was in many ways a great asset but could sometimes be detrimental: as Fitzgerald noted, 'the best acting must be based on profound study, but the study should be subsidiary to the acting; whereas Kemble too often exhibited the fruits of his study'.[65] Scott put it even more succinctly: 'John Kemble . . . certainly is a great artist. It is a pity he shows too much of his machinery.'[66] The visibility of Kemble's 'machinery' may have contributed to the perception of artifice in his acting. The review of Kemble's final performance in *Bell's Weekly Messenger* provides a nuanced consideration of the place of nature and art in Kemble's acting: 'We perceived that his whole performance was an art, and that this art consisted of rules which he had closely studied, and by considerable skill had made them his own; that he had departed intentionally from simple nature, because he had seen that nature, artificially combined, would produce a greater effect.'[67] Kemble's departure from nature in his acting was, then, not a failure of technique but a calculated performance method.

Hazlitt's review of Kemble's final performance for the *Times* concluded that 'the distinguishing excellence of his acting may be summed up in one word – *intensity;* in the seizing upon some one feeling or idea, in insisting upon it, in never letting it go, and in working it up, with a certain graceful consistency, and conscious grandeur of conception, to a very high degree of pathos or sublimity'.[68] Boaden implied that Kemble's lofty character on stage was very much a persona, adopted to go with his strikingly dignified looks: 'Mr. Kemble, as to his person, might be said to be majestic by effort rather than habit – he could become so in a moment. His ordinary gait was careless, his look rather kind than penetrating. He did not, except professionally, strive to be considered the noble creature that he was.'[69] Dobson notes that Kemble's presentation of Shakespeare's tragic heroes as larger than life has now fallen out of favour to be replaced by a preference for 'domesticating and psychologizing' such characters, 'making them more familiar rather than more astonishing'.[70]

Kemble's status as theatre manager as well as actor, of course, gave him a broader sphere of influence than Siddons, to whom participation in this aspect of the stage was not open. His managerial efforts focused on Shakespeare, staging twenty-five revivals of his plays in twenty-nine years. Kemble's 'determined efforts for scenic accuracy and effect' made him a 'pioneer of the movement towards historical realism' that would culminate in the nineteenth century with Charles Kean and Herbert Beerbohm Tree.[71] But this tendency to favour the visual played into the trend for spectacle that was increasingly taking hold of the early-nineteenth-century theatre and that was seen by some as detrimental to the drama and particularly to Shakespeare. As Baker puts it (and as we saw in Chapter 2), 'the spectacle he deplored he himself had fostered, perhaps unconsciously, through his own elaborate revivals'.[72] As his career drew to a close, Kemble lamented, 'I am only beginning thoroughly to understand my art', but his dedication to developing and portraying a unified concept for each play he staged has become foundational to directorial practice.[73]

'Blended kindred fame'[74]

In evaluating the acting of the siblings, several critics divided their roles into two main categories: the grand and the emotional.[75] For Kemble, characters of the first type included his Shakespearean heroes and the Roman roles in which he excelled. Characters of the latter type that displayed 'melancholy pride and rooted sentiments' included Cardinal Wolsey, Zanga, the Stranger and Penruddock.[76] Siddons's grand characters were also largely Shakespearean: Lady Macbeth, Queen Katherine, Constance and Volumnia. Her more pathetic roles were generally in eighteenth-century tragedy, for example, Euphrasia in *The Grecian Daughter* and Jane Shore in the play of the same name.[77] Although predominantly known as tragedians, both Siddons and Kemble could succeed in certain comic characters. Siddons mastered the 'dignified Shakspearian comedy' of Hermione in *The Winter's Tale*; her Portia in *The Merchant of Venice* was 'inexpressibly delightful'; and she continued to perform in contemporary comedy throughout her career.[78] As we saw in Chapter 1, Kemble was an excellent Petruchio in *The Taming of the Shrew* and Charles Lamb claimed of his performances in Restoration comedy that 'no man could deliver brilliant dialogue – the dialogue of Congreve or of Wycherley – because none understood it – half so well as John Kemble'.[79] Kemble himself believed that 'with pains and study an actor ought to succeed in both' forms but neither of the siblings did so to the extent that their predecessors, David Garrick and Hannah Pritchard, had achieved.[80]

While Kemble may have drawn the most recognition, in part because of his contributions as theatre manager as well as performer, Siddons was regarded as the better actor. Indeed, Lawrence told Farington that '*Kemble* had often acknowledged that He never played with Mrs. Siddons witht. feeling Her superiority'.[81] *Oxberry's Dramatic Biography* claimed that Kemble 'was originally bolstered up by the genius of his sister', and Boaden makes clear that this support applied not just to acting but to management, calling Siddons the 'great partner of his toil; and by whom alone he could have accomplished the distinguishing object of his management'.[82] That acting was thought to come more naturally to Siddons than to Kemble can be seen in Boaden's comment that 'upon ... all occasions, Mrs.

Siddons was uniformly graceful. But she was not graceful by *effort*, and sacrificed nothing to become so. In this, she widely differed from her brother, Mr. Kemble'.[83] Scott also noted that Kemble's acting sometimes involved 'a sacrifice of energy of action to grace'.[84]

Siddons herself implied that Kemble tended to focus on decorum at the expense of portraying emotion: 'My brother John in his most impetuous bursts is always careful to avoid any discomposure of his dress or deportment; but in the whirlwind of passion I lose all thought of such matters.'[85] Critics agreed that Siddons's total absorption in her roles was praiseworthy. Fellow actor Charles Mayne Young commented that 'from the first moment to the last, she was, according to theatric parlance, "*in the character*"'.[86] But he also suggested another aspect of the superiority of Siddons's acting over Kemble's in stating that 'you never caught her slumbering through some scenes, in order to produce, by contrast, an exaggerated effect in others'.[87] As we saw in the case of *King Lear* in Chapter 1, Kemble was often thought to conserve his energy (and particularly his voice) in order to make a strong impression in key scenes, probably largely because of his physical weaknesses; hence, reviewers remarked on how, unusually, he pulled out all the stops during his final appearance: 'We never saw him perform the character of *Coriolanus* with more animation, strength, and spirit, than on this occasion, as if he was determined to leave a full impression of his merits on the public mind, and a model of his art for his successors.'[88] Young evidently considered Kemble's tendency towards restraint in order to create an impact by subsequently unleashing his strength a defect of the actor's performance and deemed Siddons's ability to remain firmly in character throughout the play a major strength of her acting style.

Both Siddons and Kemble fended off challenges from younger performers later in their careers. While this new generation of actors came to assume many of the siblings' crucial roles, no single performer filled all of the characters in which each had excelled. Scott hypothesized that Kemble's 'resolution to retire' was expedited by the prospect of 'a contest with a rival in all the vigour of youth'.[89] This rival was Kean, who made his Drury Lane debut less than two weeks after Kemble's triumphant return to Covent Garden in 1814. Kean did take on some of Kemble's great Shakespearean characters, such as Hamlet and Macbeth, and was a better Shylock and Richard III than Kemble. But the older actor remained unrivalled in the Roman roles that he had worked so hard to emphasize in his repertoire. A challenge in those plays did come, however, in the form of Young, though as we have seen, he perpetuated Kemble's performance style when acting Coriolanus rather than innovating in the part. According to Rogers, late in her career Siddons felt that 'the public had a sort of pleasure in mortifying their old favourites', including herself, 'by setting up new idols' but defiantly asserted, 'I am not yet extinguished'.[90] Sarah Smith (later Bartley) and Louisa Brunton were her only direct challengers but did not make much of a mark while Siddons was still on the stage. After Siddons's retirement, Eliza O'Neill eventually took over most of her pathetic roles, including Mrs Beverley, Belvidera and Isabella. She also differentiated herself from Siddons by achieving great success as Juliet. But her career was markedly short. Siddons's grand Shakespearean roles like Lady Macbeth and Constance were subsequently performed by Bartley, a Mrs Ogilvie and Harriet Faucit (mother of the more famous Helen). Although Siddons's and Kemble's most significant parts continued to be performed after their retirements, when each actor left the stage there was a sense that the roles they had made famous had left as well: Boaden wrote of Siddons that the final performance of each of her famous parts 'seemed almost a withdrawing of the character itself from the stage', and the *Morning Chronicle* commented of Kemble that his major roles 'must be considered, now that he has ceased to impart life and animation to them, as lost to the stage – their resuscitation may be wished, but cannot be hoped for'.[91]

When Kemble died in 1823, Hazlitt's obituary for the actor worried how Siddons would take the news, underscoring how closely the siblings were linked in the public imagination: 'To Mrs. Siddons the loss must be indeed poignant, irreparable! She, and her brother John Kemble, had seen the same sun rise upon their fame – had gathered laurels from the same tree! – They lived in glory together.'[92] Kemble was buried in Lausanne, where he was residing at the time of his death. Siddons lived on for another eight years, until 1831. Both performers were memorialized in Westminster Abbey with statues in white marble. Kemble's monument, depicting him as Cato in classical drapery (Figure 11), appeared in 1826. But Siddons's statue was erected much later, in

FIGURE 11 *John Flaxman and J. E. Hinchliffe*, Statue of John Philip Kemble *(1826). Westminster Abbey, London. © Dean and Chapter of Westminster.*

FIGURE 12 *Thomas Campbell,* Statue of Sarah Siddons *(1845). Westminster Abbey, London. © Dean and Chapter of Westminster.*

1849, perhaps because objections had been voiced to Kemble's commemoration in this way on the grounds that 'a mere player' was not entitled to 'a distinction so exalted' and almost certainly because of the double standard women in public life faced, which Siddons herself had identified.[93] Siddons's effigy (Figure 12) is also classical and, as Heather McPherson has convincingly demonstrated, 'eschews the particular, elevating her to the universal realm of myth'.[94] Furthermore, Siddons's statue is larger than life, over 7 feet tall (compared to that of her brother, which stands a life-sized 6 feet high), an appropriate recognition of their relative status in public opinion, both in their lifetimes and subsequently.

Appendix

Siddons's and Kemble's performances together in London

This list of plays in which Siddons and Kemble appeared together on the London stage is arranged chronologically. The title of the play is given along with the author for non-Shakespearean drama. Entries in bold are works by Shakespeare. These were sometimes adapted by Kemble and his predecessors (as discussed in the text). The parts played by each actor are included in parentheses. I have listed all seasons in which the siblings are known to have acted together in the play in question, with the date of first performance in parentheses after the first season. Where a play has two entries, it is because one or other of the siblings subsequently acted a different role. I have used the *Biographical Dictionary*, the *London Stage Database* (for performances until the end of the 1799–1800 season), the *London Stage Calendar* (for performances from the 1800–1 season onwards) and Genest's *Some Account of the English Stage*, as well as some cross-checking in newspaper databases, to make this list as detailed as possible, but I make no claims as to its completeness. Nevertheless, I hope it will serve as a useful tool to further understanding of Siddons's and Kemble's collaborative acting.

The Gamester, by Edward Moore (Siddons as Mrs Beverley, Kemble as Mr Beverley)

1783–4 (22 November 1783), 1784–5, 1785–6, 1786–7, 1787–8, 1788–9, 1790–1, 1791–2, 1792–3, 1794–5, 1795–6, 1796–7, 1797–8, 1798–9, 1799–1800, 1800–1, 1801–2, 1803–4, 1805–6, 1808–9

King John (Siddons as Constance, Kemble as King John)
1783–4 (10 December 1783), 1785–6, 1791–2, 1792–3, 1794–5, 1795–6, 1800–1, 1801–2, 1803–4, 1805–6, 1809–10, 1810–11, 1811–12

The Countess of Salisbury, by Hall Hartson (Siddons as the Countess of Salisbury, Kemble as Alwin)
1783–4 (13 April 1784), 1797–8

Tancred and Sigismunda, by James Thomson (Siddons as Sigismunda, Kemble as Tancred)
1783–4 (24 April 1784), 1784–5, 1785–6, 1786–7

The Carmelite, by Richard Cumberland (Siddons as Matilda, Kemble as Montgomeri)
1784–5 (2 December 1784), 1785–6, 1787–8

The Maid of Honour, by Philip Massinger, adapted by Kemble (Siddons as Camiola, Kemble as Adorni)
1784–5 (27 January 1785)

Othello (Siddons as Desdemona, Kemble as Othello)
1784–5 (8 March 1785), 1785–6; 1786–7, 1787–8, 1790–1, 1791–2, 1792–3, 1794–5, 1796–7, 1797–8, 1803–4

Macbeth (Siddons as Lady Macbeth, Kemble as Macbeth)
1784–5 (31 March 1785), 1788–9, 1791–2, 1792–3, 1793–4, 1794–5, 1795–6, 1796–7, 1797–8, 1798–9, 1800–1, 1801–2, 1803–4, 1805–6, 1808–9, 1809–10, 1810–11, 1811–12, 1815–16, 1816–17

Venice Preserved, by Thomas Otway (Siddons as Belvidera, Kemble as Jaffier)
1785–6 (8 October 1785), 1786–7, 1787–8, 1788–9, 1791–2, 1792–3, 1795–6, 1801–2, 1803–4, 1805–6

The Grecian Daughter, by Arthur Murphy (Siddons as Euphrasia, Kemble as Philotas)
1785–6 (15 October 1785), 1786–7

Braganza, by Robert Jephson (Siddons as the Duchess of Braganza, Kemble as the Duke of Braganza)
1785–6 (20 October 1785)

The Jubilee, by David Garrick (Siddons as the Tragic Muse, Kemble as Richard III)
1785–6 (18 November 1785)

As You Like It (Siddons as Rosalind, Kemble as Orlando)
1785–6 (18 February 1786), 1786–7, 1787–8

The Distressed Mother, by Ambrose Philips (Siddons as Hermione, Kemble as Orestes)
1785–6 (4 March 1786), 1786–7, 1793–4, 1794–5, 1801–2, 1803–4

Percy, by Hannah More (Siddons as Elvina, Kemble as Douglas)
1785–6 (25 March 1786), 1786–7

The Merchant of Venice (Siddons as Portia, Kemble as Bassanio)
1785–6 (6 April 1786), 1787–8

Hamlet (Siddons as Ophelia, Kemble as Hamlet)
1785–6 (15 May 1786)

Cleone, by Robert Dodsley (Siddons as Cleone, Kemble as Sifroy)
1786–7 (22 November 1786)

Cymbeline (Siddons as Imogen, Kemble as Posthumus)
1786–7 (29 January 1787), 1800–1, 1801–2

The Count of Narbonne, by Robert Jephson (Siddons as Hortensia, Kemble as Raymond)
1786–7 (8 March 1787), 1792–3, 1797–8, 1807–8

All in the Wrong, by Arthur Murphy (Siddons as Lady Restless, Kemble as Beverley)
1786–7 (29 March 1787), 1788–9

Julia, by Robert Jephson (Siddons as Julia, Kemble as Mentevole)
1786–7 (14 April 1787), 1787–8

King Lear (Siddons as Cordelia, Kemble as Lear)
1787–8 (21 January 1788), 1791–2, 1792–3, 1795–6, 1800–1

The Fate of Sparta, by Hannah Cowley (Siddons as Chelonice, Kemble as Cleombrotus)
1787–8 (31 January 1788)

Jane Shore, by Nicholas Rowe (Siddons as Jane Shore, Kemble as Hastings)
1787–8 (13 March 1788), 1788–9, 1790–1, 1791–2, 1792–3, 1794–5, 1795–6, 1797–8, 1798–9, 1799–1800, 1800–1, 1801–2, 1803–4

Catharine and Petruchio (adaptation of *The Taming of the Shrew*) (Siddons as Catharine, Kemble as Petruchio)
1787–8 (13 March 1788), 1788–9

The Regent, by Bertie Greatheed (Siddons as Dianora, Kemble as Manuel)
1787–8 (29 March 1788), 1788–9, 1791–2, 1792–3, 1801–2

All for Love, by John Dryden (Siddons as Cleopatra, Kemble as Marc Antony)
1787–8 (5 May 1788)

Isabella; or, The Fatal Marriage, by Thomas Southerne, adapted by David Garrick (Siddons as Isabella, Kemble as Biron)
1788–9 (28 October 1788), 1790–1, 1791–2, 1792–3, 1793–4, 1794–5, 1795–6, 1796–7, 1797–8, 1798–9, 1799–1800, 1800–1, 1801–2, 1803–4, 1805–6, 1806–7, 1807–8, 1808–9, 1809–10, 1810–11, 1811–12

The Fair Penitent, by Nicholas Rowe (Siddons as Calista, Kemble as Sciolto)
1788–9 (11 November 1788)

Henry VIII (Siddons as Queen Katharine, Kemble as Cromwell)
1788–9 (25 November 1788), 1791–2, 1792–3

Douglas, by John Home (Siddons as Lady Randolph, Kemble as Norval/Douglas)
1788–9 (9 December 1788), 1791–2, 1792–3, 1793–4, 1794–5, 1795–6, 1796–7

The Mourning Bride, by William Congreve (Siddons as Zara, Kemble as Osmyn)
1788–9 (6 January 1789), 1790–1, 1792–3, 1794–5, 1795–6, 1796–7, 1798–9, 1801–2, 1803–4, 1804–5, 1808–9

The Merchant of Venice (Siddons as Portia, Kemble as Shylock)
1788–9 (17 January 1789), 1791–2, 1792–3, 1794–5, 1796–7, 1797–8, 1798–9, 1799–1800, 1800–1, 1810–11

Henry VIII (Siddons as Queen Katharine, Kemble as Cardinal Wolsey)
1788–9 (3 February 1789), 1805–6, 1806–7, 1807–8, 1808–9, 1810–11, 1811–12, 1815–16

Coriolanus (Siddons as Volumnia, Kemble as Coriolanus)
1788–9 (7 February 1789), 1791–2, 1792–3, 1795–6, 1796–7, 1806–7, 1807–8, 1811–12

The Law of Lombardy, by Robert Jephson (Siddons as the Princess, Kemble as Paladore)
1788–9 (16 February 1789)

Mary Queen of Scots, by John St John (Siddons as Queen Mary, Kemble as the Duke of Norfolk)
1788–9 (21 March 1789), 1791–2, 1792–3, 1795–6, 1796–7, 1800–1, 1803–4

Romeo and Juliet (Siddons as Juliet, Kemble as Romeo)
1788–9 (11 May 1789)

Richard III (Siddons as Queen Elizabeth, Kemble as Richard)
1791–2 (7 February 1792), 1796–7, 1811–12

The Jealous Wife, by George Colman the Elder (Siddons as Mrs Oakly, Kemble as Mr Oakly)
1791–2 (28 April 1792), 1792–3

The Rival Sisters, by Arthur Murphy (Siddons as Ariadne, Kemble as Perithous)
1792–3 (18 March 1793)

Emilia Galotti, by Joseph Berington, translated from Gotthold Ephraim Lessing (Siddons as Countess Orsina, Kemble as Duke of Gustalla)
1794–5 (28 October 1794)

The Roman Father, by William Whitehead, adapted from Corneille (Siddons as Horatia, Kemble as Publius Horatius)
1794–5 (15 November 1794)

Measure for Measure (Siddons as Isabella, Kemble as the Duke)
1794–5 (30 December 1794), 1795–6, 1796–7, 1797–8, 1798–9, 1799–1800, 1801–2, 1803–4, 1811–12

The Fair Penitent, by Nicholas Rowe (Siddons as Calista, Kemble as Horatio)
1794–5 (3 March 1795), 1801–2, 1803–4, 1805–6

Edwy and Elgiva, by Frances Burney d'Arblay (Siddons as Elgiva, Kemble as Edwy)
1794–5 (21 March 1795)

Mahomet the Imposter, by James Miller, adapted from Voltaire (Siddons as Palmyra, Kemble as Zaphna)
1794–5 (27 April 1795)

Alexander the Great, by Nathaniel Lee, adapted by Kemble (Siddons as Roxana, Kemble as Alexander)
1795–6 (23 November 1795)

Almeyda: Queen of Granada, by Sophia Lee (Siddons as Almeyda, Kemble as Alonzo)
1795–6 (20 April 1796)

***Hamlet* (Siddons as Gertrude, Kemble as Hamlet)**
1795–6 (29 April 1796)

Julia; or, Such Things Were, by Prince Hoare (Siddons as Julia, Kemble as Edward Clifford)
1795–6 (2 May 1796)

The Grecian Daughter, by Arthur Murphy (Siddons as Euphrasia, Kemble as Evander)
1796–7 (13 October 1796), 1797–8, 1798–9, 1803–4, 1805–6

Edward and Eleanora, by James Thomson (Siddons as Eleanora, Kemble as Edward)
1796–7 (22 October 1796)

The Conspiracy, by Robert Jephson (Siddons as Vitellia, Kemble as Sextus)
1796–7 (15 November 1796)

Theodosius, by Nathaniel Lee (Siddons as Athenais, Kemble as Varenes)
1796–7 (20 January 1797)

Tamerlane, by Nicholas Rowe (Siddons as Arpasia, Kemble as Bajazet)
1796–7 (3 February 1797), 1797–8

Fatal Curiosity, by George Lillo (Siddons as Agnes, Kemble as Old Wilmot)
1796–7 (1 May 1797)

The Rivals, by Richard Brinsley Sheridan (Siddons as Julia, Kemble as Faulkland)
1797–8 (24 November 1797)

The Stranger, by Benjamin Thompson, translated from August von Kotzebue (Siddons as Mrs Haller, Kemble as the Stranger) 1798–9 (24 March 1798), 1798–9, 1799–1800, 1800–1, 1801–2, 1803–4, 1805–6, 1808–9, 1811–12

Aurelio and Miranda, by James Boaden (Siddons as Miranda, Kemble as Aurelio)
1798–9 (29 December 1798)

The Castle of Montval, by Thomas Sedgwick Whalley (Siddons as the Countess of Montval, Kemble as the Old Count)
1798–9 (23 April 1799)

Trials of the Heart, by unknown author (Siddons as Eliza[?], Kemble as Norman[?])
1798–9 (24 April 1799)

Pizarro, by Richard Brinsley Sheridan, adapted from August von Kotzebue (Siddons as Elvira, Kemble as Rolla)
1798–9 (24 May 1799), 1799–1800, 1800–1, 1801–2, 1803–4, 1804–5, 1805–6, 1806–7, 1807–8, 1808–9, 1810–11, 1811–12

Adelaide, by Henry James Pye (Siddons as Adelaide, Kemble as Prince Richard)
1799–1800 (25 January 1800)

De Montfort, by Joanna Baillie (Siddons as Jane De Montfort, Kemble as De Montfort)
1799–1800 (29 April 1800)

Antonio; or, the Soldier's Return, by William Godwin (Siddons as Helena, Kemble as Antonio)
1800–1 (13 December 1800)

Julian and Agnes, by William Sotheby (Siddons as Agnes, Kemble as Alfonso/Julian)
1800–1 (25 April 1801)

The Winter's Tale (Siddons as Hermione, Kemble as Leontes)
1801–2 (25 March 1802), 1807–8, 1811–12

Douglas, by John Home (Siddons as Lady Randolph, Kemble as Old Norval/the Stranger)
1802–3 (6 October 1803), 1809–10, 1811–12

The Merchant of Venice (Siddons as Portia, Kemble as Antonio)
1803–4 (19 November 1803)

Jane Shore, by Nicholas Rowe (Siddons as Jane Shore, Kemble as the Duke of Gloster)
1805–6 (16 October 1805)

Venice Preserved, by Thomas Otway (Siddons as Belvidera, Kemble as Pierre)
1805–6 (7 November 1805), 1811–12

NOTES

Introduction

1 Hanna Flint, 'Why Lady Macbeth Is Literature's Most Misunderstood Villain', *BBC Culture*, 10 January 2022, https://www.bbc.com/culture/article/20220110-why-lady-macbeth-is-literatures-most-misunderstood-villain.

2 Ibid.

3 Ibid.

4 According to the playbill, Miss Kemble also sang between the acts of the play. The siblings had probably been acting before this time. Siddons's first known role was as Ariel in *The Tempest* on 22 December 1766 with her father's company in Coventry. Kemble may have played Stephano in this performance. Biographical information given here is taken from the entries for the Kemble family (particularly those for Roger Kemble, Sarah Siddons and John Philip Kemble) in Philip H. Highfill Jr, Kalman A. Burnim and Edward A. Langhans, *A Biographical Dictionary of Actors, Actresses, Musicians, Dancers, Managers & Other Stage Personnel in London, 1660–1800*, 16 vols. (Carbondale: Southern Illinois University Press, 1973–93).

5 Highfill et al., *BD*, 8:389.

6 Qtd in Roger Manvell, *Sarah Siddons: Portrait of an Actress* (London: William Heinemann Ltd, 1970), 23.

7 Ibid.

8 The list is reprinted in ibid., 25–6.

9 Qtd in Thomas Campbell, *Life of Mrs. Siddons*, 2 vols. (London: Effingham Wilson, 1834), 1:60.

10 James Boaden, *Memoirs of Mrs. Siddons*, 2 vols. (London: Henry Colburn, 1827), 1:32.

11 Ibid., 1:33. He posits that Juliet would have been a more suitable role for Siddons's debut.

12 Boaden, *Memoirs of Siddons*, 1:34.

13 See Campbell, *Life of Siddons*, 1:61. The play was revived on 26 December 1775 but the cast is not recorded. However, I assume that Siddons played Venus throughout the season. Unless otherwise noted, all London performance information for the period to 1800 is taken from the *London Stage Database*, https://londonstagedatabase.uoregon.edu/.

14 Qtd in Campbell, *Life of Siddons*, 1:75.

15 Frances Burney, journal for 30 May 1772, in *The Early Journals and Letters of Fanny Burney*, gen. ed. Lars E. Troide, 5 vols. (Oxford: Clarendon Press, 1987–2012), 1:225.

16 Campbell, *Life of Siddons*, 1:73.

17 John Genest, *Some Account of the English Stage, from the Restoration in 1660 to 1830*, 10 vols. (Bath: H. E. Carrington, 1832), 6:236. Henry was seven, Sally was six and Maria was three. A fourth child, Frances, had died in infancy and Siddons was pregnant with a fifth.

18 Campbell, *Life of Siddons*, 1:156.

19 Boaden, *Memoirs of Siddons*, 1:298.

20 Ibid., 1:309; Campbell, *Life of Siddons*, 1:168–9.

21 Boaden, *Memoirs of Siddons*, 1:327.

22 Campbell, *Life of Siddons*, 1:176.

23 Ibid., 1:56.

24 Ibid., 1:57.

25 *Morning Post*, 16 December 1782.

26 Qtd in Campbell, *Life of Siddons*, 1:190.

27 Highfill et al., *BD*, 14:8; Campbell, *Life of Siddons*, 1:191; James Boaden, *Memoirs of the Life of John Philip Kemble, Esq.*, 2 vols. (London: Longman, Hurst, Rees, Orme, Brown, and Green, 1825), 1:119; Siddons qtd in Campbell, *Life of Siddons*, 1:163.

28 *Morning Herald*, 31 March 1783.

29 Boaden, *Memoirs of Kemble*, 1:117–18.

30 Robert Shaughnessy, 'Siddons [née Kemble], Sarah (1755–1831), Actress', *Oxford Dictionary of National Biography* (Oxford: Oxford University Press, 2004), http://www.oxforddnb.com/view/article/25516.

31 Qtd in Campbell, *Life of Siddons*, 1:159, 161, 162.

32 Ibid., 1:157; Boaden, *Memoirs of Siddons*, 1:291.

33 Boaden, *Memoirs of Kemble* 1:90–1. Boaden must mean not that Kemble was older than Siddons but that he was the oldest of her male siblings.

34 See Herschel Baker, *John Philip Kemble: The Actor in His Theatre* (Cambridge: Harvard University Press, 1942), 30–1; Highfill et al., *BD*, 8:337.

35 Ibid.

36 Percy Fitzgerald, *The Kembles: An Account of the Kemble Family, Including the Lives of Mrs. Siddons and Her Brother John Philip Kemble*, 2 vols. (London: Tinsley Brothers, 1871), 1:150.

37 Qtd in Boaden, *Memoirs of Kemble*, 1:91.

38 Fitzgerald, *The Kembles*, 1:155. Fitzgerald's account of the siblings is not a first-hand one but is useful as one of the few works to treat them together.

39 Ibid.

40 *Morning Chronicle*, 1 October 1783.

41 Boaden, *Memoirs of Kemble*, 1:90.

42 Ibid., 1:93.

43 Ibid., 1:116.

44 Ibid., 1:98.

45 Linda Kelly, *The Kemble Era: John Philip Kemble, Sarah Siddons, and the London Stage* (London: Bodley Head, 1980), 35.

46 *Morning Herald*, 21 October 1783.

47 Ibid.

48 Boaden, *Memoirs of Kemble*, 1:132.

49 Ibid., 1:131.

50 Ibid.

51 Ibid., 1:132.

52 *Morning Chronicle*, 23 January 1783.

53 Ibid.

54 *Gentleman's Magazine* 53, pt 1, April 1783, 310.

55 Ibid.

56 Campbell, *Life of Siddons*, 1:204–5.

57 Boaden, *Memoirs of Siddons*, 2:54, 55. The quotation is from *The Tempest*, 1.2.198.

58 *European Magazine* 4, November 1783, 388; *Gazetteer*, 24 November 1783. The *European Magazine* noted, however, that Kemble had 'too much manliness in the features of his countenance' to play the scenes requiring Beverley to display 'the womanly pathetic'.

59 *Morning Chronicle*, 8 March 1784.

60 Information on box office receipts in the period to 1800, including those for benefit performances, is taken from *LSD*.

61 *New Spectator*, no. 13, 27 April 1784, 4.

62 See Boaden, *Memoirs of Kemble*, 1:152; Campbell, *Life of Siddons*, 1:228.

63 *Morning Chronicle*, 13 April 1784.

Chapter 1

1 *Town and Country Magazine* 16, October 1784, 509.

2 Ellen Donkin, 'Mrs. Siddons Looks Back in Anger: Feminist Historiography for Eighteenth-Century British Theatre', in *Critical Theory and Performance*, revised and enlarged edn., ed. Janelle G. Reinelt and Joseph R. Roach (Ann Arbor: University of Michigan Press, 2007), 321.

3 *Town and Country Magazine* 16, October 1784, 509.

4 Ibid., 510.

5 Ibid.

6 Donkin, 'Siddons Looks Back in Anger', 326.

7 Ibid., 322.

8 Boaden, *Memoirs of Kemble*, 1:115.

9 Campbell, *Life of Siddons*, 1:206–7. Boaden makes a similar claim (*Memoirs of Kemble*, 1:133).

10 *Morning Herald*, 11 December 1783.

11 *Public Advertiser*, 15 December 1783.

12 *General Evening Post*, 9–11 December 1783.

13 Campbell, *Life of Siddons*, 1:208.

14 Ibid.

15 David Rostron, 'John Philip Kemble's *King Lear* of 1795', in *Essays on the Eighteenth-Century English Stage*, ed. Kenneth Richards and Peter Thomson (London: Methuen, 1972), 152. The comment in the *Times* of 31 October 1815 is quoted from Rostron. The lack of variation facilitated a quick rehearsal process when plays were revived.

16 Maarten Van Dijk, 'John Philip Kemble as King John: Two Scenes', *Theatre Notebook* 29, no. 1 (1975): 22.

17 Campbell, *Life of Siddons*, 1:209–10.

18 Boaden, *Memoirs of Kemble*, 1:133.

19 Qtd in Campbell, *Life of Siddons*, 1:215–16.

20 Highfill et al., *BD*, 3:279.

21 Boaden, *Memoirs of Kemble*, 1:133.

22 Van Dijk, 'Kemble as King John', 22, 23.

23 Siddons qtd in Campbell, *Life of Siddons*, 1:216; *Opera Glass*, 20 January 1827, qtd in Arthur Colby Sprague, *Shakespeare and the Actors: The Stage Business in His Plays (1660–1905)* (Cambridge: Harvard University Press, 1948), 112.

24 Siddons qtd in Campbell, *Life of Siddons*, 1:214. Lines from the Shakespeare text are here cited from Charles H. Shattuck's edition of Kemble's promptbook, which I take to be closest to the text the actors spoke in performance for most of their careers. *John Philip Kemble Promptbooks*, 11 vols. (Charlottesville: University of Virginia Press for the

Folger Shakespeare Library, 1974), vol. 5, *King John*, 23. Each play is paginated individually and no line numbers are given.

25 Ibid., 25.

26 *The British Theatre . . . With Biographical and Critical Remarks by Mrs. Inchbald*, 25 vols. (London: Longman, Hurst, Rees, and Orme, 1808), vol. 1, 'Remarks on *King John*', 4. The remarks and plays in each volume are paginated individually.

27 Shattuck, *Kemble Promptbooks*, vol. 5, *King John*, 25; Boaden, *Memoirs of Siddons*, 2:61.

28 Qtd in Campbell, *Life of Siddons*, 1:216.

29 Boaden, *Memoirs of Siddons*, 2:61.

30 Qtd in Campbell, *Life of Siddons*, 1:218.

31 Ibid., 1:221.

32 Ibid.

33 Had Henry Siddons acted Arthur (as he had appeared as Siddons's child in *Isabella* several times in the previous season), Siddons's identity as a mother would have been further cemented for the audience. Siddons later acted Constance while heavily pregnant with her sixth child, George, leading the press to express concern: 'It hurts us not a little to be drawn off from the *fictitious* sufferings of a dramatick personage to the *real* sufferings of the performer on the stage.' I am indebted to Chelsea Phillips for this reference from the *Morning Chronicle*, 24 November 1785.

34 Campbell, *Life of Siddons*, 1:209–10.

35 *Examiner*, no. 467, 8 December 1816, 776.

36 Ibid.

37 Ibid.

38 *Morning Post*, 23 April 1817; *Monthly Mirror* 10, December 1800, 395.

39 Van Dijk, 'Kemble as King John', 26.

40 Inchbald, *British Theatre*, vol. 1, 'Remarks on *King John*', 3.

NOTES

41 *Sun*, 23 April 1817. See Shattuck, *Kemble Promptbooks*, vol. 5, *King John*, for details of the staging of Kemble's production at Covent Garden from 1810.

42 *Sun*, 23 April 1817.

43 Van Dijk, 'Kemble as King John', 31.

44 Boaden, *Memoirs of Kemble*, 1:261.

45 Boaden, *Memoirs of Siddons*, 2:154; Campbell, *Life of Siddons*, 2:59.

46 *Morning Post*, 9 March 1785.

47 Qtd in Fitzgerald, *The Kembles*, 1:216.

48 *Morning Post*, 9 March 1785.

49 Boaden, *Memoirs of Kemble*, 1:292.

50 Ibid., 1:259.

51 Shattuck, *Kemble Promptbooks*, vol. 7, *Othello*, 54; Boaden, *Memoirs of Kemble*, 1:259.

52 Ibid.

53 *Morning Chronicle*, 19 September 1785.

54 Ibid.

55 Boaden, *Memoirs of Kemble*, 1:292.

56 Ibid.

57 Ibid.

58 *Morning Chronicle*, 21 January 1804.

59 Campbell, *Life of Siddons*, 2:117–18.

60 Ibid., 2:119.

61 Boaden, *Memoirs of Siddons*, 2:234.

62 Ibid., 2:237.

63 Shattuck, *Kemble Promptbooks*, vol. 5, *King Lear*, 60.

64 Rostron, 'Kemble's *King Lear*', 164.

65 Boaden, *Memoirs of Kemble*, 1:378–9.

66 *Times*, 15 October 1810.

67 Ibid.

68 Rostron, 'Kemble's *King Lear*', 164.

69 *Examiner*, no. 21, 22 May 1808, 333.

70 Rostron, 'Kemble's *King Lear*', 163.

71 Shattuck, *Kemble Promptbooks*, vol. 5, *King Lear*, opposite 8.

72 Ibid., opposite 70.

73 Ibid., opposite 71.

74 *Universal Magazine* 9, no. 54, May 1808, 425.

75 *Morning Chronicle*, 8 April 1786.

76 Ibid.

77 Qtd in Campbell, *Life of Siddons*, 2:109.

78 *Morning Chronicle*, 8 April 1786.

79 Boaden, *Memoirs of Siddons*, 2:239; Campbell, *Life of Siddons*, 2:123; *World*, 7 May 1788.

80 Qtd in Manvell, *Sarah Siddons*, 23. I have found no evidence that Kemble acted in *As You Like It* before coming to London.

81 Ibid.

82 Qtd in Campbell, *Life of Siddons*, 2:70.

83 Boaden, *Memoirs of Siddons*, 2:168.

84 Qtd in Campbell, *Life of Siddons*, 2:69.

85 William Windham, diary for 7 June 1786, *The Diary of the Right Hon. William Windham, 1784 to 1810*, ed. Mrs Henry Baring (London: Longmans, Green, and Co., 1866), 79.

86 Kemble had already played the character opposite Jordan as Imogen on 21 November 1785, but this was Siddons's first appearance in the play in London.

87 Boaden, *Memoirs of Kemble*, 1:343.

88 Qtd in Campbell, *Life of Siddons*, 2:104.

89 Boaden, *Memoirs of Siddons*, 2:221.

90 Ibid., 2:220.

91 Campbell, *Life of Siddons*, 2:103.

92 Boaden, *Memoirs of Kemble*, 1:343.

93 Ibid., 1:344.

94 Ibid.

95 *Morning Chronicle*, 1 February 1787.

- 96 See Boaden, *Memoirs of Kemble*, 1:222. Boaden specifically pinpointed Siddons's role in the success of the play. Indeed, when the play was printed, Cumberland included a dedication to the actress.
- 97 The parallels between the two plays are explored in Campbell, *Life of Siddons*, 2:290–3 and by Paula R. Backscheider, 'In Their Blood: The Eighteenth-Century Gothic Stage', in *The Cambridge History of the Gothic. Volume 1: Gothic in the Long Eighteenth Century*, ed. Angela Wright and Dale Townshend (Cambridge: Cambridge University Press, 2020), 198–221. I am grateful to Paula Backscheider for pointing me to *The Carmelite* as a vehicle for Siddons.
- 98 Boaden, *Memoirs of Siddons*, 2:123–4.
- 99 Boaden, *Memoirs of Kemble*, 1:223.
- 100 Richard Cumberland, *Memoirs*, 2 vols. (London: Lackington, Allen, and Co., 1807), 2:219.
- 101 Boaden, *Memoirs of Kemble*, 1:223; *Public Advertiser*, 27 January 1785.
- 102 Boaden, *Memoirs of Kemble*, 1:223.
- 103 Boaden described the staging of *The Count of Narbonne* as 'the precursor' of Jephson's new tragedy (*Memoirs of Siddons*, 2:224). Jephson's *Braganza* had been revived on 20 October 1785 with both actors in the lead roles, leading the press to comment that the main characters had 'representatives far better than ever' (*Public Advertiser*, 22 October 1785).
- 104 *Morning Herald*, 16 April 1787.
- 105 Boaden, *Memoirs of Kemble*, 1:349; Campbell, *Life of Siddons*, 2:113.
- 106 *Morning Herald*, 16 April 1787.
- 107 Campbell, *Life of Siddons*, 1:294.
- 108 *London Magazine* 4, February 1785, 138.
- 109 Boaden, *Memoirs of Siddons*, 2:125.
- 110 *London Magazine* 4, February 1785, 138.
- 111 *Morning Chronicle*, 28 January 1785.
- 112 Boaden, *Memoirs of Kemble*, 1:238; Campbell, *Life of Siddons*, 1:299.

113 *Gazetteer*, 3 December 1784; *London Magazine* 4, February 1785, 138.

114 Siddons qtd in *Athenaeum*, no. 2320, 13 April 1872, 472. The quotation is from a letter to an unnamed recipient dated 1 November 1805. The ellipsis is in the source. Siddons and Kemble had acted in *Venice Preserved* on 31 October 1805.

115 Ibid.

116 Fitzgerald, *The Kembles*, 2:364. For Kemble's acting version of *Venice Preserved*, see Shattuck, *Kemble Promptbooks*, vol. 10.

117 Boaden, *Memoirs of Siddons*, 1:321.

118 Campbell, *Life of Siddons*, 2:114.

119 *World*, 15 March 1788.

120 Boaden, *Memoirs of Kemble*, 2:421.

121 Ibid., 2:422.

122 Ibid., 2:424.

123 Campbell, *Life of Siddons*, 1:173.

124 Boaden, *Memoirs of Siddons*, 1:324.

125 Ibid., 1:326. Siddons also used the stage door to great effect in *Macbeth*, as we shall see in Chapter 4.

126 Campbell, *Life of Siddons*, 1:174.

127 Ibid., 1:424.

128 *Oracle*, 17 November 1794.

129 Ibid.

130 Boaden, *Memoirs of Siddons*, 2:315. A run of six or nine consecutive nights was considered successful for a new play.

131 Campbell, *Life of Siddons*, 2:192.

132 *Sun*, 30 April 1800.

133 *Star*, 1 May 1800.

134 *Sun*, 30 April 1800.

135 *Lloyd's Evening Post*, 12–15 December 1800.

136 *E. Johnson's British Gazette, and Sunday Monitor*, no. 1102, 14 December 1800.

137 Boaden, *Memoirs of Siddons*, 2:315.

Chapter 2

1 John Philip Kemble, 'Professional Memoranda, 1788–1815', 4 vols., British Library, London, Add. MSS 31, 972–5, vol. 1, 23 September 1788. Kemble's diary records the play titles and takings for each night's performance, as well as notes on other matters related to the theatre.

2 David Francis Taylor, *Theatres of Opposition: Empire, Revolution, and Richard Brinsley Sheridan* (Oxford: Oxford University Press, 2012), 163.

3 Boaden, *Memoirs of Kemble*, 1:426.

4 Boaden, *Memoirs of Siddons*, 2:251.

5 In the first three weeks of his management, Kemble staged six Shakespeare plays (*The Merry Wives of Windsor*, *Hamlet*, *As You Like It*, *Twelfth Night*, *Macbeth* and *Richard III*), appearing in all but two of them (*The Merry Wives of Windsor* and *Twelfth Night*).

6 George C. D. Odell, *Shakespeare from Betterton to Irving*, 2 vols. (New York: Dover Publications, 1966), 2:85; Boaden, *Memoirs of Siddons*, 2:249, 252.

7 *LSD*.

8 Francis Gentleman, note on *Henry VIII*, in *Bell's Edition of Shakespeare's Plays*, 2nd. edn., 5 vols. (London: John Bell, 1774), 4:344.

9 Walter Scott, Review of *Memoirs of the Life of John Philip Kemble* by James Boaden, *Quarterly Review* 34, June 1826, 228; Boaden, *Memoirs of Kemble*, 1:423.

10 *LSD*; *Morning Post*, 26 November 1788; *World*, 26 November 1788. Kemble was a close friend of Charles Este, the theatre critic for the *World*, and had even invested financially in the paper (Baker, *John Philip Kemble*, 127).

11 Ibid., 129.

12 Kemble, 'Professional Memoranda', vol. 1, 25 November 1788; *Examiner*, no. 236, 5 July 1812, 429.

13 Campbell, *Life of Siddons*, 2:143. This moment takes place in the second scene of the play.

14 Qtd in ibid.

15 Ibid., 2:145, 146.

16 Ibid., 2:147; Boaden, *Memoirs of Siddons*, 2:265.

17 Qtd in Campbell, *Life of Siddons*, 2:149.

18 Ibid., 2:150.

19 Ibid.

20 Ibid., 2:151; Boaden, *Memoirs of Siddons*, 2:265–6.

21 Boaden, *Memoirs of Kemble*, 1:422.

22 Ibid. The source of the words in quotation marks is not clear.

23 *Morning Chronicle*, 27 November 1788; *Morning Post*, 26 November 1788.

24 *Public Advertiser*, 29 November 1788.

25 Boaden, *Memoirs of Kemble*, 1:422.

26 *Bell's Weekly Messenger*, 5 October 1806, qtd in Baker, *John Philip Kemble*, 286.

27 Qtd in Campbell, *Life of Siddons*, 2:144.

28 Ibid.

29 G. J. Bell, 'Mrs. Siddons as Queen Katharine, Mrs. Beverley, and Lady Randolph', in *Papers Literary, Scientific, &c, by Fleeming Jenkin*, ed. Sidney Colvin and J. A. Ewing, 2 vols. (London: Longmans, Green, and Co, 1887), 1:76.

30 Terry qtd in Campbell, *Life of Siddons*, 2:145.

31 Shattuck, *Kemble Promptbooks*, vol. 4, *King Henry the Eighth*, 34.

32 Ibid.

33 Scott, Review of *Memoirs of Kemble*, 228.

34 Ibid.

35 Shattuck, Introduction, *Kemble Promptbooks*, vol. 4, *King Henry the Eighth*, ii.

36 *Sale-Room* 14, 5 April 1817, 106. Kemble played Wolsey on 18 March. He had first acted the role in Edinburgh on 4 February 1813.

37 *Sale-Room* 14, 5 April 1817, 106–7.

38 Ibid., 107.

39 Ibid.

40 Shattuck, *Kemble Promptbooks*, vol. 4, *King Henry the Eighth*, 41; *Sale-Room* 14, 5 April 1817, 107–8.

41 Ibid., 108.

42 Ibid.

43 Shattuck, *Kemble Promptbooks*, vol. 4, *King Henry the Eighth*, 44; *Sale-Room* 14, 5 April 1817, 108.

44 Ibid.

45 Ibid.

46 James C. Dibdin, *The Annals of the Edinburgh Stage* (Edinburgh: Richard Cameron, 1888), 266.

47 *Caledonian Mercury*, 14 March 1812.

48 Dibdin, *Annals of the Edinburgh Stage*, 273. Similarly, when Siddons acted Queen Katharine in a benefit performance at Covent Garden on 31 May 1816, a reviewer reported that in the trial scene, the actress 'recalled to us the SIDDONS of 25 years ago', although the reviewer noted 'some slight change in the mode of articulation', possibly because she had lost some of her teeth (*Times*, 1 June 1816).

49 *Caledonian Mercury*, 25 November 1815.

50 Fitzgerald, *The Kembles*, 2:161.

51 Ibid., 2:174.

52 Ibid.

53 *London Magazine*, April 1823, 455.

54 George Henry Harlow, *The Court for the Trial of Queen Katharine* (1817), Walter Morrison Collection, Sudeley Castle, Winchcombe, Gloucestershire. I have found no record of Stephen Kemble acting Henry VIII. Highfill et al note of the painting that though the Kembles 'form the central focus of the picture, the scene does not represent an actual performance, for Harlow painted many of his friends into it' (*BD*, 8:402). The casting of Stephen may be a form of wish fulfilment or perhaps even a visual joke: Stephen was known for his corpulence, which may have suggested a comparison with the monarch,

and apparently his mother, Sarah Kemble, acted Anne Bullen in *Henry VIII* on the night of his birth.

55 *LSD*.

56 Jonathan Bate, 'The Romantic Stage', in *Shakespeare: An Illustrated Stage History*, ed. Jonathan Bate and Russell Jackson (Oxford: Oxford University Press, 1996), 99.

57 *World*, 9 February 1789.

58 *Times*, 9 January 1789.

59 For a summary of the changes made by Kemble in his adaptation, see David George, *A Comparison of Six Adaptations of Shakespeare's Coriolanus, 1681–1962* (Lewiston: Edwin Mellen Press, 2008), 48–9. No versions of *Coriolanus* had been performed in London for the previous twenty years.

60 Shattuck, Introduction, *Kemble Promptbooks*, vol. 2, *Coriolanus; or, The Roman Matron*, ii. The emphasis on Volumnia is evident in the subtitle of Kemble's adaptation, derived from Sheridan.

61 *Examiner*, no. 312, 19 December 1813, 810; *Oracle and Public Advertiser*, 4 October 1796.

62 Inga-Stina Ewbank, Introduction, *Coriolanus: J. P. Kemble 1789* (facs. edn., London: Cornmarket Press, 1970), n.p.; Campbell, *Life of Siddons*, 2:154.

63 Jane Moody, 'Romantic Shakespeare', in *The Cambridge Companion to Shakespeare on Stage*, ed. Stanley Wells and Sarah Stanton (Cambridge: Cambridge University Press, 2002), 43.

64 John Howard Payne, *Life and Writings* (Albany: Joel Munsell, 1875), 47.

65 Boaden, *Memoirs of Kemble*, 2:427.

66 John Ripley, *Coriolanus on Stage in England and America, 1609–1994* (Madison: Fairleigh Dickinson University Press, 1998), 141.

67 Kemble, 'Professional Memoranda', vol. 1, 7 February 1789.

68 Boaden, *Memoirs of Kemble*, 2:426.

69 Qtd in Dibdin, *Annals of the Edinburgh Stage*, 277.

70 Jonathan Sachs, *Romantic Antiquity: Rome in the British Imagination, 1789–1832* (Oxford: Oxford University Press, 2009), 193. Sachs supports this point with box office receipts from 1811, 1813 and 1814.

71 Ripley, *Coriolanus on Stage*, 345. The Manchester performance was of Sheridan's adaptation. Sheridan followed Thomson in renaming Volumnia (the mother of Coriolanus in Shakespeare's play), Veturia. This is the role that Siddons played. Volumnia in Thomson and Sheridan is the wife of Coriolanus. Although Kemble was in the Manchester company at this time, he did not act on this occasion (see the cast list printed in the *Manchester Mercury*, 4 February 1777).

72 Boaden, *Memoirs of Kemble*, 1:425.

73 Ibid.

74 John Ambrose Williams, *Memoirs of John Philip Kemble Esqr. With an Original Critique of his Performance* (London: T. Holt, 1823), 77.

75 David Rostron, 'John Philip Kemble's *Coriolanus* and *Julius Caesar*: An Examination of the Prompt Copies', *Theatre Notebook* 23, no. 1 (1968): 27.

76 Sheridan's version was published in 1755 with a title page that advertised the Order of the Ovation. A list of the supernumeraries and props employed in this scene is given before the text of the play. *Coriolanus; or, the Roman Matron* (London: A. Millar, 1755). The 1789 edition of Kemble's *Coriolanus* followed Sheridan in advertising this key scene on the title page. Kemble's staging of the Ovation is detailed in an appendix in Shattuck, *Kemble Promptbooks*, vol. 2, *Coriolanus*.

77 Julian Charles Young, *A Memoir of Charles Mayne Young, Tragedian*, 2 vols. (London and New York: Macmillan and Co., 1871), 1:62.

78 Young, *Memoir*, 62.

79 William Robson, *The Old Play-Goer* (London: Joseph Masters, 1846), 35.

80 Young, *Memoir*, 63.

81 Ibid., 62–3.

82 Ibid., 63.

83 Ripley, *Coriolanus on Stage*, 122.

84 Shattuck, *Kemble Promptbooks*, vol. 2, *Coriolanus*, 59.

85 *Dramatic Censor*, November 1811, 476.

86 Ibid.

87 *Star*, 4 October 1796.

88 Williams, *Memoirs of Kemble*, 80.

89 Rostron, 'Kemble's *Coriolanus* and *Julius Caesar*', 32. Rostron bases his analysis on a promptbook held by the Garrick Club Library. The promptbook held by the Folger Shakespeare Library and reproduced by Shattuck appears to be broadly similar.

90 Scott, Review of *Memoirs of Kemble*, 224.

91 Ibid.

92 Ibid.; Bertram Joseph, *The Tragic Actor* (New York: Theatre Arts Books, 1959), 192.

93 Henry Crabb Robinson, *Diary, Reminiscences, and Correspondence*, ed. Thomas Sadler, 3 vols. (London: Macmillan and Co., 1869), 1:384.

94 Ripley, *Coriolanus on Stage*, 140; Shattuck, *Kemble Promptbooks*, vol. 2, *Coriolanus*, 62.

95 Ibid., 63.

96 Bate, 'Romantic Stage', 98.

97 Sachs, *Romantic Antiquity*, 194–5.

98 Ripley, *Coriolanus on Stage*, 141.

99 Jonathan Bate, *Shakespearean Constitutions: Politics, Theatre, Criticism, 1730–1830* (Oxford: Clarendon Press, 1989), 64.

100 Inchbald, *British Theatre*, vol. 5, 'Remarks on *Coriolanus*', 5.

101 Sachs, *Romantic Antiquity*, 181. As both Sachs and Ripley have noted, Kemble's Rome was, though visually striking, in many ways anachronistic.

102 These performances are detailed in Ripley's helpful 'Chronological Handlist of Performances, 1609–1994' (*Coriolanus on Stage*, 343–66).

103 George, *Adaptations of Coriolanus*, 66.

104 Genest, *Some Account of the English Stage*, 8:480. Kemble makes no mention of the substitution in his 'Professional Memoranda'. The *Morning Post* noted the replacement and commented that Conway 'acquitted himself throughout in a very credible and effective style' (16 May 1816).

105 Ripley, *Coriolanus on Stage*, 348–53.

106 George, *Adaptations of Coriolanus*, 58.

107 John Finlay, 'Kemble in Coriolanus', in *Miscellanies* (Dublin: John Cumming, 1835), 257.

108 Shattuck, Introduction, *Kemble Promptbooks*, vol. 2, *Coriolanus*, i.

109 Ripley, *Coriolanus on Stage*, 115, 141.

110 George reads this image as representative of performance but Ripley sees it as idealized. George, *Adaptations of Coriolanus*, 52; John Ripley, 'Kemble's *Coriolanus* and the Folger Painting: A Second Look', *Theatre Notebook* 49, no. 3 (1995): 173–6.

111 Kemble, 'Professional Memoranda', vol. 1, opposite 8 June 1789.

112 Qtd in Campbell, *Life of Siddons*, 1:198.

113 Ibid.

114 By the 1796 season, Sheridan owed Kemble £1,367 in back salary and by November 1799, he owed Siddons £2,100, not including her benefit earnings from the previous season (Highfill et al., *BD*, 8:353, 14:23).

115 Boaden, *Memoirs of Kemble*, 2:185. Kemble's resignation was reported in the *Gazetteer* on 18 April 1796.

116 Peter Thomson, for example, writes: 'With the grand new theatre opened in March 1794, and the style of spectacular staging that its massiveness demanded launched, Kemble was approaching the end of his tether.' Kemble, John Philip (1757–1823), actor', *Oxford Dictionary of National Biography* (Oxford University Press, 2004), http://www.oxforddnb.com/view/article/15322.

117 Qtd in Fitzgerald, *The Kembles*, 1:310.

118 Qtd in Campbell, *Life of Siddons*, 2:183–4. *Macbeth* opened on 21 April 1794. In addition to his detailed attention to scenery

and costume, Kemble followed William Davenant's innovations in having the witches sing in chorus and fly above the stage.

119 *Courier*, 10 June 1794.

120 Thomson, *ODNB* Kemble; Highfill et al., *BD*, 8:350.

121 Boaden, *Memoirs of Kemble*, 2:126.

122 'Collection of Drawings of Theatrical Scenery with some Manuscript Comments' (late-eighteenth or early-nineteenth century), Folger Shakespeare Library, Washington D.C., Art Vol. d21, 87v-88r, images 163893 and 163894. The note states that the scenery was painted by Thomas Malton, assisted by Thomas Frederick Luppino and James De Maria. I am very grateful to Daniel O'Quinn for drawing my attention to this source.

123 Michael Kelly, *Reminiscences*, 2 vols. (London: Henry Colburn, 1826), 2:67.

124 Campbell, 'Life of Siddons', 2:246; Boaden, *Memoirs of Kemble*, 2:240. Selena Couture and Alexander Dick note that the collapsing bridge may have been inspired by Kemble's innovations in staging but do not posit *Lodoiska* as a specific influence. Introduction, *Pizarro: A Tragedy in Five Acts*, by Richard Brinsley Sheridan (Peterborough: Broadview Press, 2017), 49.

125 Qtd in Boaden, *Memoirs of Kemble*, 2:239.

126 Taylor, *Theatres of Opposition*, 130.

127 Selena Couture, 'Siddons's Ghost: Celebrity and Gender in Sheridan's *Pizarro*', *Theatre Journal* 65, no. 2 (2013): 186.

128 Ibid., 193.

129 Shattuck, *Kemble Promptbooks*, vol. 11, *Pizarro*, 60.

130 Boaden, *Memoirs of Kemble*, 2:242.

131 Taylor, *Theatres of Opposition*, 150.

132 Shattuck, *Kemble Promptbooks*, vol. 11, *Pizarro*, opposite 23.

133 Taylor, *Theatres of Opposition*, 151.

134 Couture and Dick, Introduction, 40. Robert Dighton's images may not reflect stage practice with complete accuracy but given their widespread circulation in the form of engravings, they do suggest how the public conceived of the characters.

135 *Morning Chronicle*, 22 September 1808. Kemble wrote in his diary 'we have not been able to discover the cause of this misfortune' (Kemble, 'Professional Memoranda', vol. 4, 20 September 1808). For more on the fire, see Chapter 4.

136 Boaden, *Memoirs of Siddons*, 2:360.

137 For the terms Sheridan proposed to Kemble, see Thomas Moore, *Memoirs of the Life of the Right Honourable Richard Brinsley Sheridan*, 3rd. edn., 2 vols. (London: Longman, Hurst, Rees, Orme, Brown, and Green, 1825), 2:304–8.

138 Boaden, *Memoirs of Kemble*, 2:314.

139 Ibid.

140 Kemble, 'Professional Memoranda', vol. 3, 25 March 1802.

141 Qtd in Boaden, *Memoirs of Kemble*, 2:290. Thomas Greenwood was one of the scene painters. Boaden reprints other notes of a similar nature.

Chapter 3

1 See Jeffrey Kahan, *Reforging Shakespeare: The Story of a Theatrical Scandal* (Bethlehem: Lehigh University Press, 1998), 56. I am indebted to Kahan's excellent book for many of the details about *Vortigern* and the Irelands provided in this chapter.

2 A drawing of Vortigern and Rowena executed by Samuel (after John Hamilton Mortimer's painting) hung prominently in the Irelands' home and William Henry claimed this was his inspiration. *The Confessions of William-Henry Ireland* (London: Ellerton and Byworth, 1805), 132–3. Rowena, the daughter of Hengist, with whom Vortigern became infatuated, had played a key role in depictions of the historical legend such as this image but curiously enough, the character was not central to William Henry's play. Jack Lynch cautions us to be on our guard when approaching William Henry's writing as his compulsion to lie persistently means 'that almost everything we think we know about Ireland may be wrong'. 'William Henry Ireland's Authentic Forgeries', *Princeton University Library Chronicle* 66, no. 1 (2004): 87.

3 The letters are reprinted and discussed in Kahan, *Reforging Shakespeare*, 63–4.

4 See Ireland's account of the play's composition in *Confessions*, 133–4. This piecemeal method of writing is not as outrageous as it might seem in the theatrical context of the time: a few years later, Sheridan employed a similar technique in finishing *Pizarro* (see Kelly, *Reminiscences*, 2:159, 162–3).

5 Ireland, *Confessions*, 136.

6 In fact, while William Henry later claimed to be the sole author of the Shakespeare Papers (including *Vortigern*), others have implicated Samuel in their creation. See Ireland, *Confessions*, 131; Kahan, *Reforging Shakespeare*, 108–23.

7 Kahan contends that Malone deliberately timed the publication of his *Inquiry* to coincide with the performance. The work 'was not seen as an attack on the papers but a "treatise on the play of *Vortigern*"' (ibid., 168; the quotation is from a clipping from an unnamed newspaper dated 4 April 1796 found in British Library, London, Add. MS 30349, fol. 70r.).

8 William Henry later wrote: 'My father would often lavish his usual praises on *Shakspear*, and frequently add, that he would give all his curious books to become possessed of a single line of his hand writing.' *An Authentic Account of the Shaksperian Manuscripts, &c* (London: J. Debrett, 1796), 7.

9 Antonia Forster, 'Seeing is Believing: External vs. Internal Evidence in the Controversy Over the Ireland Forgeries', in *Early British Drama in Manuscript*, ed. Tamara Atkin and Laura Estill (Turnhout, Belgium: Brepols, 2019), 298–9.

10 Ibid., 304.

11 Ireland, *Confessions*, 146–7.

12 The *Gazetteer* of 4 April 1796 commented on *Vortigern*'s parallels with various works of Shakespeare in negative terms, noting that the 'parodies and plagiarisms are so palpable, so much weakened by the variation from their prototypes, that instead of charming and surprising the greedy ear, they pall upon the sense, teize and torment the recollection'.

13 In a later edition of the play with a new preface, it was William Henry that accused Kemble of wanting to present the premiere

of *Vortigern* as an April Fool, but his account may, of course, be suspect. Preface, *Vortigern* (London: Joseph Thomas, 1832), vi.

14 Michael Dobson, 'John Philip Kemble', in *Great Shakespeareans: Garrick, Kemble, Siddons, Kean*, ed. Peter Holland (London: Bloomsbury, 2010), 87.

15 Ibid.

16 Kemble corroborated this assessment of Sheridan's attitude in his later account of *Vortigern* qtd in Charles Marsh, *The Clubs of London*, 2 vols. (London: Henry Colburn, 1828), 2:107–8.

17 Ireland, *Confessions*, 158.

18 Bernard Grebanier, *The Great Shakespeare Forgery* (New York: Norton, 1965), 221.

19 *Times*, 4 April 1796. The same report appeared in *Lloyd's Evening Post*, 1–4 April 1796.

20 Joseph Farington, diary for 17 December 1795 and 3 April 1796, in *The Diary of Joseph Farington*, ed. Kenneth Garlick, Angus Macintyre, Kathryn Cave and Evelyn Newby, 17 vols. (New Haven: Yale University Press, 1978–98), 2:446, 518.

21 Qtd in Marsh, *Clubs of London*, 2:107.

22 Ibid., 2:108–9.

23 For example, Kemble claims that Phillimore played Vortigern, the role that Kemble himself played, and that Jordan acted Rowena, not Flavia (ibid., 2:109).

24 Qtd in Percy Fitzgerald, *The Lives of the Sheridans*, 2 vols. (London: Richard Bentley and Son, 1886), 2:15.

25 Qtd in Campbell, *Life of Siddons*, 2:197.

26 W. H. Ireland, MS note, *An Authentic Account of the Shaksperian Manuscripts, &c.*, ed. W. H. Ireland (London: J. Debrett, 1796), Harvard Theatre Collection, Houghton Library, Harvard University, Cambridge, MA, TS 680.23.5, fol. 107r. I am extremely grateful to Jack Lynch for sharing with me his extensive transcriptions of manuscript material related to *Vortigern*, many of which are cited here, and for pointing me to numerous additional print sources.

NOTES

27 T. Nixon, letter to ? [March] 1796, in 'Collections on the Ireland Forgeries of the Play *Vortigern*', Shakespeare Birthplace Trust Collections, Stratford-upon-Avon, ER1/114/3, fol. 55.

28 Ibid.

29 Samuel Ireland, letter to John Philip Kemble, 28 December 1795, in 'Correspondence of Samuel Ireland with the Managers of Drury Lane Theatre, Relating to the Production of the Play of *Vortigern*', 1794–8, British Library, London, Add. MS 30348, fols. 63r.–v.

30 Samuel Ireland, letter to William Powell, 23 March 1796, in ibid., fol. 88r.

31 Samuel Ireland, letter to Richard Brinsley Sheridan, 28 March [1796], in ibid., fol. 89r.

32 *Oracle*, 28 March 1796.

33 Qtd in Hester Lynch Thrale Piozzi, *Autobiography, Letters, and Literary Remains*, ed. A. Hayward, 2 vols., 2nd. edn. (London: Longman, Green, Longman, and Roberts, 1861), 2:239.

34 Ibid.

35 Highfill et al., *BD*, 14:22.

36 Thomas Gilliland, *Jack in Office* (London: C. Chapple, 1804), 20.

37 Qtd in Marsh, *Clubs of London*, 2:107.

38 James Boaden, *The Life of Mrs. Jordan*, 2 vols. (London: Edward Bull, 1831), 1:297.

39 Farington, diary for 2 April 1796, 2:518.

40 Boaden, *Life of Jordan*, 1:297.

41 Kemble qtd in Marsh, *Clubs of London*, 2:110; Ireland, *Confessions*, 153, 152.

42 Nick Groom, *The Forger's Shadow: How Forgery Changed the Course of Literature* (London: Picador, 2002), 227.

43 Samuel Ireland, letter to Richard Brinsley Sheridan, 17 November 1795, in 'Correspondence', fols. 48r.-49r. (AL). Samuel subsequently threatened not to relinquish the manuscript of the play until he had confirmation that the scenery was being prepared. Letter to Richard Brinsley Sheridan, 7 December 1795, in ibid., fol. 58r. (AN).

44 *LSD*, 2 April 1796.

45 *Vortigern* was not performed again until a revival which had a short run at the Bridewell theatre in London in 1997 (see Kahan, *Reforging Shakespeare*, 223–4). On the other side of the Atlantic, a staged reading took place at the American Shakespeare Center during their 2013–14 season.

46 Thomson, *ODNB* Kemble.

47 Taylor, *Theatres of Opposition*, 185; *Oracle*, 18 February 1796.

48 Michael Gamer and Robert Miles, 'Gothic Shakespeare on the Romantic Stage', in *Gothic Shakespeares*, ed. John Drakakis and Dale Townshend (Abingdon: Routledge, 2008), 139.

49 *True Briton*, 14 March 1796.

50 *Whitehall Evening Post*, 12–15 March 1796.

51 *Oracle*, 14 March 1796. For comments on the play's flaws, see the *Star* of the same date.

52 George Colman the Younger, Preface, *The Iron Chest* (London: W. Woodfall, 1796), x.

53 Ibid., vii.

54 Ibid., x. For another account of Kemble's opium use, see Fitzgerald, *The Kembles*, 1:331.

55 Ibid., 1:325.

56 Ireland, *Confessions*, 157–8. Ireland's chronology is confused here as *Vortigern* was performed after *The Iron Chest*, not before.

57 Boaden, *Memoirs of Kemble*, 2:162. See also Fitzgerald, *The Kembles*, 1:338, 340–1.

58 Colman, Preface, *The Iron Chest*, xv.

59 Ibid., vii–viii. The drama proved more successful when it was later cut down.

60 Samuel Ireland, Preface, *Vortigern* (London: J. Barker, 1799), vi.

61 Qtd in Ireland, *Confessions*, 136.

62 Samuel Ireland, Preface, *Vortigern*, vi.

63 Ibid.

64 Ibid.

65 Much later, Chatterton would be depicted by Henry Wallis on his deathbed (he died from an overdose of arsenic and opium at the age of seventeen) with manuscripts spilling from a trunk at his side.

66 Ireland, *Confessions*, 63.

67 John Nixon, *The Oaken Chest or the Gold Mines of Ireland a Farce* (1796), British Museum, London, K,64.72.

68 Ibid.

69 Ibid.

70 David Worrall notes that 'while there is nothing to suggest that Ireland Jr's family assisted him, they were certainly talented enough, and capable enough, to do so'. *The Politics of Romantic Theatricality, 1787–1832: The Road to the Stage* (Basingstoke: Palgrave Macmillan, 2007), 114.

71 *Herald*, 12 January 1796, qtd in Jack Lynch, *Deception and Detection in Eighteenth-Century Britain* (Aldershot: Ashgate Publishing Limited, 2008), 37.

72 A further dramatic connection is found in the print's subtitle, which in addition to emphasizing the avarice of the Irelands, both highlighted the genre of the entertainment they provided ('a Farce') and recalled John O'Keefe's comic opera *The Lad of the Hills; or, the Wicklow Gold Mine* (performed on 9 April 1796), which referred to the discovery of gold in the Wicklow mountains in October 1795. Several farces that mocked the Irelands and featured documents appearing from trunks, boxes or chests appeared in 1796, including Frederick Reynolds's *Fortune's Fool* and Walley Chamberlain Oulton's *Precious Relics; or the Tragedy of Vortigern Rehearsed*. William Henry also told his father that Mr H. wanted to 'preserv[e] the manuscript of the unknown play, *Vortigern*, by having made for it an iron case to be covered with crimson velvet, studded with gold, and to be embroidered with Shakespeare's arms' (Grebanier, *Great Shakespeare Forgery*, 135).

73 Brean Hammond, 'Shakespeare Discoveries and Forgeries', in *Shakespeare in the Eighteenth Century*, ed. Fiona Ritchie and Peter Sabor (Cambridge: Cambridge University Press, 2012), 78–96; Lynch, *Deception and Detection*, 85.

74 Kahan, *Reforging Shakespeare*, 215.

75 Genest, *Some Account of the English Stage*, 6:163, 210.

76 *Morning Advertiser*, 23 March 1795.

77 *Morning Herald*, 23 March 1795.

78 *Oracle*, 23 March 1795.

79 Campbell, *Life of Siddons*, 2:190. See the reviews in the *Observer*, 22 March 1795 and *Morning Herald*, 23 March 1795 for a more detailed description.

80 *Morning Herald*, 23 March 1795.

81 Dobson, 'John Philip Kemble', 85. Dobson also sees 'shades of the de Camp affair' in Vortigern's lustful pursuit of Rowena ('John Philip Kemble', 88).

82 Williams, *Memoirs of Kemble*, 24.

83 Ibid.

84 Qtd in ibid., 25. The apology is dated 27 January 1795. For Kemble's private apology to De Camp, see Highfill et al., *BD*, 8:326.

85 Qtd in Williams, *Memoirs of Kemble*, 25.

86 Highfill et al., *BD*, 8:351, 326. Kelly notes that the reaction of Kemble's wife to this scandal is unrecorded (*The Kemble Era*, 105). In 1787, Kemble had married Priscilla Brereton, widow of the actor who was one of his early rivals and daughter of the Drury Lane prompter, William Hopkins.

87 Williams, *Memoirs of Kemble*, 25.

88 Campbell, *Life of Siddons*, 2:199.

89 'M. H.', letter to Samuel Ireland, 25 July 1795, British Library, London, Add. MS 30346, fol. 54r.

90 W. H. Ireland, 'A Full and Explanatory Account of the Shaksperian Forgery by Myself the Writer William Henry Ireland', Houghton Library, Harvard University, Cambridge, MA, MS Hyde 60 (3), 252. Like William Henry's other confessional works, this text should not be taken at face value.

91 John Philip Kemble, letter to W. H. Ireland, 5 February 1801, Centre for Research Collections, University of Edinburgh, H. -P. Coll. 321, fol. 17r.

92 W. H. Ireland, letter to John Philip Kemble, [February 1801], Centre for Research Collections, University of Edinburgh, H. -P. Coll. 321, fol. 17r.

93 John Philip Kemble, letter to W. H. Ireland, 14 April 1801, qtd in Ireland, *Full and Explanatory Account*, opposite 255.

94 Grebanier, *Great Shakespeare Forgery*, 287.

95 W. H. Ireland, *Mutius Scævola; or, the Roman Patriot* (London: D. N. Shury, 1801), n.p.

96 Ibid., 72.

97 Ibid., 83.

98 *Observer*, 3 April 1796.

99 Jack Lynch, 'England's Ireland, Ireland's England: William Henry Ireland's National Offense', in *Literary Forgery in Early Modern Europe, 1450–1800*, ed. Walter Stephens and Earle A. Havens (Baltimore: Johns Hopkins University Press, 2018), 266.

100 Jonathan Bate, 'Faking It: Shakespeare and the 1790s', *Essays and Studies* 46 (1993): 77. Bate also notes how this claim 'replicates the debate on the French Revolution which . . . so dominated the printing-presses throughout the 1790s'.

101 George Chalmers, *An Apology for the Believers in the Shakspeare-Papers* (London: Thomas Egerton, 1797), 2, 608.

Chapter 4

1 Baker, *John Philip Kemble*, 274.

2 Fitzgerald, *The Kembles*, 2:51–2.

3 Boaden, *Memoirs of Siddons*, 2:330.

4 See Frances Burney, journal for 3 November 1797, in *The Journals and Letters of Fanny Burney (Madame d'Arblay)*, gen. ed. Joyce Hemlow, 12 vols. (Oxford: Oxford University Press, 1972–84), 4:24. Burney expressed surprise about 'so extraordinary a combination – so degrading a one, indeed, that of the first Tragic Actress, the living Melpomene, & something so burlesque as Sadler's Wells'. William Siddons owned a quarter share in Sadler's Wells from 1792 to 1802, purchased

with funds from Siddons. Like all married women in the period, Siddons's income 'legally belonged to and was managed by her husband' who 'proved to be quite inept in his handling of the finances' (Shaughnessy, *ODNB* Siddons).

5 Boaden, *Memoirs of Siddons*, 2:337.

6 Ibid., 2:338.

7 See Campbell, *Life of Siddons*, 2:298 for details of Siddons's salary at Covent Garden.

8 Boaden, *Memoirs of Kemble*, 2:374.

9 Boaden, *Memoirs of Siddons*, 2:343.

10 Siddons 'maintained a cold reserve upon the subject' of Betty, 'being convinced herself that the effect was delusive' and left her daughter-in-law, Harriet Siddons, to play her major roles opposite the young actor (ibid., 2:350). Kemble regarded Betty as 'a passing novelty' (Boaden, *Memoirs of Kemble*, 2:408).

11 *Theatrical Recorder* 2, no. 11, 1805, 348. *Othello* was, indeed, being performed at Covent Garden in November 1805 when Holcroft was writing, but with Sarah Smith as Desdemona. Siddons had last played the part (with Cooke as Iago and Kemble as Othello) on 17 May 1804. In 1807–8, Kemble played Iago to Cooke's Othello.

12 *Theatrical Recorder* 2, no. 11, 1805, 347.

13 Baker, *John Philip Kemble*, 288. Productions of *Cymbeline* (January 1806) and *The Two Gentlemen of Verona* (April 1808) were somewhat less successful.

14 *Monthly Mirror* 22, November 1806, 346.

15 The situation is recounted in Boaden, *Memoirs of Kemble*, 2:428–9.

16 Ibid., 2:452.

17 Sarah Siddons, letter to Lady Perceval, after 20 September 1808, Philbrick Library Collection of Theater Letters, Honnold Mudd Library, Special Collections, Claremont Colleges, CA, phl00210, https://ccdl.claremont.edu/digital/collection/phl/id/1319/rec/16.

18 Thomson, *ODNB* Kemble.

19 J. Britton and A. Pugin, *Illustrations of the Public Buildings of London*, 2 vols. (London: J. Taylor, 1825), 1:217.

20 Ibid.

21 Ibid., 1:218. Plate V (after 226) shows the staircase and the statue.

22 *Examiner*, no. 91, 24 September 1809, 618.

23 Elaine Hadley, 'The Old Price Wars: Melodramatizing the Public Sphere in Early-Nineteenth-Century England', *PMLA* 107, no. 3 (1992): 525.

24 Boaden, *Life of Kemble*, 2:492. The figure of £300 is from Terry F. Robinson, 'National Theatre in Transition: The London Patent Theatre Fires of 1808–1809 and the Old Price Riots', March 2016, *BRANCH: Britain, Representation and Nineteenth-Century History*, ed. Dino Franco Felluga, http://www.branchcollective.org/?ps_articles=terry-f-robinson-national-theatre-in-transition-the-london-patent-theatre-fires-of-1808-1809-and-the-old-price-riots. Robinson also notes that these boxes, because of their privacy, 'were said to promote immoral behaviors such as prostitution and gambling'. Boaden claims that such accusations of immorality were 'a pretence' and that the real objection to the private boxes was the fact that they enabled 'the absolute seclusions of a PRIVILEGED ORDER from all *vulgar contact*' (*Memoirs of Kemble*, 2:492). These issues had been contentious since Kemble joined the theatre in 1803, when sixteen private boxes had been added (Baker, *John Philip Kemble*, 275).

25 Marc Baer, *Theatre and Disorder in Late Georgian London* (Oxford: Clarendon Press, 1992), 2.

26 Kemble, 'Professional Memoranda', vol. 1, after 26 June 1791.

27 J. J. Stockdale, *The Covent Garden Journal* (London: J. J. Stockdale, 1810), 153 (hereafter *CGJ*).

28 Ibid., 29.

29 Ibid., 309–10.

30 Gillian Russell, 'Playing at Revolution: The Politics of the O. P. Riots of 1809', *Theatre Notebook* 44, no. 1 (1990): 20.

31 Stockdale, *CGJ*, 152. The *Covent Garden Journal* was first published in weekly instalments but I cite from the edition collected and reprinted in 1810.

32 Ibid., 239, 243.

33 Ibid., 163.

34 David Worrall, *Theatric Revolution: Drama, Censorship, and Romantic Period Subcultures 1773–1832* (Oxford: Oxford University Press, 2006), 58.

35 Stockdale, *CGJ*, 215.

36 Russell, 'Playing at Revolution', 20.

37 Stockdale, *CGJ*, 170.

38 For the audience's response to the committee's findings, see ibid., 172–6.

39 See ibid., 136–7.

40 Ibid., 290. Rioting broke out again in September 1810 after a misunderstanding by Kemble, whether wilful or innocent it is hard to determine, over the number of private boxes to be retained. The managers had to yield to audience demands once more in order for peace to be restored.

41 Scott, Review of *Memoirs of Kemble*, 239.

42 Qtd in Campbell, *Life of Siddons*, 2:329.

43 *Life of John Philip Kemble* (London: J. Johnston, 1809), 42.

44 Ibid., 42–3.

45 Ibid., 43.

46 Stockdale, *CGJ*, 149–50.

47 Thomas Lawrence, letter to Joseph Farington, 19 September 1809, in *Sir Thomas Lawrence's Letter-Bag*, ed. George Somes Layard (London: George Allen, 1906), 64.

48 Indeed, Boaden claims that before Covent Garden reopened, there was 'but little expectation that our great actress would herself act in the new theatre. She really wished to retire' (*Memoirs of Siddons* 2:358).

49 Ibid., 2:373.

50 Sarah Siddons, letter to Harriet Siddons, [25 October 1809], Folger Shakespeare Library, Washington D.C., Y.c.432 (14).

51 According to Manvell, Siddons was in Edinburgh in March and April 1810 (*Sarah Siddons*, 295).

52 Qtd in Stockdale, *CGJ*, 152.

53 Fitzgerald, *The Kembles*, 2:137. Fitzgerald's numbers do not quite add up. See also Stockdale, *CGJ*, 168; *Life of Kemble*, 50.

54 Stockdale, *CGJ*, 78.

55 Ibid., 150.

56 Ibid., 217.

57 Lawrence, letter to Farington, 23 September 1809, in *Lawrence's Letter-Bag*, 66.

58 Stockdale, *CGJ*, 83.

59 Qtd in Campbell, *Life of Siddons*, 2:329. Scott confirmed that attacks were made on the family's home and that they particularly targeted the Kemble women (Review of *Memoirs of Kemble*, 239).

60 James Boaden, *Memoirs of Mrs. Inchbald*, 2 vols. (London: Richard Bentley, 1833), 2:144.

61 Sean McEvoy, *Theatrical Unrest: Ten Riots in the History of the Stage, 1601–2004* (Abingdon: Routledge, 2016), 61.

62 The lines below the image importantly refer to 'the Princely income which my Family have long enjoyed', invoking Kemble's siblings as well.

63 Qtd in Stockdale, *CGJ*, 198.

64 Qtd in ibid., 157.

65 Baer, *Theatre and Disorder*, 79.

66 '*John Kemble, in the Character of Coriolanus, Addressing the Plebeians*', in Stockdale, *CGJ*, 691.

67 Qtd in Stockdale, *CGJ*, 196.

68 A further placard linked Kemble with another tyrannical ruler, *Richard III* (a part he had played since early in his career but had recently handed over to Cooke). See Thomas Tegg, *The Rise, Progress, and Termination of the O. P. War, in Poetic Epistles* (London: Thomas Tegg, 1810), 114.

69 Stockdale, *CGJ*, 195, 205, 210.

70 *Life of Kemble*, 44.

71 Russell, 'Playing at Revolution', 22.

72 Qtd in Stockdale, *CGJ*, 645.

73 Qtd in ibid., 183.

74 Ibid., 208.

75 Ibid., 218.

76 Ibid.

77 Bate, *Shakespearean Constitutions*, 43.

78 Qtd in Russell, 'Playing at Revolution', 17.

79 Shattuck, *Kemble Promptbooks*, vol. 5, *Macbeth*, opposite 9. 'The Blasted Heath, with Bridge, &c.' painted by Thomas Greenwood was one of the new scenes included in Kemble's 1794 production of the play, again suggesting the visual importance of this moment. See the review in the *World*, 22 April 1794. Shattuck reprints as an appendix pages from a second promptbook which show even more details of the staging of this scene.

80 Williams claims that Brandon was later reinstated (*Memoirs of Kemble*, 53).

81 Tegg, *O. P. War*, 169.

82 John Ashton, *The Dawn of the XIXth Century in England*, 2 vols. (London: T. Fisher Unwin, 1886), 2:153. Ashton says this occurrence took place on 19 December but Kemble did not appear as Hamlet on that night (though he did on 18 and 20 December).

83 Boaden, *Memoirs of Kemble*, 2:120.

84 Ibid., 1:21; Highfill et al., *BD*, 14:7. For Siddons learning the role as a young actress, see her comments to Campbell (*Life of Siddons*, 2:35). She played Lady Macbeth in Cheltenham in her early twenties (Shaughnessy, *ODNB* Siddons).

85 Reiko Oya, *Representing Shakespearean Tragedy: Garrick, the Kembles, and Kean* (Cambridge: Cambridge University Press, 2007), 68.

86 Sarah Siddons, 'Remarks on the Character of Lady Macbeth', in Campbell, *Life of Siddons*, 2:10–39; John Philip Kemble, *Macbeth Reconsidered* (London: T. and J. Egerton, 1786). Kemble later expanded his work as *Macbeth, and King Richard*

the Third (London: John Murray, 1817). Campbell's biography was published in 1834 but the author wrote that 'Mrs. Siddons shewed me these Remarks on the character of *Lady Macbeth* some nineteen years ago', so around 1815 (*Life of Siddons*, 2:44).

87 Qtd in Dennis Bartholomeusz, *Macbeth and the Players* (Cambridge: Cambridge University Press, 1969), 102.

88 Joseph W. Donohue, Jr, 'Kemble and Mrs. Siddons in *Macbeth*: The Romantic Approach to Tragic Character', *Theatre Notebook* 22, no. 2 (1967/8): 67.

89 Bartholomeusz, *Macbeth and the Players*, 137. Kemble was, indeed, explicitly writing in response to Thomas Whately's pamphlet published the previous year which claimed that, unlike Richard III, Macbeth is a coward.

90 Chelsea Phillips offers a rich consideration of one important example: she examines the implications of Siddons's performances of Lady Macbeth while heavily pregnant in 1785 and 1794, when the actress's gravid state would have been visible to the audience and would have had a significant impact on their reception of the character. *Carrying All Before Her: Celebrity Pregnancy and the London Stage, 1689–1800* (Newark: University of Delaware Press, 2022), 136–41.

91 Donohue, 'Kemble and Siddons in *Macbeth*', 65, 76.

92 Shaughnessy, *ODNB* Siddons.

93 *Macbeth*, 5.9.35. This line about the protagonists was in fact excised from Kemble's version of the play.

94 G. J. Bell, 'Mrs. Siddons as Lady Macbeth', in *Papers Literary and Scientific*, ed. Fleeming Jenkin, 2 vols. (London: Longmans, Green and Co, 1887), 1:53.

95 Boaden, *Memoirs of Siddons*, 2:158. In this discussion, I quote the lines from the play as they are rendered in the source I am citing.

96 Bell, 'Siddons as Lady Macbeth', 54.

97 Ibid.

98 Ibid.; J. H. Siddons, 'Random Recollections of a Life', *Harper's New Monthly Magazine* 26, December 1862, 71. For more on J. H. Siddons (a.k.a. Stocqueler), see below.

NOTES

99 Bell, 'Siddons as Lady Macbeth', 55–6.

100 Ibid., 56.

101 Ibid.

102 Ibid.

103 Ibid., 57.

104 Ibid.

105 *Tatler* 3, no. 370, 9 November 1831, 446.

106 J. H. Stocqueler, *Memoirs of a Journalist* (Bombay and London: Offices of the Times of India, 1873), 17. This performance took place in 1816 (after Siddons's official retirement). Stocqueler, who claimed to be the illegitimate child of the actress's son, George, and who often used the name J. H. Siddons (as mentioned earlier), was a teenager at the time. The house was full and he had been allowed to watch from backstage after entreating Siddons in a letter. His account is corroborated by Bell's notes, which record that Siddons 'breathes with difficulty, hearkens towards the door' and delivers the line '*He is about it*' in a 'whisper horrible ('Siddons as Lady Macbeth', 58).

107 Shattuck, *Kemble Promptbooks*, vol. 5, *Macbeth*, 23. In general, Kemble's promptbooks (which date from some time after the 1808 fire) are geared towards documenting the stage placement and movement of the whole cast rather than recording the interpretations of individual actors. They therefore contain very few details of Siddons's and Kemble's acting.

108 Bell, 'Siddons as Lady Macbeth', 59.

109 Ibid., 60.

110 Ibid.

111 Ibid.

112 Ibid.; Thomas Beach, *John Philip Kemble and Sarah Siddons in Macbeth* (1786), Garrick Club, London, G0390 (see cover image).

113 Bell, 'Siddons as Lady Macbeth', 60–1.

114 Donohue, 'Kemble and Siddons in *Macbeth*', 82.

115 Bell, 'Siddons as Lady Macbeth', 63.

116 Ibid., 63, 64.

117 *Tatler*, 9 November 1831; Boaden, *Memoirs of Kemble*, 1:177.
118 Bell, 'Siddons as Lady Macbeth', 64.
119 Ibid.
120 Ibid.
121 Donohue, 'Kemble and Siddons in *Macbeth*', 84. Donohue takes this detail (which is not found in the Shattuck promptbook) from annotations to a part book for Macduff held by the Garrick Club, London.
122 Farington, diary for 10 November 1811, 11:4029.
123 Ibid.
124 *Times*, 19 September 1811.
125 Dobson, 'John Philip Kemble', 95.
126 Campbell, *Life of Siddons*, 2:39. Sheridan apparently tried to dissuade her from this departure from tradition (which, as I have argued elsewhere, was a direct challenge to her predecessor, Hannah Pritchard) but she persisted in her interpretation and was ultimately vindicated.

Chapter 5

1 Shattuck, Introduction, *Kemble Promptbooks*, vol. 2, *Hamlet*, i.
2 Qtd in Manvell, *Sarah Siddons*, 23.
3 Amy Muse, 'Actresses and the Making of the Modern Hamlet', in *Text and Presentation, 2007*, ed. Stratos E. Constantinidis, The Comparative Drama Conference Series 4 (Jefferson: McFarland & Company, Inc., 2007), 139.
4 Highfill et al., *BD*, 14:3.
5 *Manchester Mercury*, 18 March 1777.
6 Shaughnessy, *ODNB* Siddons.
7 Highfill et al., *BD*, 8:336.
8 William Siddons also sang 'an ingenious SONG . . . on a Manufacturing Town' at the end of the fourth Act of *Hamlet* 'by particular Desire' and appeared in the afterpiece, *The Man of Quality*, as Dr Bull (*Manchester Mercury*, 18 March 1777).

NOTES

9 R. J. Broadbent, *Annals of the Liverpool Stage* (Liverpool: Edward Howell, 1908), 70.

10 Qtd in Boaden, *Memoirs of Inchbald*, 2:363.

11 Ibid. Younge had acted in London since 1768 and appeared at various regional theatres in the 1770s; at Liverpool in the summer of 1777 she earned over £10 per night (Highfill et al., *BD*, 12:68). She was one of the actresses with whom Siddons had to compete when she debuted at Drury Lane in 1775.

12 Siddons visited Liverpool in 1783, 1785, 1786, 1789, 1793, 1796 and 1797 (see Highfill et al., *BD*). She also acted there in 1809 (Broadbent, *Annals of the Liverpool Stage*, 122).

13 Baker, *John Philip Kemble*, 31.

14 'A Collection of Playbills from Theatre Royal, Liverpool, 1773–1781', 2 vols., British Library, London, Playbills 225 (1).

15 Genest, *Some Account of the English Stage*, 6:211.

16 Frances had been introduced to the Bath stage by Siddons in September 1780 (Highfill et al., *BD*, 8:30).

17 Qtd in F. W. Price, 'Ann Radcliffe, Mrs. Siddons and the Character of Hamlet', *Notes & Queries* 23, no. 4 (1976): 167.

18 Muse, 'Actresses and the Modern Hamlet', 146.

19 Qtd in Price, 'Radcliffe, Siddons and Hamlet', 167.

20 Celestine Woo, 'Sarah Siddons's Performances as Hamlet: Breaching the Breeches Part', *European Romantic Review* 18, no. 5 (1007): 573–4. When Bate scouted Siddons for Garrick in 1775, he cautioned the manager of her Hamlet: 'nay beware yourself *Great Little* Man', a gentle jibe at his celebrity status in the part and his short stature (qtd in Manvell, *Sarah Siddons*, 23).

21 Woo, 'Breaching the Breeches Part', 573.

22 Muse, 'Actresses and the Modern Hamlet', 146.

23 *Manchester Mercury*, 10 March 1778.

24 Genest, *Some Account of the English Stage*, 6:209.

25 Ibid., 6:211. According to Genest, 'Mrs. Piozzi allowed that her friend Mrs. Siddons did not shine in Comedy, but observed that she played Mrs. Candour [in Sheridan's *The School for Scandal*] very well' (ibid., 6:115).

26 Muse, 'Actresses and the Modern Hamlet', 146–7.

27 Charlotte Charke, *A Narrative of the Life* (London: W. Reeve, 1755), 207–8; 'Addenda and Corrigenda to *The Dublin Stage, 1720–1745*, in *Theatre in Dublin, 1745–1820: A Calendar of Performances*, ed. John C. Greene, 6 vols. (Lanham: Lehigh University Press, 2011), 6:4562.

28 Howard, *Women as Hamlet*, 38–9.

29 Charles Lee Lewes, *Memoirs*, 4 vols. (London: Richard Phillips, 1805), 1:87. William 'Canterbury' Smith ran a circuit in Kent in the 1750s and 1760s (Highfill et al., *BD*, 14:187–8).

30 *Memoirs of Lee Lewes*, 1:88.

31 Greene, *Theatre in Dublin, 1745–1820*, 5:3317.

32 Robert Rainey, diary for 27 July 1802, 'Journal Kept in Dublin', vol. 6, Royal Irish Academy, Dublin, MS 24 K 15, fol. 247.

33 Judith Pascoe, *The Sarah Siddons Audio Files: Romanticism and the Lost Voice* (Ann Arbor: University of Michigan Press, 2013), 85.

34 Muse, 'Actresses and the Modern Hamlet', 140.

35 *Mrs. Galindo's Letter to Mrs. Siddons* (London: Printed for the Authoress, 1809), 6–7. Pascoe considers it not unreasonable that Siddons would not want to be observed as she practised, given that this would necessarily have meant her appearing ungraceful at times (*Siddons Audio Files*, 86–7).

36 *Mrs. Galindo's Letter*, 61.

37 Ibid.

38 Charlotte Boatner-Doane, 'Sarah Siddons and the Romantic Hamlet', *Nineteenth Century Theatre and Film* 44, no. 2 (2017): 217. This article reprints the image, which is very rare (218).

39 Rainey, diary for 27 July 1802, fol. 246.

40 Ibid., fol. 246.

41 *Hamlet*, 1.5.20; Rainey, diary for 27 July 1802, fol. 246–7.

42 Ibid., fol. 247.

43 Ibid., fol. 246.

44 Woo, 'Breaching the Breeches Part', 576.

45 Qtd in Manvell, *Sarah Siddons*, 23.

46 Howard, *Women as Hamlet*, 40.

47 Rainey, diary for 27 July 1802, fol. 246.

48 Ibid., fol. 247.

49 Ibid.

50 Boaden, *Memoirs of Kemble*, 1:96–7.

51 Sprague, *Shakespeare and the Actors*, 47. Dobson notes that Kemble's choice of Hamlet for his Drury Lane debut was a deliberate challenge to the memory of Garrick's performance ('John Philip Kemble', 70).

52 Boaden, *Memoirs of Kemble*, 1:98.

53 Ibid.

54 Ibid.

55 Inchbald, *British Theatre*, vol. 1, 'Remarks on *Hamlet*', 3.

56 Elizabeth Inchbald, '*Hamlet* [Autograph Manuscript of an Essay on John Philip Kemble's Portrayal of Hamlet]' (c. 1805), Huntington Library, San Marino, CA, HM 63342.

57 Ibid.

58 Ibid.

59 Ibid.

60 Ibid.

61 Ibid.

62 Ibid.

63 *Morning Chronicle*, 19 November 1785; *Public Advertiser*, 7 October 1783.

64 Augustus Bozzi Granville, *Critical Observations on Mr. Kemble's Performances at the Theatre Royal, Liverpool* (Liverpool: M. Galway, 1811). Kemble acted Hamlet in Liverpool on 8 July 1811 (Broadbent, *Annals of the Liverpool Stage*, 127).

65 *Critical Observations*, 5.

66 Ibid., 7.

67 Ibid., 8.

68 Boaden, *Memoirs of Kemble*, 2:107.

69 Ibid.

70 For these regional performances, see Highfill et al., *BD*. There were probably many others as well.

71 *Gentleman's Magazine* 53, pt 1, April 1783, 309. The writer also praised Kemble's performance in *The Count of Narbonne*, which ran for thirty nights over the course of the season.

72 Other regional performances of Hamlet include Edinburgh (1792, 1817), Dublin (1795), Bath (1803), Bristol (1803) (see Highfill et al., *BD*). Again, this is surely not an exhaustive list.

73 'Seventh Anniversary of the Shakespeare Club, November 30, 1825', in *Proceedings of the Sheffield Shakespeare Club* (Sheffield: Printed for the Editor by H. and G. Crookes, 1829), 79.

74 Ibid.

75 Ibid.

76 Ibid.

77 Dobson, 'John Philip Kemble', 58.

78 Boaden, *Memoirs of Kemble*, 1:91–2.

79 *Morning Chronicle*, 1 October 1783.

80 Boatner-Doane, 'Siddons and the Romantic Hamlet', 224.

81 Ibid., 213.

82 Rainey, diary for 27 July 1802, fol. 246.

83 *New Monthly Magazine and Literary Journal* 16, pt 1, 1826, 147. These comments appear in a conversation between two characters and Radcliffe is therefore not writing in her own voice.

84 *Times*, 25 June 1817.

85 Boaden, *Memoirs of Siddons*, 1:282.

86 Boatner-Doane, 'Siddons and the Romantic Hamlet', 227.

87 Howard, *Women as Hamlet*, 41.

88 Boaden, *Memoirs of Siddons*, 1:282.

89 Ibid.

90 Ibid., 1:282–3.

91 Rainey, diary for 27 July 1802, fol. 247.

92 Harriet Martin, *Remarks on Mr. John Kemble's Performance of Hamlet and Richard the Third* (London: G. and J. Robinson), 6–7.

93 Raymond Mander and Joe Mitchenson, *Hamlet Through the Ages: A Pictorial Record from 1709* (London: Rockliff, 1952), 93.

94 Alan R. Young, *Hamlet and the Visual Arts, 1709–1900* (Newark: University of Delaware Press, 2002), 358.

95 Woo, 'Breaching the Breeches Part', 580.

96 This is Siddons's only recorded performance of Ophelia in London. I have found no evidence of Siddons performing the part before this and Ophelia was not included on the list of roles she sent to Bate to share with Garrick.

97 *Public Advertiser*, 17 May 1786.

98 Ibid.

99 Boaden, *Memoirs of Kemble*, 1:330.

100 *Theatrical Recorder* 2, no. 12, 1805, 412.

101 *Examiner*, no. 325, 20 March 1814, 190.

102 Campbell, *Life of Siddons*, 2:87. Elizabeth Hopkins (mother of Kemble's wife, Priscilla) played Gertrude in Siddons's one London performance as Ophelia.

103 This appears to be Siddons's only London performance in the role. For her appearances as Gertrude outside London, see Highfill et al., *BD*, 14:6.

104 Although generally renowned as a comic actress, Jordan was a successful Ophelia and played the part from 1796. Jane Powell took over the role of Gertrude and also became the first recorded female Hamlet on the London stage, acting the character in 1796, 1797 and 1802.

105 Bell, 'Siddons as Lady Macbeth', 58.

106 *New Monthly Magazine and Literary Journal* 32, pt 2, 1831, 31. Boatner-Doane connects this comment to the Romantic antitheatrical tendency ('Siddons and the Romantic Hamlet', 229).

Conclusion

1 Frances Ann Kemble, *Record of a Girlhood*, 3 vols. (London: Richard Bentley and Son, 1878), 3:12. Shaughnessy makes the connection with Hamlet (Shaughnessy, *ODNB* Siddons).

2 Samuel Rogers, *Recollections of the Table-Talk of Samuel Rogers* (London: Edward Moxon, 1856), 186.

3 Kemble, *Record of a Girlhood*, 1:57; *London Magazine* 7, April 1823, 450.

4 Siddons's farewell address, qtd in Campbell, *Life of Siddons*, 2:339.

5 Qtd in Fitzgerald, *The Kembles*, 2:305.

6 Boaden, *Memoirs of Kemble*, 2:546.

7 For details of Siddons's earnings in her final seasons, see Fitzgerald, *The Kembles*, 2:144. Siddons had originally set out to earn the sum of £10,000 to make herself 'perfectly at ease with respect to fortune' but she had achieved this by 1786 and by the time of her retirement had 'more than doubled that sum' (ibid., 1:258, 2:145).

8 *The London Stage Calendar 1800–1844. Part I: 1800–1832*, https://londonstage.bodleian.ox.ac.uk/.

9 Boaden, *Memoirs of Siddons*, 2:378.

10 Campbell enumerates the parts and the number of times Siddons acted them in her final season (*Life of Siddons*, 2:335).

11 Qtd in Manvell, *Sarah Siddons*, 298.

12 Farington, diary for 29 June 1812, 11:4151. Genest pronounced this 'an absurdity' (*Some Account of the English Stage*, 8:297).

13 Farington, diary for 29 June 1812, 11:4151; *Oxberry's Dramatic Biography, and Histrionic Anecdotes* 1, no. 7, 12 February 1825, 136. Kemble also appeared in costume (as Coriolanus) to speak his farewell address five years later (see later).

14 Farington, diary for 29 June 1812, 11:4151.

15 Ibid.

16 Manvell, *Sarah Siddons*, 298; Highfill et al., *BD*, 14:31.

17 For a full list of these post-retirement appearances, see ibid., 14:31–2.

18 Campbell, *Life of Siddons*, 2:364.

19 Qtd in Manvell, *Sarah Siddons*, 306.

20 Qtd in Campbell, *Life of Siddons*, 2:361.

21 *Examiner*, no. 442, 16 June 1816, 378.

22 Boaden, *Memoirs of Siddons*, 2:383.

23 Ibid., 2:384.

24 Benjamin Robert Haydon, *Autobiography and Memoirs . . . (1786–1846)*, ed. Tom Taylor, 2 vols (London: Peter Davies, 1926), 1:299.

25 Qtd in Campbell, *Life of Siddons*, 2:351.

26 Qtd in ibid., 2:354.

27 Kemble's farewell address, qtd in *An Authentic Narrative of Mr. Kemble's Retirement from the Stage* (London: John Miller, 1817), 6.

28 Thomson, *ODNB* Kemble.

29 Boaden, *Memoirs of Kemble*, 2:541–2, 543.

30 Ibid., 2:549–50; Baker, *John Philip Kemble*, 318. Thomson notes that Kemble acted in Liverpool, Edinburgh, Dublin, Bath and Bristol and states that he did so in order to make money as he prepared for retirement. He had previously taken a similar absence from the London stage when he travelled to the continent in 1802–3. (*ODNB* Kemble)

31 *Monthly Museum*, November 1813, 114; Irving qtd in Manvell, *Sarah Siddons*, 305.

32 Lisa A. Freeman, 'Mourning the "Dignity of the Siddonian Form"', *Eighteenth-Century Fiction* 27, no. 3–4 (2015): 618.

33 Kemble gave 'a somewhat pathetic farewell performance' of *Othello* in Dublin in the summer of 1816, then acted in Liverpool and Bristol before going on to Edinburgh (Highfill et al., *BD*, 8:360). The address was co-written with Scott.

34 *LSC*. Like Siddons, Kemble often performed roles again after they had been advertised as acted for the last time. For a list of the parts he played in his final season and the number of times

he performed each one, see *Authentic Narrative*, 2–3. Siddons joined him for a performance of *Macbeth* on 5 June 1817.

35 Qtd in Farington, diary for 7 June 1817, 14:5031.

36 *Authentic Narrative*, 78.

37 Dobson, 'John Philip Kemble', 99; *Sun*, 24 June 1817.

38 *Times*, 25 June 1817.

39 *Bell's Weekly Messenger*, no. 1109, 29 June 1817, 1.

40 *Times*, 25 June 1817.

41 Qtd in *Authentic Narrative*, 6.

42 Boaden, *Memoirs of Kemble*, 2:561.

43 Thomson, *ODNB* Kemble. There had been a rehearsal for this dinner in Edinburgh too.

44 Qtd in *Authentic Narrative*, 55.

45 Ibid., 68.

46 Rogers, *Table-Talk*, 186–7.

47 Highfill et al., *BD*, 14:36.

48 Fitzgerald, *The Kembles*, 2:240.

49 Qtd in *Authentic Narrative*, 9.

50 The quotations are from Hazlitt's comments on Siddons's career (*Examiner*, no. 442, 16 June 1816, 378) and the ode written by Campbell and spoken by Young at Kemble's retirement dinner (qtd in *Authentic Narrative*, 59).

51 Boaden, *Memoirs of Siddons*, 2:379.

52 Ibid., 2:380. Campbell commented that Siddons gave these roles 'a charm that was absolutely marvellous in the person of an actress of fifty-six' (*Life of Siddons*, 2:336).

53 Russ McDonald, 'Sarah Siddons', in *Great Shakespeareans: Garrick, Kemble, Siddons, Kean*, ed. Peter Holland (London: Bloomsbury, 2010), 130, 131.

54 Campbell, *Life of Siddons*, 2:381.

55 *Oxberry's Dramatic Biography* 1, no. 8, 19 February 1825, 137.

56 Ibid., 2:374.

57 *Standard*, 8 October 1829.

58 *LSC*.

59 *Morning Post*, 28 April 1832.

60 *More About All About Eve: A Colloquy by Gary Carey with Joseph L. Mankiewicz Together with His Screenplay: All About Eve* (New York: Random House, 1972), 116.

61 Sarah Siddons Society website, https://sarahsiddonssociety.org/about. Originally only for actresses, the award now considers actors as well.

62 David Román, 'The Afterlife of Sarah Siddons; or, The Archives of Performance', in *Representing the Passions: Histories, Bodies, Visions*, ed. Richard Meyer (Los Angeles: Getty Research Institute, 2003), 167.

63 Ibid.

64 *Oxberry's Dramatic Biography* 1, no. 7, 12 February 1825, 122.

65 Fitzgerald, *The Kembles*, 2:314.

66 Qtd in J. G. Lockhart, *Memoirs of the Life of Sir Walter Scott, Bart.*, 7 vols (Edinburgh: Robert Cadell, 1837), 3:50.

67 *Bell's Weekly Messenger*, no. 1109, 29 June 1817, 1.

68 *Times*, 25 June 1817.

69 Boaden, *Memoirs of Kemble*, 2:584.

70 Dobson, 'John Philip Kemble', 104.

71 Baker, *John Philip Kemble*, 334.

72 Ibid., 333.

73 Qtd in ibid., 334. Unable to dispose of his one-sixth share in Covent Garden (valued at £45,000), he eventually gifted it to his brother, Charles (Highfill et al., *BD*, 8:362). But according to Fanny Kemble it became a financial liability for her father (Thomson, *ODNB* Kemble).

74 The quotation is from Campbell's ode, qtd in *Authentic Narrative*, 58.

75 See, for example, Fitzgerald, *The Kembles*, 2:378.

76 *London Magazine* 7, April 1823, 455.

77 Fitzgerald, *The Kembles*, 2:161. In fact, Fitzgerald makes a further distinction between roles that required 'classical dignity

... combined with modern ... emotion' (e.g. Euphrasia) and those that were 'purely melodramatic' (e.g. Mrs Haller).
78 Ibid.; Godwin qtd in Campbell, *Life of Siddons*, 2:109.
79 *London Magazine* 5, April 1822, 309.
80 Qtd in Fitzgerald, *The Kembles*, 2:317.
81 Farington, diary for 7 January 1817, 14:4953.
82 *Oxberry's Dramatic Biography*,1, no. 7, 12 February 1825, 120–1; Boaden, *Memoirs of Siddons*, 2:380.
83 Ibid., 2:387.
84 Scott, Review of *Memoirs of Kemble*, 216.
85 Qtd in William Charles Macready, *Reminiscences, and Selections from his Diaries and Letters*, ed. Frederick Pollock, 2 vols (London: Macmillan and Co, 1875), 1:149.
86 Qtd in Campbell, *Life of Siddons*, 2:383.
87 Ibid.
88 *Sun*, 24 June 1817.
89 Scott, Review of *Memoirs of Kemble*, 240.
90 Rogers, *Table-Talk*, 187. Siddons apparently favoured a Miss Dance, who became her pupil; indeed, Siddons 'pledged her reputation for Miss Dance's abilities' (Genest, *Some Account of the English Stage*, 9:109).
91 Boaden, *Memoirs of Siddons*, 2:378; *Morning Chronicle*, 24 June 1817.
92 *London Magazine* 7, April 1823, 459.
93 Qtd in *John Bull* 4, no. 34, 23 August 1824, 278.
94 Heather McPherson, *Art & Celebrity in the Age of Reynolds & Siddons* (University Park: Pennsylvania State University Press, 2017), 176.

BIBLIOGRAPHY

Appleton, Alexandra. 'In Search of an Identity: The Changing Fortunes of Liverpool's Theatre Royal, 1772–1855'. PhD dissertation, Royal Holloway, University of London, 2015.

Ashton, John. *The Dawn of the XIXth Century in England: A Social Sketch of the Times*. 2 vols. London: T. Fisher Unwin, 1886.

Asleson, Robyn, ed. *A Passion for Performance: Sarah Siddons and Her Portraitists*. Los Angeles: J. Paul Getty Museum, 1999.

Athenaeum: Journal of English and Foreign Literature, Science, the Fine Arts, Music and the Drama, no. 2320, 13 April 1872.

An Authentic Narrative of Mr. Kemble's Retirement from the Stage. London: John Miller, 1817.

Backscheider, Paula R. 'In Their Blood: The Eighteenth-Century Gothic Stage'. In *The Cambridge History of the Gothic. Volume 1: Gothic in the Long Eighteenth Century*, edited by Angela Wright and Dale Townshend, 198–221. Cambridge: Cambridge University Press, 2020.

Baer, Marc. *Theatre and Disorder in Late Georgian London*. Oxford: Clarendon Press, 1992.

Baker, Herschel. *John Philip Kemble: The Actor in His Theatre*. Cambridge: Harvard University Press, 1942.

Bartholomeusz, Dennis. *Macbeth and the Players*. Cambridge: Cambridge University Press, 1969.

Bate, Jonathan. 'Faking It: Shakespeare and the 1790s'. *Essays and Studies* 46 (1993): 63–80.

Bate, Jonathan. 'The Romantic Stage'. In *Shakespeare: An Illustrated Stage History*, edited by Jonathan Bate and Russell Jackson, 92–111. Oxford: Oxford University Press, 1996.

Bate, Jonathan. *Shakespearean Constitutions: Politics, Theatre, Criticism, 1730–1830*. Oxford: Clarendon Press, 1989.

Bell, G. J. 'Annotations by George Joseph Bell on Plays from Mrs. Inchbald's *British Theatre*'. (*c.* 1808). 3 vols. Folger Shakespeare Library, Washington D.C., W.a.70–72. Digitized version in Gale

Primary Sources, document numbers CYVVKW761979138, CYXASB922066573, CYSKJC614346657.

Bell, G. J. 'Mrs. Siddons as Lady Macbeth'. In *Papers Literary, Scientific, &c, by Fleeming Jenkin*, edited by Sidney Colvin and J. A. Ewing. 2 vols, 1: 45–66. London: Longmans, Green, and Co., 1887.

Bell, G. J. 'Mrs. Siddons as Queen Katharine, Mrs. Beverley, and Lady Randolph'. In *Papers Literary, Scientific, &c, by Fleeming Jenkin*, edited by Sidney Colvin and J. A. Ewing, 2 vols, 1: 67–86. London: Longmans, Green, and Co., 1887.

Bell's Weekly Messenger, no. 1109, 29 June 1817.

Boaden, James. *The Life of Mrs. Jordan; Including Original Private Correspondence, and Numerous Anecdotes of Her Contemporaries*. 2 vols. London: Edward Bull, 1831.

Boaden, James. *Memoirs of the Life of John Philip Kemble, Esq., Including a History of the Stage, from the Time of Garrick to the Present Period*. 2 vols. London: Longman, Hurst, Rees, Orme, Brown, and Green, 1825.

Boaden, James. *Memoirs of Mrs. Inchbald: Including Her Familiar Correspondence With the Most Distinguished Persons of Her Time, to Which Are Added The Massacre, and A Case of Conscience; Now First Published from Her Autograph Copies*. 2 vols. London: Richard Bentley, 1833.

Boaden, James. *Memoirs of Mrs. Siddons. Interspersed with Anecdotes of Authors and Actors*. 2 vols. London: Henry Colburn, 1827.

Boatner-Doane, Charlotte. 'Sarah Siddons and the Romantic Hamlet'. *Nineteenth Century Theatre and Film* 44, no. 2 (2017): 212–35.

Britton, J., and A. Pugin. *Illustrations of the Public Buildings of London: With Historical and Descriptive Accounts of Each Edifice*. 2 vols. London: J. Taylor, 1825.

Broadbent, R. J. *Annals of the Liverpool Stage from the Earliest Period to the Present Time, Together with Some Account of the Music Halls in Bootle and Birkenhead*. Liverpool: Edward Howell, 1908.

Burney, Frances. *The Early Journals and Letters of Fanny Burney*. General editor Lars E. Troide. 5 vols. Oxford: Clarendon Press, 1987–2012.

Burney, Frances. *The Journals and Letters of Fanny Burney (Madame d'Arblay)*. General editor Joyce Hemlow. 12 vols. Oxford: Oxford University Press, 1972–84.

Caledonian Mercury, 14 March 1812.
Caledonian Mercury, 25 November 1815.
Campbell, Thomas. *Life of Mrs. Siddons*. 2 vols. London: Effingham Wilson, 1834.
Chalmers, George. *An Apology for the Believers in the Shakspeare-Papers*. London: Thomas Egerton, 1797.
Charke, Charlotte. *A Narrative of the Life of Mrs. Charlotte Charke: (Youngest Daughter of Colley Cibber, Esq.) . . . Written by Herself*. London: W. Reeve, 1755.
'Collection of Drawings of Theatrical Scenery with some Manuscript Comments' (late-eighteenth or early-nineteenth century). Folger Shakespeare Library, Washington D.C., Art Vol. d21.
'A Collection of Playbills from Theatre Royal, Liverpool, 1773–1781'. 2 vols. British Library, London, Playbills 225.
Colman the Younger, George. Preface. *The Iron Chest*, i–xx. London: W. Woodfall, 1796.
'Correspondence of Samuel Ireland with the Managers of Drury Lane Theatre, Relating to the Production of the Play of Vortigern', 1794–8. British Library, London, Add. MS 30348.
Courier, and Evening Gazette, 10 June 1794.
Couture, Selena. 'Siddons's Ghost: Celebrity and Gender in Sheridan's *Pizarro*'. *Theatre Journal* 65, no. 2 (2013): 183–96.
Couture, Selena, and Alexander Dick. 'Introduction'. In *Pizarro: A Tragedy in Five Acts*, edited by Richard Brinsley Sheridan, 11–57. Peterborough: Broadview Press, 2017.
Crochunis, Thomas C. 'Women Theatre Managers'. In *The Oxford Handbook of the Georgian Theatre*, edited by Julia Swindells and David Francis Taylor, 569–84. Oxford: Oxford University Press, 2014.
Cruikshank, Isaac. *King John and John Bull* (1809), British Museum, London, 1865,1111.2052.
Cumberland, Richard. *Memoirs of Richard Cumberland, Written by Himself: Containing an Account of His Life and Writings, Interspersed with Anecdotes and Characters of Several of the Most Distinguished Persons of His Time, with Whom He Has Had Intercourse and Connection*. 2 vols. London: Lackington, Allen, and Co., 1807.
Dibdin, James C. *The Annals of the Edinburgh Stage with an Account of the Rise and Progress of Dramatic Writing in Scotland*. Edinburgh: Richard Cameron, 1888.

Dighton, Robert. *We Serve a King Whom We Love (John Philip Kemble as Rolla) and Hold! – Pizarro – Hear Me! (Mrs. Siddons as Elvira in Pizarro)* (1799). British Museum, London, 1848,1221.55 and 1848,1221.51.

Dobson, Michael. 'John Philip Kemble'. In *Great Shakespeareans: Garrick, Kemble, Siddons, Kean*, edited by Peter Holland, 55–104. London: Bloomsbury, 2010.

Dobson, Michael. *The Making of the National Poet: Shakespeare, Adaptation and Authorship, 1660–1769*. Oxford: Clarendon Press, 1992.

Donkin, Ellen. 'Mrs. Siddons Looks Back in Anger: Feminist Historiography for Eighteenth-Century British Theatre'. In *Critical Theory and Performance*, revised and enlarged edition, edited by Janelle G. Reinelt and Joseph R. Roach, 317–33. Ann Arbor: University of Michigan Press, 2007.

Donohue, Jr, Joseph W. 'Kemble and Mrs. Siddons in *Macbeth*: The Romantic Approach to Tragic Character'. *Theatre Notebook* 22, no. 2 (1967/8): 65–85.

The Dramatic Censor: or, Critical and Biographical Illustration of the British Stage, November 1811.

Engel, Laura. *Fashioning Celebrity: Eighteenth-Century British Actresses and Strategies for Image Making*. Columbus: Ohio State University Press, 2011.

European Magazine, and London Review 4, November 1783.

Ewbank, Inga-Stina. 'Introduction'. In *Coriolanus: J. P. Kemble, 1789*, facs. edn, n.p. London: Cornmarket Press, 1970.

Examiner, no. 21, 22 May 1808.

Examiner, no. 91, 24 September 1809.

Examiner, no. 236, 5 July 1812.

Examiner, no. 312, 19 December 1813.

Examiner, no. 325, 20 March 1814.

Examiner, no. 442, 16 June 1816.

Examiner, no. 467, 8 December 1816.

Farington, Joseph. *The Diary of Joseph Farington*. Edited by Kenneth Garlick, Angus Macintyre, Kathryn Cave and Evelyn Newby. 17 vols. New Haven: Yale University Press, 1978–98.

Feibel, Juliet. 'Vortigern, Rowena, and the Ancient Britons: Historical Art and the Anglicization of National Origin'. *Eighteenth-Century Life* 24, no. 1 (2000): 1–22.

Finlay, John. *Miscellanies: The Foreign Relations of the British Empire: The Internal Resources of Ireland: Sketches of Character: Dramatic Criticism*. Dublin: John Cumming, 1835.

Fitzgerald, Percy. *The Kembles: An Account of the Kemble Family, Including the Lives of Mrs. Siddons, and Her Brother John Philip Kemble*. 2 vols. London: Tinsley Brothers, 1871.

Fitzgerald, Percy. *The Lives of the Sheridans*. 2 vols. London: Richard Bentley and Son, 1886.

Flint, Hanna. 'Why Lady Macbeth Is Literature's Most Misunderstood Villain'. *BBC Culture*. 10 January 2022. https://www.bbc.com/culture/article/20220110-why-lady-macbeth-is-literatures-most-misunderstood-villain

Forster, Antonia. 'Seeing is Believing: External vs. Internal Evidence in the Controversy over the Ireland Forgeries'. In *Early British Drama in Manuscript*, edited by Tamara Atkin and Laura Estill, 298–9. Turnhout, Belgium: Brepols, 2019.

Freeman, Lisa A. 'Mourning the "Dignity of the Siddonian Form"'. *Eighteenth-Century Fiction* 27, no. 3–4 (2015): 597–629.

Galindo, Catherine. *Mrs. Galindo's Letter to Mrs. Siddons: Being a Circumstantial Detail of Mrs. Siddons's Life for the Last Seven Years, with Several of Her Letters*. London: Printed for the Authoress, 1809.

Gamer, Michael, and Robert Miles. 'Gothic Shakespeare on the Romantic Stage'. In *Gothic Shakespeares*, edited by John Drakakis and Dale Townshend, 131–52. Abingdon: Routledge, 2008.

Gazetteer and New Daily Advertiser, 24 November 1783.

Gazetteer and New Daily Advertiser, 3 December 1784.

Gazetteer and New Daily Advertiser, 4 April 1796.

Gazetteer and New Daily Advertiser, 18 April 1796.

General Evening Post, 9–11 December 1783.

Genest, John. *Some Account of the English Stage, from the Restoration in 1660 to 1830*. 10 vols. Bath: H. E. Carrington, 1832.

Gentleman, Francis. 'Notes'. In *Bell's Edition of Shakespeare's Plays, As They Are Performed at the Theatres Royal in London; Regulated from the Prompt Books of Each House by Permission; with Notes Critical and Illustrative; by the Authors of the Dramatic Censor*. 2nd. edn. 5 vols. London: John Bell, 1774.

Gentleman's Magazine, And Historical Chronicle 53, pt 1, April 1783.

George, David. *A Comparison of Six Adaptations of Shakespeare's Coriolanus, 1681–1962*. Lewiston: Edwin Mellen Press, 2008.

George, Mary Dorothy. *Catalogue of Political and Personal Satires Preserved in the Department of Prints and Drawings in the British Museum*. Vol. 8. London: Printed by Order of the Trustees, 1947.

Gilliland, Thomas. *Jack in Office; Containing Remarks on Mr. Braham's Address to the Public, with a Full and Impartial Consideration of Mr. Kemble's Conduct with Respect to the Above Gentleman*. London: C. Chapple, 1804.

Granville, Augustus Bozzi. *Critical Observations on Mr. Kemble's Performances at the Theatre Royal, Liverpool*. Liverpool: M. Galway, 1811.

Grebanier, Bernard. *The Great Shakespeare Forgery*. New York: Norton, 1965.

Greene, John C. *Theatre in Dublin, 1745–1820: A Calendar of Performances*. 6 vols. Lanham: Lehigh University Press, 2011.

Griffiths, Trevor. '*A Midsummer Night's Dream* and *The Tempest* on the London Stage, 1789–1914'. PhD dissertation, University of Warwick, 1974.

Groom, Nick. 'Chatterton, Thomas (1752–1770), Poet'. Oxford Dictionary of National Biography. Oxford University Press, 2004. http://www.oxforddnb.com/view/article/5189

Groom, Nick. *The Forger's Shadow: How Forgery Changed the Course of Literature*. London: Picador, 2002.

Hadley, Elaine. 'The Old Price Wars: Melodramatizing the Public Sphere in Early-Nineteenth-Century England'. *PMLA* 107, no. 3 (1992): 524–37.

Hammond, Brean. 'Shakespeare Discoveries and Forgeries'. In *Shakespeare in the Eighteenth Century*, edited by Fiona Ritchie and Peter Sabor, 78–96. Cambridge: Cambridge University Press, 2012.

Harlow, George Henry. *The Court for the Trial of Queen Katharine* (1817), Walter Morrison Collection, Sudeley Castle, Winchcombe, Gloucestershire.

Haydon, Benjamin Robert. *The Autobiography and Memoirs of Benjamin Robert Haydon (1786–1846)*. Edited by Tom Taylor. 2 vols. London: Peter Davies, 1926.

Highfill, Philip H., Jr, Kalman A. Burnim and Edward A. Langhans. *A Biographical Dictionary of Actors, Actresses, Musicians, Dancers, Managers & Other Stage Personnel in London, 1660–1800*. 16 vols. Carbondale: Southern Illinois University Press, 1973–93.

Howard, Tony. *Women As Hamlet: Performance and Interpretation in Theatre, Film and Fiction*. Cambridge: Cambridge University Press, 2007.

Inchbald, Elizabeth. 'Hamlet [Autograph Manuscript of an Essay on John Philip Kemble's Portrayal of Hamlet]'. (*c.* 1805). Huntington Library, San Marino, CA, HM 63342.

Inchbald, Elizabeth, ed. *The British Theatre; or, a Collection of Plays, Which Are Acted at the Theatres Royal, Drury Lane, Covent Garden, and Haymarket. Printed Under the Authority of the Managers from the Prompt Books. With Biographical and Critical Remarks, by Mrs. Inchbald*. 25 vols. London: Longman, Hurst, Rees and Orme, 1808.

Ireland, Samuel. 'Preface'. In *Vortigern, an Historical Tragedy, in Five Acts; Represented at the Theatre Royal, Drury Lane, on Saturday, April 2, 1796*, edited by W. H. Ireland, iii–vii. London: J. Barker, 1799.

Ireland, W. H. *An Authentic Account of the Shaksperian Manuscripts, &c*. London: J. Debrett, 1796.

Ireland, W. H. *The Confessions of William-Henry Ireland. Containing the Particulars of his Fabrication of the Shakspeare Manuscripts; Together with Anecdotes and Opinions (Hitherto Unpublished) of Many Distinguished Persons in the Literary, Political, and Theatrical World*. London: Ellerton and Byworth, 1805.

Ireland, W. H. 'A Full and Explanatory Account of the Shaksperian Forgery by Myself the Writer William Henry Ireland'. Houghton Library, Harvard University, Cambridge, MA, MS Hyde 60 (3).

Ireland, W. H. Letter to John Philip Kemble, [February 1801]. Centre for Research Collections, University of Edinburgh, H. -P. Coll. 321, fol. 17r.

Ireland, W. H. 'MS Note'. In *An Authentic Account of the Shaksperian Manuscripts, &c.*, edited by W. H. Ireland. London: J. Debrett, 1796. Harvard Theatre Collection, Houghton Library, Harvard University, Cambridge, MA, TS 680.23.5, fol. 107r.

Ireland, W. H. *Mutius Scævola; or, the Roman Patriot: An Historical Drama*. London: D. N. Shury, 1801.

Ireland, W. H. 'Preface'. In *Vortigern: An Historical Play, with an Original Preface*, edited by W. H. Ireland. Represented at the Theatre Royal, Drury Lane, on Saturday, April 2, 1796, as a Supposed Newly-Discovered Drama of Shakspeare, i–xiii. London: Joseph Thomas, 1832.

John Bull 4, no. 34, 23 August 1824.

E. Johnson's British Gazette, and Sunday Monitor, no. 1102, 14 December 1800.

Joseph, Bertram. *The Tragic Actor*. New York: Theatre Arts Books, 1959.

Kahan, Jeffrey. *Reforging Shakespeare: The Story of a Theatrical Scandal*. Bethlehem: Lehigh University Press, 1998.

Kelly, Linda. *The Kemble Era: John Philip Kemble, Sarah Siddons, and the London Stage*. London: Bodley Head, 1980.

Kelly, Michael. *Reminiscences of Michael Kelly, of the King's Theatre, and Theatre Royal Drury Lane, Including a Period of Nearly Half a Century; with Original Anecdotes of Many Distinguished Persons, Political, Literary, and Musical*. 2 vols. London: Henry Colburn, 1826.

Kemble, Frances Ann. *Record of a Girlhood*. 3 vols. London: Richard Bentley and Son, 1878.

Kemble, John Philip. Letter to W. H. Ireland, 5 February 1801. Centre for Research Collections, University of Edinburgh, H. -P. Coll. 321, fol. 17r.

Kemble, John Philip. Letter to W. H. Ireland, 14 April 1801. In 'A Full and Explanatory Account of the Shaksperian Forgery by Myself the Writer William Henry Ireland' by W. H. Ireland. Houghton Library, Harvard University, Cambridge, MA, MS Hyde 60 (3).

Kemble, John Philip. *Macbeth, and King Richard the Third: An Essay, in Answer to Remarks on Some of the Characters of Shakspeare*. London: John Murray, 1817.

Kemble, John Philip. *Macbeth Reconsidered: An Essay Intended as an Answer to Part of the Remarks on Some of the Characters of Shakspeare*. London: T. and J. Egerton, 1786.

Kemble, John Philip. 'Professional Memoranda, 1788–1815'. 4 vols. British Library, London, Add. MSS 31,972–31,975.

Lawrence, Thomas. *John Philip Kemble as Coriolanus* (1798). Guildhall Art Gallery, London, 844.

Lawrence, Thomas. *John Philip Kemble as Hamlet* (1801). Tate, London, N00142.

Lawrence, Thomas. *Sir Thomas Lawrence's Letter-Bag, With Recollections of the Artist by Miss Elizabeth Croft*. Edited by George Somes Layard. London: G. Allen, 1906.

Lewes, Charles Lee. *Memoirs of Charles Lee Lewes, Containing Anecdotes, Historical and Biographical, of the English and Scottish Stages, during a Period of 40 Years, Written by Himself*. 4 vols. London: Richard Phillips, 1805.

The Life of John Philip Kemble, Esquire, a Proprietor, and Stage Manager of Covent Garden Theatre, Interpersed with Family and Theatrical Anecdotes. London: J. Johnston, 1809.

Lloyd's Evening Post, 1–4 April 1796.

Lloyd's Evening Post, 12–15 December 1800.

Lockhart, J. G. *Memoirs of the Life of Sir Walter Scott, Bart*. 7 vols. Edinburgh: Robert Cadell, 1837.

London Magazine, Enlarged and Improved 4, February 1785.

London Magazine 5, April 1822.

London Magazine 7, April 1823.

The London Stage Calendar, 1800–1844. Part I: 1800–1832. https://londonstage.bodleian.ox.ac.uk/

London Stage Database [1660–1800]. https://londonstagedatabase.uoregon.edu/

Lynch, Jack. 'England's Ireland, Ireland's England: William Henry Ireland's National Offense'. In *Literary Forgery in Early Modern Europe, 1450–1800*, edited by Walter Stephens and Earle A. Havens, assisted by Janet E. Gomez, 255–73. Baltimore: Johns Hopkins University Press, 2018.

Lynch, Jack. 'William Henry Ireland's Authentic Forgeries'. *Princeton University Library Chronicle* 66, no. 1 (2004): 79–96.

Macready, William Charles. *Macready's Reminiscences, and Selections from his Diaries and Letters*. Edited by Frederick Pollock. 2 vols. London: Macmillan and Co., 1875.

Mair, John. *The Fourth Forger: William Ireland and the Shakespeare Papers*. London: Cobden-Sanderson, 1938.

Manchester Mercury and Harrop's General Advertiser, 4 February 1777.

Manchester Mercury and Harrop's General Advertiser, 18 March 1777.

Manchester Mercury and Harrop's General Advertiser, 10 March 1778.

Mander, Raymond, and Joe Mitchenson. *Hamlet Through the Ages: A Pictorial Record from 1709*. London: Rockliff, 1952.

Manvell, Roger. *Sarah Siddons: Portrait of an Actress*. London: William Heinemann Ltd, 1970.

Marsden, Jean I. *Theatres of Feeling: Affect, Performance, and the Eighteenth-Century Stage*. Cambridge: Cambridge University Press, 2019.

Marsh, Charles. *The Clubs of London, with Anecdotes of their Members, Sketches of Character, and Conversations*. 2 vols. London: Henry Colburn, 1828.

Martin, Harriet. *Remarks on Mr. John Kemble's Performance of Hamlet and Richard the Third*. London: G. and J. Robinson, 1802.

Martin, Robert Bernard. 'Kemble [*married name* Butler], Frances Anne [Fanny] (1809–1893), actress and author'. In *Oxford Dictionary of National Biography*. Oxford University Press, 2004. http://www.oxforddnb.com/view/article/15318

McDonald, Russ. 'Sarah Siddons'. In *Great Shakespeareans: Garrick, Kemble, Siddons, Kean*, edited by Peter Holland, 105–37. London: Bloomsbury, 2010.

McEvoy, Sean. *Theatrical Unrest: Ten Riots in the History of the Stage, 1601–2004*. Abingdon: Routledge, 2016.

McGirr, Elaine. 'New Lines: Mary Ann Yates, *The Orphan of China*, and the New She-Tragedy'. *ABO: Interactive Journal for Women in the Arts, 1640–1830* 8, no. 2 (2018): https://scholarcommons.usf.edu/abo/vol8/iss2/1.

McPherson, Heather. *Art & Celebrity in the Age of Reynolds & Siddons*. University Park: Pennsylvania State University Press, 2017.

'M. H.' Letter to Samuel Ireland, 25 July 1795. British Library, London, Add. MS 30346, fols. 54r.-55r.

Moody, Jane. 'Romantic Shakespeare'. In *The Cambridge Companion to Shakespeare on Stage*, edited by Stanley Wells and Sarah Stanton, 37–57. Cambridge: Cambridge University Press, 2002.

Moore, Thomas. *Memoirs of the Life of the Right Honourable Richard Brinsley Sheridan*, 3rd edition. 2 vols. London: Longman, Hurst, Rees, Orme, Brown and Green, 1825.

Monthly Mirror: Reflecting Men and Manners: With Strictures on Their Epitome, the Stage, 10, December 1800.

Monthly Mirror: Reflecting Men and Manners: With Strictures on Their Epitome, the Stage 22, November 1806.

Monthly Museum; or, Dublin Literary Repertory, November 1813.
More About All About Eve: A Colloquy by Gary Carey with Joseph L. Mankiewicz, Together with His Screenplay All About Eve. New York: Random House, 1972.
Morning Advertiser, 23 March 1795.
Morning Chronicle, 21 January 1804.
Morning Chronicle, 22 September 1808.
Morning Chronicle, 24 June 1817.
Morning Chronicle, and London Advertiser, 23 January 1783.
Morning Chronicle, and London Advertiser, 1 October 1783.
Morning Chronicle, and London Advertiser, 8 March 1784.
Morning Chronicle, and London Advertiser, 13 April 1784.
Morning Chronicle, and London Advertiser, 28 January 1785.
Morning Chronicle, and London Advertiser, 19 September 1785.
Morning Chronicle, and London Advertiser, 19 November 1785.
Morning Chronicle, and London Advertiser, 24 November 1785
Morning Chronicle, and London Advertiser, 8 April 1786.
Morning Chronicle, and London Advertiser, 1 February 1787.
Morning Chronicle, and London Advertiser, 27 November 1788.
Morning Herald, 16 April 1787.
Morning Herald, 23 March 1795
Morning Herald, and Daily Advertiser, 31 March 1783.
Morning Herald, and Daily Advertiser, 21 October 1783.
Morning Herald, and Daily Advertiser, 11 December 1783.
Morning Post, 16 May 1816.
Morning Post, 23 April 1817.
Morning Post, 28 April 1832.
Morning Post, and Daily Advertiser, 16 December 1782.
Morning Post, and Daily Advertiser, 9 March 1785.
Morning Post, and Daily Advertiser, 26 November 1788.
Muse, Amy. 'Actresses and the Making of the Modern Hamlet'. In *Text and Presentation, 2007*, edited by Stratos E. Constantinidis, The Comparative Drama Conference Series 4, 137–42. Jefferson: McFarland & Company, Inc., 2007.
New Monthly Magazine and Literary Journal 16, pt 1, 1826.
New Monthly Magazine and Literary Journal 32, pt 2, 1831.
New Spectator, with the Sage Opinions of John Bull, no. 13, 27 April 1784.
Nixon, John. *The Oaken Chest or the Gold Mines of Ireland a Farce* (1796). British Museum, London, K,64.72.

Nixon, T. Letter to ? [March] 1796. In 'Collections on the Ireland Forgeries of the Play *Vortigern*'. Shakespeare Birthplace Trust Collections, Stratford-upon-Avon, ER1/114/3, fol. 55.

Observer, 22 March 1795.

Observer, 3 April 1796.

Odell, George C. D. *Shakespeare from Betterton to Irving*. 2 vols. New York: Dover Publications, 1966.

O'Quinn, Daniel. 'Insurgent Allegories: Staging *Venice Preserv'd, The Rivals*, and *Speculation* in 1795'. Literature Compass 1, no. 1 (2004): 1–31. https://doi-org.proxy3.library.mcgill.ca/10.1111/j.1741-4113.2004.00088.x

Oracle, 17 November 1794.

Oracle, and Public Advertiser, 23 March 1795.

Oracle, and Public Advertiser, 18 February 1796.

Oracle, and Public Advertiser, 14 March 1796.

Oracle, and Public Advertiser, 28 March 1796.

Oracle, and Public Advertiser, 4 October 1796.

Oxberry's Dramatic Biography, and Histrionic Anecdotes 1, no. 7, 12 February 1825.

Oxberry's Dramatic Biography, and Histrionic Anecdotes 1, no. 8, 19 February 1825.

Oya, Reiko. *Representing Shakespearean Tragedy: Garrick, the Kembles, and Kean*. Cambridge: Cambridge University Press, 2007.

Pascoe, Judith. *The Sarah Siddons Audio Files: Romanticism and the Lost Voice*. Ann Arbor: University of Michigan Press, 2013.

Payne, John Howard, and Gabriel Harrison. *The Life and Writings of John Howard Payne, the Author of Home, Sweet Home; The Tragedy of Brutus; and Other Dramatic Works*. Albany: Joel Munsell, 1875.

Phillips, Chelsea. *Carrying All Before Her: Celebrity Pregnancy and the London Stage, 1689–1800*. Newark: University of Delaware Press, 2022.

Pierce, Patricia. *The Great Shakespeare Fraud: The Strange, True Story of William-Henry Ireland*. Stroud: Sutton Publishing, 2014.

Piozzi, Hester Lynch Thrale. *Autobiography, Letters, and Literary Remains of Mrs. Piozzi (Thrale)*. Edited by A. Hayward. 2 vols. London: Longman, Green, Longman and Roberts, 1861.

Price, F. W. 'Ann Radcliffe, Mrs. Siddons and the Character of Hamlet'. *Notes & Queries* 23, no. 4 (1976): 164–7.

Public Advertiser, 7 October 1783.
Public Advertiser, 15 December 1783.
Public Advertiser, 27 January 1785.
Public Advertiser, 22 October 1785.
Public Advertiser, 14 February 1786.
Public Advertiser, 17 May 1786.
Public Advertiser, 29 November 1788.
Rainey, Robert. 'Journal Kept in Dublin'. Vol. 6. Royal Irish Academy, Dublin, MS 24 K 15.
Reynolds, Joshua. *Sarah Siddons as the Tragic Muse* (1783–84). Huntington Library, Art Museum and Botanical Gardens, San Marino, CA, 21.2.
Ripley, John. *Coriolanus on Stage in England and America, 1609–1994*. Madison: Fairleigh Dickinson University Press, 1998.
Ripley, John. 'Kemble's *Coriolanus* and the Folger Painting: A Second Look'. *Theatre Notebook* 49, no. 3 (1995): 173–6.
Ritchie, Fiona. *Women and Shakespeare in the Eighteenth Century*. New York: Cambridge University Press, 2014.
Roach, Joseph. *It*. Ann Arbor: University of Michigan Press, 2007.
Robinson, Henry Crabb. *Diary, Reminiscences, and Correspondence of Henry Crabb Robinson, Barrister-at-Law, F. S. A.* Selected and edited by Thomas Sadler. 3 vols. London: Macmillan and Co., 1869.
Robinson, Terry F. 'National Theatre in Transition: The London Patent Theatre Fires of 1808–1809 and the Old Price Riots'. In *BRANCH: Britain, Representation and Nineteenth-Century History*, edited by Dino Franco Felluga. March 2016. https://www.branchcollective.org/?ps_articles=terry-f-robinson-national-theatre-in-%09transition-the-london-patent-theatre-fires-of-1808-1809-and-the-old-price-riots
Robson, William. *The Old Play-Goer*. London: Joseph Masters, 1846.
Rogers, Samuel. *Recollections of the Table-Talk of Samuel Rogers, to Which Is Added Porsoniana*. London: Edward Moxon, 1856.
Román, David. 'The Afterlife of Sarah Siddons; or, The Archives of Performance'. In *Representing the Passions: Histories, Bodies, Visions*, edited by Richard Meyer, 163–74. Los Angeles: Getty Research Institute, 2003.
Rosenthal, Laura J. 'The Sublime, The Beautiful, "The Siddons"'. In *The Clothes That Wear Us: Essays on Dressing and Transgressing*

in Eighteenth-Century Culture, edited by Jessica Munns and Penny Richards, 56–79. Newark: University of Delaware Press, 1999.

Rostron, David. 'Contemporary Political Comment in Four of J. P. Kemble's Shakespearean Productions'. *Theatre Research = Recherches théâtrales* 12 (1972): 113–19.

Rostron, David. 'John Philip Kemble's *Coriolanus* and *Julius Caesar*: An Examination of the Prompt Copies'. *Theatre Notebook* 23, no. 1 (1968): 26–35.

Rostron, David. 'John Philip Kemble's *King Lear* of 1795'. In *Essays on the Eighteenth-Century English Stage*, edited by Kenneth Richards and Peter Thomson, 149–70. London: Methuen, 1972.

Russell, Gillian. 'Killing Mrs. Siddons: The Actress and the Adulteress in Late Georgian Britain'. *Studies in Romanticism* 51, no. 3 (2012): 419–48.

Russell, Gillian. 'Playing at Revolution: The Politics of the O. P. Riots of 1809'. *Theatre Notebook* 44, no. 1 (1990): 16–25.

Sachs, Jonathan. *Romantic Antiquity: Rome in the British Imagination, 1789–1832*. Oxford: Oxford University Press, 2009.

Sale-Room 14, 5 April 1817.

Sarah Siddons Society website. https://sarahsiddonssociety.org/about

Scott, Walter. Review of *Memoirs of the Life of John Philip Kemble* by James Boaden and *Reminiscences of Michael Kelly*. *Quarterly Review* 34, June 1826, 196–248.

'Seventh Anniversary of the Shakespeare Club, November 30, 1825', in *Proceedings of the Sheffield Shakespeare Club, from its Commencement, in 1819, to January 1829. By a Member of the Club*, 71–89. Sheffield: Printed for the Editor by H. and G. Crookes, 1829.

Shattuck, Charles H. *John Philip Kemble Promptbooks*, 11 vols. Charlottesville: University of Virginia Press for the Folger Shakespeare Library, 1974.

Shaughnessy, Robert. 'Siddons [*née* Kemble], Sarah (1755–1831), actress'. In *Oxford Dictionary of National Biography*. Oxford University Press, 2004. http://www.oxforddnb.com/view/article/25516

Sheridan, Thomas. *Coriolanus: or, the Roman Matron*. London: A. Millar, 1755.

A Short Criticism on the Performance of Hamlet by Mr. Kemble. London: T. Hookham, 1789.

Siddons, J. H. 'Random Recollections of a Life'. *Harper's New Monthly Magazine* 26, December 1862, 71–80.

Siddons, Sarah. Letter to Harriet Siddons, [25 October 1809]. Folger Shakespeare Library, Washington D.C., Y.c.432 (14).

Siddons, Sarah. Letter to Lady Perceval, after 20 September 1808. Philbrick Library Collection of Theater Letters, Honnold Mudd Library, Special Collections, Claremont Colleges, CA, phl00210. https://ccdl.claremont.edu/digital/collection/phl/id/1319/rec/16

Siddons, Sarah. 'Remarks on the Character of Lady Macbeth'. In *Life of Mrs. Siddons*, edited by Thomas Campbell, 2 vols, 2: 10–39. London: Effingham Wilson, 1834.

Sprague, Arthur Colby. *Shakespeare and the Actors: The Stage Business in His Plays (1660–1905)*. Cambridge: Harvard University Press, 1948.

Standard, 8 October 1829.

Star, 14 March 1796.

Star, 4 October 1796.

Star, 1 May 1800.

Stockdale, J. J. *The Covent Garden Journal*. London: J. J. Stockdale, 1810.

Stocqueler, J. H. *Memoirs of a Journalist*. Bombay and London: Offices of the Times of India, 1873.

Sun, 30 April 1800.

Sun, 23 April 1817.

Sun, 24 June 1817.

Tatler: A Daily Paper of Literature, Fine Arts, Music, and the Stage 3, no. 370, 9 November 1831.

Taylor, David Francis. *Theatres of Opposition: Empire, Revolution, and Richard Brinsley Sheridan*. Oxford: Oxford University Press, 2012.

Taylor, Miles. 'Bull, John (supp. fl. 1712–), fictitious epitomist of Englishness and British imperialism'. In *Oxford Dictionary of National Biography*. Oxford University Press, 2004. http://www.oxforddnb.com/view/article/68195

Tegg, Thomas. *The Rise, Progress, and Termination of the O. P. War, in Poetic Epistles*. London: Thomas Tegg, 1810.

Theatrical Recorder 2, no. 11, 1805.

Theatrical Recorder 2, no. 12, 1805.

Thomson, Peter. 'Kemble, John Philip (1757–1823), actor'. *Oxford Dictionary of National Biography*. Oxford University Press, 2004. http://www.oxforddnb.com/view/article/15322

Times, 9 January 1789.
Times, 4 April 1796.
Times, 30 April 1800.
Times, 15 October 1810.
Times, 19 September 1811.
Times, 1 June 1816.
Times, 25 June 1817.
True Briton, 14 March 1796.
Town and Country Magazine; or Universal Repository of Knowledge, Instruction and Entertainment 16, October 1784.
Universal Magazine. New Series. Containing Original Communications in History, Philosophy, the Belles Lettres, Politics, Amusements, &c, &c 9, no. 54, May 1808.
Van Dijk, Maarten. 'John Philip Kemble as King John: Two Scenes'. *Theatre Notebook* 29, no. 1 (1975): 22–32.
Walford Davies, Damian. 'Models of Betrayal and Flight: Vortigern'. In *Presences that Disturb: Models of Romantic Identity in the Literature and Culture of the 1790s*, 55–94. Cardiff: University of Wales Press, 2002.
Walford Davies, Damian. 'The Politics of Allusion: *Caleb Williams*, *The Iron Chest*, *Middlemarch*, and the *Armoire De Fer*'. *Review of English Studies* new ser. 53, no. 212 (2002): 526–43.
Wallis, Henry. *Chatterton* (1856). Tate, London, N01685.
West, Shearer. 'Siddons, Celebrity and Regality: Portraiture and the Body of the Aging Actress'. In *Theatre and Celebrity in Britain, 1660–2000*, edited by Mary Luckhurst and Jane Moody, 191–213. New York: Palgrave Macmillan, 2005.
Whitehall Evening Post, 12–15 March 1796.
Williams, John Ambrose. *Memoirs of John Philip Kemble Esqr. With an Original Critique of his Performance*. London: T. Holt, 1823.
Windham, William. *The Diary of the Right Hon. William Windham, 1784 to 1810*. Edited by Henry Baring. London: Longmans, Green, and Co., 1866.
Woo, Celestine. 'Sarah Siddons as Hamlet: Three Decades, Five Towns, Absent Breeches, and Rife Critical Confusion'. *ANQ: A Quarterly Journal of Short Articles, Notes and Reviews* 20, no. 1 (2007): 37–44.
Woo, Celestine. 'Sarah Siddons's Performances as Hamlet: Breaching the Breeches Part'. *European Romantic Review* 18, no. 5 (2007): 573–95.

World, 15 March 1788.
World, 7 May 1788.
World, 26 November 1788.
World, 9 February 1789.
World, 22 April 1794.
Worrall, David. *The Politics of Romantic Theatricality, 1787–1832: The Road to the Stage.* Basingstoke: Palgrave Macmillan, 2007.
Worrall, David. *Theatric Revolution: Drama, Censorship, and Romantic Period Subcultures 1773–1832.* Oxford: Oxford University Press, 2006.
Young, Alan R. *Hamlet and the Visual Arts, 1709–1900.* Newark: University of Delaware Press, 2002.
Young, Julian Charles. *A Memoir of Charles Mayne Young, Tragedian, with Extracts from His Son's Journal.* 2 vols. London and New York: Macmillan and Co., 1871.

INDEX

Abington, Frances 7
Addision, Joseph 14
Adelaide (Pye) 172
afterpiece 7, 35, 68, 115, 207 n.8
Aickin, James 43
Alexander the Great (N. Lee) 170
All About Eve 157
All For Love (Dryden) 35, 168. *See also Antony and Cleopatra*
All in the Wrong (Murphy) 168
Almeyda (S. Lee) 171
androgyny 134. *See also* breeches roles; cross-dressing
anti-Semitism 114
Antonio (Godwin) 46–7, 172
Antony and Cleopatra (Shakespeare) 35. *See also All For Love*
Argyll Rooms 146
As You Like It (Shakespeare) 36–7, 80, 167, 184 n.5
audience 11, 14, 17, 38, 63, 70, 85, 87, 88, 92, 102, 103, 114
  addressed by Kemble 81, 109, 111, 152
  addressed by Siddons 8, 19, 26, 156
  behaviour of 101, 117
  in London 7, 12, 28
  and OP Riots 102–4, 106, 111, 116, 123, 202 n.38
  hostile response 106, 107, 109, 113, 115
  and politics 63, 64
  in provinces 5, 125, 129
  response to Kemble 26, 27, 39, 43, 54, 123, 137, 153
  response to Siddons 8–10, 36, 51, 52, 55, 60, 70, 107
    final performance 148, 149
    as Hamlet 127, 128, 131, 141, 146
    maternity 26, 205 n.90
    post-retirement 150, 152
  response to Siddons and Kemble 12–13, 101, 117, 140
    acting together 30, 31, 40, 44, 46, 47
    as Hamlet 127, 132, 140, 144, 145
  taste of 6, 7, 15, 26, 32
    emotion 6, 9, 10, 21, 27, 55, 63, 118
    novelty 16, 28, 43, 127
    spectacle 68, 96
  and *Vortigern* 75, 77, 78, 81, 82, 84, 88, 97

Aurelio and Miranda
(Boaden) 172
Authentic Narrative of Mr. Kemble's Retirement from the Stage, An 153, 154

Baer, Marc 111
Baillie, Joanna 46, 86, 172
Baker, Herschel 51, 159
bardolatry 78, 79, 85
Barry, William 126
Barrymore, William 86
Bartholomeusz, Dennis 118
Bate, Henry 12, 212 n.96
 evaluates Siddons for Garrick in the provinces 5, 36, 125, 129, 134, 208 n.20
Bate, Jonathan 63, 115
Bath 208 n.16
 Kemble acts at 65, 211 n.72, 214 n.30
 Siddons's early career at 8, 17, 21, 37, 92, 117, 127, 129, 145
Baxter, Anne 157
Beach, Thomas 121
Beggar's Opera, The (Gay) 103, 107
Bell, G. J. 53, 119–22, 146, 206 n.106
Bell's Weekly Messenger 158
benefit performances 19, 21, 130, 148
 earnings from 16, 31, 38, 46, 67, 107, 127, 129, 144
 Siddons
  of Hamlet 126–9
  retirement and after 55–6, 149–50, 186 n.48
 Siddons and Kemble 16–17, 20, 31, 34, 35, 37, 38, 43, 46, 144
Bensley, Robert 52, 53
Berington, Joseph 170
Betty, William Henry West 100–1
Blue Beard (Colman the Younger) 152
Boaden, James
 as biographer 22
 as dramatist 172
 on Kemble's stage persona 158–9
 on Siddons and Kemble
  acting together 29, 44, 47, 117
  contrast between them as actors 160–1
  Siddons's support of Kemble's career 12, 160
  stage relationship 39–40
 on Siddons's acting style 6, 60
Boatner-Doane, Charlotte 131, 140, 141
Braganza (Jephson) 167, 182 n.103
Brandon, James 105, 116, 204 n.80
breeches roles 36, 80, 132, 134. *See also* cross-dressing
Brereton, William 13, 19, 42
Bristol
 Kemble acts at 65, 211 n.72, 214 n.30, 214 n.33
 Siddons's early career at 8, 127–9

British Theatre, The
    (Inchbald) 136
Brunton, Louisa 162
Bull, John 111, 114
Burney, Frances 8, 92, 170,
    199 n.4
Butcher, Mrs (great-
    grandmother of Siddons
    and Kemble) 4
Butcher, Stephen (great-
    grandfather of Siddons
    and Kemble) 4
Byron, George Gordon,
    Lord 149

Caledonian Mercury 55, 56
Cambridge 151
Campbell, Thomas
  as biographer 22
  on Siddons and Kemble 15,
    31
  on Siddons's acting
    methods 21–2, 156
  Siddons's recollections printed
    by 6, 117
Cardenio (Shakespeare). *See
    Double Falsehood*
caricature 90, 108, 110, 113,
    114, 131
Carmelite, The
    (Cumberland) 38–41,
    45, 166
Castle of Montval, The
    (Whalley) 172
Catalani, Angelica 103, 107,
    111, 114
Catharine and Petruchio
    (Garrick, Kemble) 35,
    168. *See also Taming of
    the Shrew, The*

Cato (Addison) 14, 163
Chalmers, George 79, 98
Chamberlain. *See* Crump and
    Chamberlain
Charke, Charlotte 130
Charlotte, Princess 149, 150
Charlotte, Queen 10
Chavalliaud, Leon 157
Cheltenham 6
  Siddons's early career at 4,
    5, 10, 36, 125, 204 n.84
Cibber, Colley 157
Cibber, Susanna 24
circuits, theatrical 4, 8, 12,
    127, 209 n.29
Clarence, Duke of 85
Cleone (Dodsley) 167
Coen, Joel 1
Colman, George, the
    Elder 170
Colman, George, the
    Younger 87–91, 93,
    152
command performances 21,
    29, 149
Congreve, William 10, 91,
    160, 169
Conspiracy, The
    (Jephson) 171
Conway, William
    Augustus 65,
    190 n.104
Cooke, George Frederick
  in *Othello* 30, 101
  takes over Kemble's
    roles 34, 42, 43,
    203 n.68
Coriolanus (Shakespeare) 14,
    30, 50, 54, 162, 169
  and Kemble

acting 60, 62–3
  farewell performance 59, 125, 153–4, 161
  productions 58–66, 70, 72, 96, 101, 152
  OP Riots 111, 112
  Siddons as Volumnia 56, 58–62, 65, 160
Corneille, Pierre 45, 170
costume 13, 41
  Kemble 154, 213 n.13
  in Kemble's productions 1, 22, 50, 100, 154–5
  Coriolanus 58, 60, 62, 64
  Macbeth 68, 70, 190–1 n.118
  Pizarro 70, 72
  Siddons 36, 37, 133–5
  Siddons and Kemble, for Hamlet 142–4
  Vortigern 75, 86, 94
Countess of Salisbury, The (Hartson) 16–17, 166
Count of Narbonne, The (Jephson) 40, 167, 182 n.103, 211 n.71
Courier 68
Couture, Selena 70, 191 n.124
Covent Garden Journal, The 104
Covent Garden theatre (London) 5, 28, 77, 91, 95, 155–7
  destroyed by fire, rebuilt and reopened 72, 101, 102, 106, 108, 152
  changes made to new theatre 102–3, 112, 115
  Kemble

  actor 34, 73, 106, 152, 162
  proprietor and manager 71, 94, 97, 99, 100, 216 n.73
  Shakespeare productions 22, 30, 53, 61, 101, 180 n.41
  OP Riots 97, 104, 105, 111, 114, 115, 123
  rival actors perform at 9, 13, 21, 52, 65
  Siddons's career at 73, 84, 100, 148, 149, 186 n.48, 202 n.48
Cowley, Hannah 8, 168
Crawford, Ann Barry 16
Critical Observations on Mr. Kemble's Performances at the Theatre Royal, Liverpool 136
cross-dressing 36–8, 134. *See also* breeches roles
Crouch, Anna Maria 68, 69
crowd scenes 1, 58, 60, 64, 96, 100, 188 n.76
Crown and Anchor tavern (London) 105
Crow Street theatre (Dublin) 130
Cruikshank, Isaac 110, 111, 114
Crump and Chamberlain 4
Cumberland, Richard 39, 166, 182 n.96
Cymbeline (Shakespeare) 37–8, 73, 134, 167, 200 n.13

Dance, Miss 217 n.90
d'Arblay, Frances. *See* Burney, Frances

Davis, Bette 157
De Camp, Maria Theresa (Mrs Charles Kemble) 93–4, 108, 198 n.81, 198 n.84
De Montfort (Baillie) 46, 47, 172
Dick, Alexander 191 n.124
Digges, West 19
Dighton, Robert 72, 191 n.134
Dignum, Charles 85, 144
Distressed Mother, The (Philips) 167
Dobson, Michael 80, 93, 123, 139, 153, 159
Dodsley, Robert 167
Donkin, Ellen 19
Donohue, Joseph W., Jr 118, 122
Double Falsehood 91–2
Douglas (Home) 16, 39, 149, 169, 173
Dover 139
Drury Lane theatre (London) 5, 25, 43, 87, 152, 162
  Kemble's career at 34, 73, 93, 130, 139
    debut season (1783) 11–14, 125, 210 n.51
    manager 49, 72, 81, 94, 95, 99, 100
    focus on Shakespeare 22, 97
  rebuilt and enlarged 67, 68
  Siddons and Kemble act together at 17, 20, 28–30
  Siddons's career at 67, 73, 149
    first engagement (1775) 5–7, 34, 36, 126, 208 n.11
    re-engaged (1782) 8–11
    Vortigern staged at 77, 78, 83, 86, 89
Dryden, John 35, 168
Dublin 131, 152
  Kemble acts at 65, 214 n.30, 214 n.33
  early career at 12, 14, 15, 17, 21, 40, 130
  Hamlet 139, 211 n.72
  Siddons acts at 19, 150
  Hamlet 129, 130, 142, 144
East India Company 70
Edgeworth, Maria 151
Edinburgh
  Kemble acts at 65, 185 n.36, 214 n.30
  farewell performances 54, 152, 154, 215 n.43
  Hamlet 139, 211 n.72
  Siddons acts at 51, 55, 203 n.51
  post-retirement performances 56, 149, 150
Edward and Eleanora (Thomson) 171
Edward the Black Prince (Shirley) 13
Edwy and Elgiva (Burney) 92, 170
Elias, Samuel 103, 114
Emilia Galotti (Lessing, Berington) 170
Examiner 58

Fair Penitent, The (Rowe) 9, 11, 156, 157, 168, 170

INDEX

Farington, Joseph   81, 85, 107, 148–9, 160
Farquhar, George   130
Farren, Elizabeth   126
Farren, William   28
Fatal Curiosity (Lillo)   171
Fate of Sparta, The (Cowley)   168
Faucit, Harriet   65, 162
Fitzgerald, Percy   107, 176 n.38
  on Kemble   42, 88, 99, 158
  on Siddons   56–7, 216–17 n.77
Flint, Hanna   1
Folger Shakespeare Library   189 n.89
Forster, Antonia   79
Freeman, Lisa A.   152
Freeman, Mrs (Anna Maria de Burgh Coppinger)   90
Freemasons' tavern   154
French Revolution   63, 79, 87, 109, 118, 199 n.100
Furnival, Elizabeth 'Fanny'   130

Galindo, Catherine   131
Galindo, Philemon   130–1
Gamester, The (Moore)   15–16, 19, 150, 157, 162, 165
Garrick, David   10, 78
  as actor   8, 14, 16
    Hamlet   128, 132, 135, 136, 210 n.51
  as dramatist   7, 8, 31, 35, 115, 167, 168
  as manager   5, 6
    sends Bate to observe Siddons   5, 36, 125, 208 n.20

Garrick Club   189 n.89, 207 n.121
General Evening Post   21
Genest, John   65, 127, 165
Gentleman, Francis   50
Gentleman's Magazine   15, 139
George, David   65
George III, King   10, 21, 34, 67, 114, 115
Gilliland, Thomas   84
Gillray, James   108
Godwin, William   10, 35, 46–7, 87, 172
Gothic   68, 86–7, 93
Greatheed, Bertie   168
Grebanier, Bernard   81, 96
Grecian Daughter, The (Murphy)   9, 11, 157, 160, 167, 171
Greenwood, Thomas   73, 204 n.79
Groom, Nick   85

Hamilton, Mary Sackville   133, 134, 142, 143
Hamilton, William   10, 37
Hamlet (Shakespeare)   14, 15, 20, 24, 100, 147, 162, 167, 171, 184 n.5
  comparisons of Siddons and Kemble as   140–4
  Kemble acts   13, 106, 116, 125, 130, 210 n.51
    commentary   136–8
    costume   143
    innovations   13, 135–6, 138
    as Laertes   126, 144

in the provinces 138–40
Siddons acts 38, 123, 151
  costume 133–5
  at Dublin 129–33
  in early career 125–9
  as Gertrude 145
  as Ophelia 144–5
  readings of 146
  significance 128–9
  women act 130, 212 n.104
Hammond, Brean 91
Handel, Georg Friedrich 153
Harlow, George Henry 57, 66
Harris, Henry 100
Harris, Thomas 77, 95, 99, 100, 105
Hartson, Hall 16, 166
Hastings, Warren 70
Haydon, Benjamin 151
Haymarket theatre (London) 5, 101
Hazlitt, William
  on Kemble 26, 57, 141, 147, 153, 158, 162
  on Siddons 146, 150
Henderson, John 13, 14, 21
Henry II (Ireland) 95
Henry VIII (Shakespeare) 58, 66, 101, 112
  Kemble's acting 52–5, 160
  Siddons and Kemble act together 53–4, 57, 112, 169
  Siddons as Queen Katharine 51–2, 55–7, 63, 151
  spectacle in Kemble's production 50–1, 57
history plays 2, 77, 92, 95
Hoare, Prince 171

Holcroft, Thomas 101, 145
Holinshed, Raphael 77
Holland, Lord 154–5
Home, John 16, 39, 169, 173
Howard, Tony 130, 134
Hull 117

Inchbald, Elizabeth 99, 109, 126
  as critic 25, 27, 64, 136–8
Inchbald, Joseph 126
Inquiry into the Authenticity of Certain Miscellaneous Papers and Legal Instruments, An (Malone) 78, 82, 96
Ireland (country) 12, 19, 129, 132, 152
Ireland, Anna Maria 90
Ireland, Jane 90
Ireland, Samuel
  as antiquarian 76, 78, 90
  and Siddons 82–4
  and *Vortigern* 77, 78, 86, 89, 90, 94, 95
Ireland, William Henry 85, 95–6
  criticism of Siddons and Kemble 81, 83
  and Shakespeare Papers 76–7, 79, 90
  and *Vortigern* 77, 79–80, 86, 88, 89, 97, 193 n.6
Ireland family 75, 77, 78, 90–1
Iron Chest, The (Colman the Younger) 86–94
Irving, Henry 158
Irving, Washington 152
Isabella (Southerne, Garrick) 9, 12, 168

and Henry Siddons 10, 179 n.33
performed by other actresses 157, 162
in Siddons's repertoire 8, 11, 129, 156
Is This a Rattle Which I See Before Me? (Cruikshank) 110

Jane Shore (Rowe) 35, 156, 160, 168, 173
Siddons and Kemble act in 42–5
in Siddons's early career 9, 11, 129
Jealous Wife, The (Colman the Elder) 170
Jephson, Robert 40, 167–9, 171, 182 n.103
Jordan, Dorothy 36, 181 n.86, 212 n.104
and *Vortigern* 80, 84–5, 194 n.23
Jubilee (event) 7, 78
Jubilee, The (Garrick) 7, 115, 167
Jubilee, The (in honour of George III) 115
Julia (Hoare) 171
Julia (Jephson) 40, 168
Julian and Agnes (Sotheby) 172

Kahan, Jeffrey 193 n.7
Kean, Charles 159
Kean, Edmund 30, 151, 152, 162
Kelly, Michael 68, 69
Kemble, Charles (brother of Siddons and Kemble) 30, 42, 53, 57, 149, 216 n.73
marriage and children 93, 117, 147
and OP Riots 107–9, 113
Kemble, Elizabeth (sister of Siddons and Kemble) 34
Kemble, Fanny (niece of Siddons and Kemble) 117, 147, 156–7, 216 n.73
Kemble, Frances (Fanny) (sister of Siddons and Kemble) 2, 43, 127, 208 n.16
Kemble, John Philip
as actor (*see* individual play titles)
acting style 12, 33, 35, 63, 86, 136, 158–60, 162
preparation for roles 15, 22, 24, 27, 30, 40, 41, 60, 135, 158
provincial performances 2–5, 12, 17, 20–1, 28, 34, 50, 125, 152
repertoire 12, 31, 34, 45, 112, 116, 139, 162
list of early roles 12, 20, 37, 41
and antiquity 60, 64, 85
and audience 12, 43, 64, 68, 81, 82, 87–8, 101, 152, 153
during OP Riots 102–3, 105, 107, 109, 111, 116, 123
death 162–3
early life 2–5, 126

family
  marriage 198 n.86
  parents and siblings 2–4
finances 16, 17, 59, 73,
    99, 107, 108, 127,
    144, 152, 184 n.1,
    190 n.114, 216 n.73
health 33, 87–8, 156, 161
as manager
  at Covent Garden 71, 94,
    97, 99, 100, 216 n.73
  as 'director' 1–2, 101, 159
  at Drury Lane 49, 67, 72,
    81, 94, 95, 99, 100
  importance of
    Shakespeare 49, 50,
    72, 79, 94, 97, 100,
    101, 154, 159
politics 64, 72, 87
retirement 147, 153–6
rivals 13, 19–21, 43, 161–2
and Shakespeare 2, 3, 14,
    75, 79, 81, 86, 98, 102,
    110, 112–13, 115, 155
and Siddons
  acting together 2–4, 5, 12,
    15–17, 20, 27–8, 29,
    30, 31, 42, 44–5, 57,
    66, 71, 110, 112, 144,
    153–4, 165–73 (see
    also individual play
    titles)
  roles created for 38, 40,
    46, 75, 80–1
  as siblings 45–7
  compared to 12, 14, 15,
    31, 45, 140–4, 146,
    151, 155, 160–1, 164
  resemblance to 12–13, 140
visual representations
  caricatures 108, 110–11,
    113, 114
  paintings 57, 65–6, 70–2,
    121, 142
  statues 163–4
Kemble, Mrs Charles. *See* De
    Camp, Maria Theresa
    (sister-in-law of Siddons
    and Kemble)
Kemble, Priscilla Hopkins
    Brereton (wife of
    Kemble) 109, 198
    n.86
Kemble, Roger (father
    of Siddons and
    Kemble) 2–4, 130
Kemble, Sarah Ward (mother
    of Siddons and
    Kemble) 2–4, 130,
    187 n.54
Kemble, Stephen (brother
    of Siddons and
    Kemble) 57
Kemble family 4, 108, 186
    n.54
King, Thomas 34
King Charles the First
    (Havard) 2
King John (Shakespeare) 29,
    32, 41, 45, 73, 80, 157,
    162
  Kemble acts in 24–7
  and OP Riots 111, 112, 114
  Siddons and Kemble act
    together in 16, 20–3,
    27–8, 112, 166
  Siddons as Constance 24–6,
    56, 57, 121, 142, 160
King John and John Bull
    (Cruikshank) 111

King Lear (Shakespeare) 11, 45, 77, 79, 116
  Kemble acts in 32–3, 161
  Kemble's text of 31–2
  Siddons and Kemble act together in 31, 33–4, 39, 168
  Siddons as Cordelia in 31, 32
King's theatre (London) 101
Kotzebue, August von 69, 70, 157, 172

Lamb, Charles 160
Lausanne 139, 163
Law of Lombardy, The (Jephson) 169
Lawrence, Thomas 66, 107, 109, 142, 143, 160
Lee, Nathaniel 170, 171
Lee, Sophia 171
Leland, Thomas 16
Lessing, Gotthold Ephraim 170
Lewes, Charles Lee 130
Life of John Philip Kemble, The (anon) 113
Lillo, George 171
Liverpool 65, 67, 214 n.30, 214 n.33
  Kemble acts Hamlet at 136, 138, 139
  Siddons acts Hamlet at 126, 127, 129
  Siddons's and Kemble's early careers at 8, 12, 20, 127, 129, 145
Lodoiska (Kemble) 68–9, 86, 191 n.124
London Magazine 8, 41
Lynch, Jack 91, 97

Macbeth (Shakespeare) 1, 80, 151, 152, 157, 162
  Kemble's productions of 68, 115, 184 n.5
  and new Covent Garden theatre 102, 106, 107
  and OP Riots 97, 105, 108–10, 112, 115, 123
  Siddons and Kemble act together in 1, 20, 27, 117–23, 146, 166, 214–15 n.34
  Siddons as Lady Macbeth 8, 142, 148, 160, 183 n.125
  compared with other roles 10, 26, 28, 32, 56, 70
  farewell performance 148–9
Macbeth Reconsidered (Kemble) 117–18
Macready, William Charles 32
Mahomet the Imposter (Voltaire, Miller) 45, 46, 170
Maid of Honour, The (Massinger, Kemble) 40–1, 45, 166
Malone, Edmond 78, 79, 96, 98, 193 n.7
  friendship with Kemble 80–2
Manchester 65, 67, 127
  Siddons's and Kemble's early careers at 8, 12, 188 n.71
  repertoire 17, 20, 28, 60, 126, 129
Manchester Mercury 126, 188 n.71

Mankiewicz, Joseph 157
Martin, Harriet 142
Mary Queen of Scots (St
    John) 169
Massinger, Philip 14, 40, 166
Mattocks, George 8, 12
McDonald, Russ 156
McDormand, Frances 1
McEvoy, Sean 109
McPherson, Heather 164
Measure for Measure
    (Shakespeare) 170
Mendoza, Daniel 103, 114
Merchant of Venice, The
    (Shakespeare) 113,
    162, 167, 169, 173
  Kemble and 14, 34, 35
  Siddons and 5–7, 9, 151,
    160
Miller, James 45, 46, 170
*Miscellaneous Papers and Legal
    Instruments Under
    the Hand and Seal of
    William Shakespeare.*
    See Shakespeare Papers
Monthly Museum 152
Moody, Jane 59
Moore, Edward 15, 165
morality 41, 70, 87, 95,
    201 n.24. *See also*
    virtue
  and Shakespeare 1, 26, 27,
    32, 62, 118, 137
More, Hannah 167
Morning Chronicle 111
  compares Siddons and
    Kemble 13, 140
  on Kemble 14, 34, 137, 162
  on Siddons 16, 35
Morning Herald 10, 21, 40

Morning Post 10, 28, 157
Mourning Bride, The
    (Congreve) 10, 169
Murphy, Arthur 9, 167, 168,
    170, 171
Muse, Amy 126, 127, 129–31
music 2, 80, 103, 104, 107,
    114
  in Kemble's productions 1,
    63, 68, 72
Mutius Scævola (Ireland) 95–6

nationalism 63, 103, 109,
    114. *See also* patriotism
Negga, Ruth 1
New Spectator 16
New Way to Pay Old Debts, A
    (Massinger) 14
Nixon, T. 83, 84
Northumberland, Duke
    of 108

Oaken Chest, The 90–1
Observer 96
Ogilvie, Mrs 162
Old Price Riots
  effect on Siddons and
    Kemble 105, 148
  Kemble and 111–12, 114,
    116, 123, 153
    attempts to quell 103, 104,
      115–16
  nationalism 104, 114
  politics 64, 109
  reasons for 102–3
  resolution of 105, 109,
    115–16
  satires of 113, 114
  and Shakespeare 97, 110,
    113–16

Siddons and 106–7, 112–13
O'Neill, Eliza 65, 162
opium 88, 89, 197 n.65
OPs (rioters)
 aims 98, 103, 115
 animosity towards Kemble
  family 107–9, 113
 placards 104, 105, 110–14
 response to *Macbeth* 105–6,
  108–9, 123
Oracle 87
*Oracle and Public
 Advertiser* 58
Othello (Shakespeare) 3, 32,
  113, 116, 214 n.33
 Siddons and Kemble act
  in 20, 28–31, 101,
  166
Otway, Thomas 10, 11, 166,
  173
*Oxberry's Dramatic
 Biography* 156, 158,
  160
Oxford 151
Oya, Reiko 117

Paddington Green
 (London) 157
Palmer, John 13
Pascoe, Judith 131
pathos
 and *Hamlet* 137, 145
 and *Henry VIII* 50, 51, 55,
  56
 and Kemble 27, 30, 158,
  177 n.58, 214 n.33
 and Siddons
  acting 9, 10, 14, 44, 149
  repertoire 6, 15, 39, 70,
   156, 160, 162
 Isabella 8–9, 129
patriotism 46, 62, 63, 104, 114–
  15. *See also* nationalism
Peake, Richard 73
Percy (More) 167
Philips, Ambrose 167
Phillimore, John 85, 194 n.23
Phillips, Chelsea 179 n.33,
  205 n.90
Piozzi, Hester Lynch Thrale 82,
  84, 208 n.25
Pizarro (R. B. Sheridan) 68–
  72, 100, 172, 193 n.4
playbills 2, 7, 75, 148, 153
playgoers. *See* audience
poetic justice 39
points 15, 25, 32–3, 56, 132
Powell, Jane 212 n.104
Powell, William 83
Pritchard, Hannah 160, 207
  n.126
promptbooks 33, 38, 53, 62,
  71, 206 n.107
 King John 178 n.24, 180
  n.41
 Macbeth 115, 121, 204
  n.79, 207 n.121
provinces 4, 5, 65
 Hamlet acted in 125–7, 129
 Kemble 21, 34, 50, 125, 152
 Siddons 8, 9, 21, 41, 46, 67,
  152
 Siddons and Kemble 2–5,
  12, 17, 20, 28
provincial theatre
 companies 2–4, 8, 10,
  126, 127, 130, 188 n.71
*Provoked Husband,
 The* (Vanbrugh,
  Cibber) 157

Public Advertiser 21, 40, 135, 137, 144
pugilists 103, 114
Pye, Henry James 172

Radcliffe, Ann 140–1, 144
Rainey, Robert 130–5, 140–2, 144
Recruiting Officer, The (Farquhar) 130
Regent, The (Greatheed) 168
regicide 80, 87, 112, 119
rehearsal 40, 49, 82, 83, 89, 131, 152, 178 n.15
'Remarks on the Character of Lady Macbeth' (Siddons) 117–18
Restoration comedy 160
Revenge, The (Young) 116, 160
revivals 7, 39, 41, 45, 47, 50, 152, 182 n.103, 196 n.45
  of Shakespeare 22, 30, 50, 52, 53, 57, 58, 72, 101, 159, 178 n.15
Reynolds, Joshua 157
Richard III (Shakespeare) 80, 167, 169, 184 n.5, 205 n.89
  early in Siddons's and Kemble's careers 8, 14
  Kemble rivalled by other actors in 43, 162
  OP Riots 113, 203 n.68
Ripley, John 64, 65, 189 n.102, 190 n.110
rivalry 9, 13, 19–21, 36, 43, 161–2, 208 n.11
Rivals, The (Sheridan) 171

Rival Sisters The (Murphy) 170
Robinson, Terry F. 201 n.24
Rogers, Samuel 147, 155, 162
roles, ownership of 6–7, 13, 20, 39, 42–4, 117
Román, David 157
Roman Father, The (Whitehead) 45–7, 170
Roman plays 45, 96
Romeo and Juliet (Shakespeare) 169
Rostron, David 22, 33, 62
Rowe, Nicholas 9, 11, 43, 168, 170, 171, 173
royal family 10, 21, 29, 34, 146, 149–51
Runaway, The (Cowley) 8
Russell, Gillian 103, 113

Sachs, Jonathan 59, 64
Sadler's Wells theatre (London) 100
St John, John 169
Salter 139
Sarah Siddons Award 157
Sarah Siddons Society 157
scenery 41, 50, 68, 69, 86, 94
  and Shakespeare 1, 51, 61, 68, 100, 155
School for Scandal, The (R. B. Sheridan) 86, 208 n.25
Scott, Walter 86, 105, 161–2, 203 n.59, 214 n.33
  on Kemble's acting 53–4, 59, 62–3, 158, 161
sculpture. *See* statuary

Shakespeare, William
  adaptations of   31–2, 35, 58, 91
  and eighteenth-century drama   11, 43, 46, 70
  imitation of   2, 14, 40, 43, 67, 79–80
  importance to Kemble as manager   49, 50, 72, 79, 94, 100, 101, 154, 159
  linked with Siddons and Kemble   2, 7, 79, 102, 110, 112–13, 115, 155
  and nationalism   79, 97, 112, 114, 115
  ownership of   97, 98, 111, 115
  scholarship   78, 79, 98, 135, 136, 155
Shakespeare Papers   79, 82, 85, 94
  Vortigern as part of   75–8, 90–1, 97
Shattuck, Charles   65, 125
Shaughnessy, Robert   11, 118, 126
Sheffield Shakespeare Club   139
Sheridan, Richard Brinsley
  as dramatist   69–72, 114, 171, 172, 193 n.4, 208 n.25
  as manager of Drury Lane theatre   8, 21, 49, 67, 68, 73, 87, 99, 100, 207 n.126
  and *Vortigern*   80, 81, 83, 84, 86, 89, 194 n.16
Sheridan, Thomas   24–5, 58, 60, 63, 188 n.71, 188 n.76

Shirley, William   13
Siddons, Cecilia (daughter of Siddons)   151
Siddons, Harriet Murray (daughter-in-law of Siddons)   56, 107, 149, 200 n.10
Siddons, Henry (son of Siddons)   56, 149
  as a child   9, 10, 175 n.17, 179 n.33
Siddons, Sarah
  as actor (*see* individual play titles)
    acting style   6, 24, 44, 56–7, 60, 70, 120–1, 141–2, 156, 157, 159–61
    preparation for roles   21–2, 60, 72, 117
    provincial performances   2–5, 8, 9, 12, 17, 20–1, 28, 41, 46, 67, 152
    Hamlet   125–7, 129
    repertoire   6, 11, 34, 45, 56, 92, 156
    list of early roles   6, 12, 20, 37, 212 n.96
  and antiquity   60, 72
  and audience   6, 8–10, 19, 26, 36, 101, 106, 107, 128, 148–9, 152, 156
  at Covent Garden   72, 73, 84, 100–2, 115, 148, 149, 186 n.48, 202 n.48
  death   163
  at Drury Lane   5–11, 17, 20, 28–30, 34, 36, 67, 73, 94, 126, 149, 208 n.11
  early life   2–5

family
  marriage 3, 4, 100, 131
  parents and siblings 2–4
  pregnancy and children 5, 8, 9, 29, 36, 56, 149, 151, 179 n.33, 205 n.90
finances 10–11, 16, 17, 31, 38, 46, 67, 73, 84, 100, 107, 127, 129, 144, 148, 151
  accused of avarice 19, 150, 152
health 67, 82–4
and Kemble
  acting together 2–4, 5, 12, 15–17, 20, 27–8, 29, 30, 31, 42, 44–5, 57, 66, 71, 110, 112, 144, 153–4, 165–73 (*see also* individual play titles)
  roles created for 38, 40, 46, 75, 80–1
  as siblings 45–7
  compared to 12, 14, 15, 31, 45, 140–4, 146, 151, 155, 160–1, 164
  resemblance to 12–13, 140
retirement 146–50, 154, 155, 162, 202 n.48, 206 n.106, 213 n.7
rivals 9, 21, 36, 65, 161–2, 208 n.11
and royal family 10, 21, 29, 146, 149–51
and sexism 34, 150, 152, 155, 164
and Shakespeare 2, 3, 5, 7, 56, 75, 79, 91–2, 98, 102, 110, 112–13, 115, 156

visual representations
  caricatures 108, 113, 131
  paintings 10, 57, 66, 70–2, 121, 157
  statues 157–8, 163–4
Siddons, William (husband of Siddons) 2, 4, 100, 126, 127, 131
Smirke, Robert 102
Smith, Sarah 30, 174, 200 n.11
Smith, William (actor) 13, 16, 20, 39, 43, 117, 122
Smith, William (manager) 130
Sotheby, William 172
Southerne, Thomas 8, 11, 168
spectacle 41, 68, 69, 72, 75, 85, 94–6, 115, 152, 159
  and Shakespeare 21, 22, 50, 57, 58, 68, 100, 138
spectators. *See* audience
Star 46
statuary 7, 60, 61, 72, 102, 155, 157, 158, 163–4
Steevens, George 135
Stockdale, John Joseph 104, 108, 109
Stocqueler, J. H. (aka Siddons) 120, 205 n.98, 206 n.106
Stranger, The (Kotzebue, Thompson) 157, 160, 172, 216–17 n.77
Stratford-upon-Avon 4, 7, 78, 155
Strolling. *See* touring
Sun 46
supernumeraries. *See* crowd scenes

sympathy   1, 27, 51, 55, 64, 109, 118

Tamerlane (Rowe)   171
Taming of the Shrew, The (Shakespeare)   35, 160, 168. *See also Catharine and Petruchio*
Tancred and Sigismunda (Thomson)   16–17, 166
Tate, Nahum   31–2, 39
Taylor, David Francis   49, 72, 87
Tegg, Thomas   116
Tempest, The (Shakespeare)   101, 174 n.4
Terry, Daniel   51–3, 56
theatre history   7, 21–2, 103
theatres, size of   6, 67–8
Theatrical Mendicants, Relieved (Gillray)   108
Theodosius (N. Lee)   171
Thompson, Benjamin   157, 172
Thomson, Henry   153
Thomson, James   16, 166, 171
  Coriolanus   58, 62, 63, 188 n.71
Thomson, Peter   151
Thorndike, Sybil   158
Times   22, 58, 81, 107, 123, 158
touring   3–6, 8, 127, 138, 139, 152, 157
Tree, Herbert Beerbohm   159
Trials of the Heart (unknown)   172
Twiss, Horace   149

Universal Magazine   34

Vanbrugh, John   91, 157
Van Dijk, Maarten   22, 27
Venice Preserved (Otway)   10, 11, 45, 148, 156, 157, 162
  Siddons and Kemble act together in   41–2, 166, 173
virtue   15, 39, 42, 70. *See also* morality
  and Shakespeare   29, 31, 32, 38, 63
Voltaire (François-Marie Arouet)   45, 170
Vortigern (Ireland)
  antiquarianism   78, 85, 90
  audience response   81, 82, 85, 86
  bardolatry   76, 78–9
  compared with *Double Falsehood*   91–2
  compared with eighteenth-century plays   87–90, 92
  compared with Shakespeare   79–80, 96–7
  Drury Lane production   75, 77, 86, 94, 95
  Gothic   86–7
  Jordan and   80, 84–5
  Kemble and   67, 75, 79–83, 85, 89, 91, 97
  nationalism   79, 97
  OP Riots   97–8
  politics   87
  satire on   90–1
  and the Shakespeare Papers   75–8, 90–1, 97

Sheridan and 80–1, 83, 84, 86, 89
  Siddons and 79–80, 82–4

Ward, Sarah 28
Ward, Sarah (mother of Siddons and Kemble). *See* Kemble, Sarah Ward
Ward, Sarah Butcher (grandmother of Siddons and Kemble) 4
Westall, Richard 66
Westminster Abbey (London) 163–4
Whalley, Thomas Sedgwick 172
Whalleys, the (Thomas and Elizabeth) 29
Whately, Thomas 205 n.89
Wheel of Fortune, The (Cumberland) 115–16, 160
Whitehead, William 45, 46, 170
Wicklow 197 n.72

Wilkinson, Tate 8, 12, 20, 41, 127
Williams, John Ambrose 60, 93
Windham, William 37
Windsor Castle 146
Winter's Tale, The (Shakespeare) 72–3, 160, 172
Wolverhampton 126
Woo, Celestine 128, 134, 144
Worcester 2, 3, 125, 126
World 36, 58, 184 n.10
Wrighten, Mary Ann 35
Wroughton, Richard 94
Wycherley, William 160

Yates, Mary Ann 7, 9, 20, 21
Yorke, Henry Redhead 114
Yorkshire 8, 12, 41, 127
Young, Charles Mayne 30, 61, 65, 161, 162, 215 n.50
Young, Edward 116
Younge, Elizabeth 7, 9, 20, 126
Younger, Joseph 8, 12, 126, 127

Printed in the USA
CPSIA information can be obtained
at www.ICGtesting.com
LVHW052335240624
783913LV00001BA/179